The Soul of Wit

G. K. Chesterton on William Shakespeare

G. K. CHESTERTON

Edited and with an Introduction by
Dale Ahlquist

DOVER PUBLICATIONS, INC.
Mineola, New York

Bibliographical Note

The Soul of Wit: G. K. Chesterton on William Shakespeare, first published
by Dover Publications, Inc., in 2012, is a new compilation edited, and with an
Introduction by, Dale Ahlquist. Inconsistencies in the text (such as spelling
and punctuation), which have been retained, reflect the wide variety of source
material.

Library of Congress Cataloging-in-Publication Data

Chesterton, G. K. (Gilbert Keith), 1874–1936.
  The soul of wit : G. K. Chesterton on William Shakespeare / edited and
with an introduction by Dale Ahlquist.
    p. cm.
  "A new compilation edited, and with an introduction, by Dale Ahlquist.
Inconsistencies in the text (such as spelling and punctuation), which have
been retained, reflect the wide variety of source material"—T.p. verso.
  ISBN-13: 978-0-486-48919-3
  ISBN-10: 0-486-48919-1
  1. Shakespeare, William, 1564–1616—Criticism and interpretation. I.
Ahlquist, Dale. II. Title. III. Title: Chesterton on William Shakespeare.

PR2899.C473 2012
822.3'.3—dc23

2012019699

Manufactured in the United States by Courier Corporation
48919102
www.doverpublications.com

CONTENTS

Contents

INTRODUCTION

Dale Ahlquist

In his *Autobiography*, G. K. Chesterton paints the following early memory:

> My father knew all his English literature backwards, and . . . I knew
> a great deal of it by heart, long before I could really get it into my
> head. I knew pages of Shakespeare's blank verse without a notion
> of the meaning of most of it; which is perhaps the right way to
> begin to appreciate verse. And it is also recorded of me that, at the
> age of six or seven, I tumbled down in the street in the act of excit-
> edly reciting the words,
>
> > Good Hamlet, cast this nighted colour off,
> > And let thine eye look like a friend on Denmark,
> > Do not for ever with thy veiléd lids
> > Seek for thy noble father in the dust,
>
> at which appropriate moment I pitched forward on my nose.

This amusing passage reveals that Chesterton enjoyed a
lifelong relationship with Shakespeare. It was a relationship
that was scheduled to continue in print, as Chesterton had
been commissioned to write a book on Shakespeare after
completing the *Autobiography*. Unfortunately, the *Autobiography* was the last book he wrote. He poetically com-
pleted his life in the flesh only a few weeks after completing
it on paper.

Anyone familiar with Chesterton's exquisite literary criticism is pained by the thought that he did not live long enough to write that promised book on Shakespeare. Each of his books on other literary figures—Dickens, Browning, Stevenson, Chaucer, St. Thomas Aquinas—has been praised by experts on those authors as the best work ever written on that subject. Chesterton always combines a profound insight with an unbelievably wide knowledge, an unfailingly fresh perspective and simply dazzling prose. The book on Shakespeare might have been his greatest book if only he had written it.

But perhaps it was not lost to us after all. Perhaps he did write the book on Shakespeare. Among the thousands of essays that Chesterton churned out over his thirty-six-year career are several devoted to Shakespeare's plays and characters and criticisms. Just over two dozen of those essays were collected by Chesterton's secretary and literary executrix, Dorothy Collins, who put them in a book called *Chesterton on Shakespeare*. But only a few copies were printed by a small, obscure press in the 1970s, which were the dark ages in terms of interest in Chesterton. Most of his books were out of print at that point, and his popularity was at an all-time low. It is a book that almost no one has read.

There has since been a wonderful revival of interest in Chesterton, thanks in no small part to our colleges and universities. As his books have returned to print, even scholars are starting to take notice. Not lost on them is the fact that Chesterton's one hundred or so books represent only a fraction of what he wrote. There is more material to be mined among his uncollected writings that first appeared in newspapers and magazines. Much more. Enough for many more books.

I have had the pleasure of attempting to complete the task promised by Chesterton and started by his secretary:

the book on Shakespeare. I am sure more good bits of Chesterton's criticism on Shakespeare will still turn up. But here is the most complete collection that you can expect to see for a while. It has at least fifty percent more material than Dorothy Collins' first go-round, drawn from over one hundred additional sources, spanning Chesterton's entire literary career. There are references to at least thirty of Shakespeare's thirty-seven plays. Interestingly, he talks more about Richard II than Richard III, talks more about Falstaff than any of the kings. There are references to *Cymbeline* but none to *The Taming of the Shrew*. And Hamlet gets the most attention, as well he should.

Some of these essays and excerpts have been buried for a long time. It was fun to dig these up. I am especially grateful to Geir Hasnes, who has done so much work in tracking down uncollected Chesterton pieces. He found the essay on *Love's Labour Lost*, the souvenir program from the Shakespeare Ball, and some other great things that appear here for the first time after being hidden for a century or more.

For the few people who have seen the earlier collection, I have followed Dorothy Collins' layout only somewhat. We begin by putting Shakespeare in his context. Chesterton compares Elizabethan drama not only with the drama that came after it—right up to our day—but with the drama that came before it—medieval drama, which most modern audiences (and critics) know nothing about. He also argues persuasively that Shakespeare, the cream of English literature, is part of the Latin tradition and not the Nordic or even distinctly Anglo tradition.

Then comes Chesterton's treatment of the tragedies and the comedies. It is possible that the superb essays "The Macbeths" and "The Tragedy of King Lear" were actually intended for the Shakespeare book that Chesterton had been commissioned to write, since they apparently were never published in his lifetime. Add to them, from the comedy section, the essay in which Chesterton gives the highest praise to *A Midsummer Night's Dream,* and we have pure literary criticism at its finest. If there were no Chesterton, and a college English student handed in an essay like one of these, any proper English professor with even a modicum of respect for his subject would properly fall to his knees and weep with joy and then retire in peace. His life would be fulfilled.

In the next section we see how Chesterton deals with the plays as plays—the staging, the costuming, the plotting. Chesterton shows how Shakespeare can be adapted to fashion but of course transcends fashion. The fashions fade, Shakespeare remains. Chesterton also muses on the intriguing idea of presenting the Shakespeare tragedies as detective stories. Who killed Desdemona? Othello would be the last one we suspect.

We then consider several essays and excerpts that cover the wide range of the elements of Shakespeare: his style, his techniques, his themes, his characters, and the reactions they elicit in us. Here we touch on the history plays as well. Chesterton is insightful and incisive in his observations, revealing a keen power of interpretation. And yet he is humble enough to admit when he is absolutely baffled by Shakespeare's rather obscure and obtuse poem, "The Phoenix and the Turtle." That Chesterton cannot figure out what it means should give comfort to all students everywhere.

The greatest living playwright in England in Chesterton's day was the Irishman George Bernard Shaw. Chesterton and Shaw were good friends and even better opponents.

Among the many topics on which they disagreed was the greatness of Shakespeare and the philosophical outlook of Shakespeare. Shaw didn't think the Swan of Avon was any great shakes. Worse still, he thought Shakespeare was a pessimist. Chesterton sets Shaw straight on both accounts. He points out that Shaw does not see what the world sees in Shakespeare, because what the world sees is not what Shaw happens to be looking for. And though Chesterton would never admit to doing so, he exposes Shaw as a bit of a lightweight.

Recently, there have been some several serious books arguing that Shakespeare was a Catholic. Chesterton joins this argument even before it starts, and seems to end it as well. As always, he draws on history, philosophy, literature, art, and common sense to make his points converge on a conclusion. It is clear that Shakespeare shares the religion of Chaucer and Dante as a fellow architect of literary cathedrals.

If there is one part of his criticism where we might have wished he had spent less time, and more time on something else, it would be in the amount of ink Chesterton devotes to refuting the folks who claimed that Bacon wrote Shakespeare. Or the Earl of Leicester. Or Sir Walter Raleigh. Or the theory that it was Shakespeare's patron, Lord Southampton, who wrote Shakespeare's works. ("Lord Southampton evidently believed in keeping a dog and then barking himself.") And yet, it is still useful to include his many arguments here because they can be used to refute the current crop of anti-Stratfordians who this week claim that Edward de Vere wrote Shakespeare. I have no doubt that, if necessary, Chesterton would update his arguments to skewer these latest challenges to the authenticity of Shakespeare, but the new arguments are surprisingly old and stale, and Chesterton's rebuttals are

still fresh and new. I admit I enjoy arguing with the
Oxfordians because they know their Shakespeare, even if
they do not know it was Shakespeare. These people puzzle
me, but I love them anyway.

It is true that a great deal of Chesterton's Shakespeare
criticism is a criticism of Shakespeare's critics. "Critics say
that little is known about 'the Man Shakespeare.' But, to
judge by the critics, even less is known about 'the Poet
Shakespeare': for he is allowed to be almost everything
except a poet." Shakespeare poetry speaks to the poetical in
all of us. Though we cannot write like Shakespeare, we
immediately recognize that what Shakespeare has written is
what we think and feel. He captures our moods like the
Psalmist. The same doubts and dreads, the same hopes and
ecstasies. The same wryness and wrath. Chesterton says the
great plays of Shakespeare are things "that nearly anybody
can obtain and anybody should enjoy." But as is often the
case, the modern critics get between Shakespeare and his
audience and make him and his plays into something other
than what the audience sees. Chesterton's main role as a
critic is to undo the damage done by other critics.
Chesterton's genius as a critic is that he tells the audience
not what it should feel but what it does feel.

But Chesterton can also take us to a sublime level that we
might not have achieved on our own. He can open our eyes,
as it were. In one of his early reviews of a book on
Shakespeare criticism, Chesterton says: "The only test that
can be adequately suggested of a critic's work on a masterpiece is whether it freshens it or makes it stale, whether, like
the inferior appreciation, it sends us to our hundredth reading of the work, or whether, like the higher appreciation, it
sends us to our first reading of it. There is one kind of criticism which reminds us that we have read a book; there is

another and better which convinces us that we have never read it."

In this sense Chesterton gets us to read Shakespeare for the first time. Of course, as he points out: when people talk about the books they would take to a desert island, they usually answer: Shakespeare and the Bible. This is because, in most cases, they would be reading Shakespeare and the Bible for the first time in their lives.

Shakespeare is a classic, which means he is quoted as opposed to being read. Though Shakespeare's popularity never goes away, very few of us have read Shakespeare. Chesterton, however, really has read Shakespeare. They were, as I said, lifelong friends. And one thing true friends do is keep their promises. Here, I hope, is the book that Chesterton promised to write about his friend.

I.
THIS BLESSED PLOT, THIS EARTH,
THIS REALM, THIS ENGLAND

The Measure of Shakespeare

S hakespeare is so big that he hides England.
   (*Daily News*, Sept. 17, 1906)

❖

English Literature and the Latin Tradition

I fear the title I have chosen is what we should call a priggish title; that is, a pompous and pedantic title. The world
has always rightly rebuked even a scholar when he appeared
as a pedant; and it may well regard with reasonable derision
a pedant who is not even a scholar. As will appear only too
clearly as I proceed, I make no remote claim to classical
scholarship; and it may well be asked why I should label this
essay with the name of classicism.

What I would here advance, very broadly, is this thesis:
first that the English are not barbarians; second, that the
division between England and Europe has been enormously
exaggerated. I admit it has sometimes been exaggerated by
the English. But that is because, quite lately, England was
dominated not only by the English who were ignorant of
Europe, but rather specially by the English who were ignorant of England. For my main thesis may appear more of a
paradox. I want specially to insist that the classical tradition,
the Latin and Greek tradition in English history was the

1

popular thing, the common thing; even the vulgar thing. All those three words, "common" and "popular" and "vulgar", are Latin words, I do not know whether the Anglo-Saxons even had a word for vulgar; the real modern Anglo-Saxons are much too refined. A culture must never be judged by its cultured people. The Latin culture lives in Britain in the uncultured people. It is not a question of English scholars who know Latin. Kamchatkan scholars know Latin; and if there are any Eskimaux scholars, of course they know Latin. They know the Latin scientific word for blubber; and possibly write the Latin odes to the walrus, addressing him the vocative as "walre".

The point is not concerned with the learned; they know Latin, and they know they know it. My point is that the populace, the common men know it without knowing it. Even the old yokel who said, "I ain't no scholar", used a term older than the Schoolmen, as old as the Roman schools. It is not a matter of a Roman pinnacle, but of a Roman pavement. Our populace in every way is such a pavement; and not least in being trampled under foot. For, as I shall try to show, it was the popular Roman tradition that was trampled under foot; and if anything was imposed by aristocrats, it was the pretence of being Anglo-Saxon. Matthew Arnold used the term Barbarian almost as a compliment to an English gentleman; and there was a time quite recently when it was very genteel to be a Barbarian. But it was never very popular, even then, and it had never been heard of before. I wish chiefly to suggest here that it will never be heard of again. The old influence of the southern civilization had sunk so deep in Britain from the beginning, that it was really almost as impossible to weed out the Latin culture from England as to weed it out from Italy. Suppose somebody tried to persuade Italians that their heritage came only from German mercenaries or English trippers or American globe-trotters. Some professors might say that; but it would not be necessary to find more sane and patriotic professors to answer. If these were silent, the very stones would cry out. Not merely ruins, but the common stones; the stones along the Roman road.

Now, in a much less degree, it is true that the very bones of Britain cried out against the myth that she was barbaric. Our country began as a Roman Province. Popular legend connected it with Brutus, proper history connected it with Caesar. It was such a Province in all common talk and tradition. Only when it ceased to be a Province did it become provincial. It is found not in judgments but in jokes; not in odes but in oaths; in common swear words. I will give one case, because it happens to sum up my thesis. I had a debate with a gentleman who denied this; he said the English were descended only from Vikings; and could therefore despise all others who were only descended from Roman soldiers or Renaissance artists or such riff-raff. He sent me a huge book refusing all Latin friendship in the title. *By Thor, No!* I delicately evaded reading his book, or the whole of his book; but I said I would prove my whole case merely from the title of the book. I said to him, in effect, "I will give a hundred pounds to the Home for Decayed Vikings, if you can name to me any kind of Englishman, at any period since there have been any kinds of Englishman, who ever in his life said, or even thought of saying, 'By Thor'. But I, on the other hand, will show you thousands and millions of Englishmen, men in clubs, men in pubs, men in trams and trains, ordinary business men grumbling at City dinners, old colonels cursing and swearing on racecourses, all sorts of perfectly ordinary Englishmen, who have habitually said, and do still sometimes say, 'By Jove'." That is the real story of English literature and life; since Caesar, before or after his British adventure, must have gone up to the throne of the Thunderer upon the Rock of the Capitol. *De Jova Principium*; the song began from Jove.

Let me give some examples. The point is that the classic may be found even in the comic; in comic songs and in those patriotic songs that are unfortunately sometimes rather like comic songs. Here is a rude rhyme about St. George and the Dragon, meant to be sung as a drinking-song in the seventeenth century, with a shout for a chorus. Note that it is full of that vagueness about a very remote past, which is the mark of hero-worship by hearsay; the ballad-monger mentions such names as he happens to have heard, heaven knows where.

> Of the deeds done by old kings
>   Is more than I can tell,
> And chiefly of the Romans
>   Who greatly did excel,
> Hannibal and Scipio
>   Had many a bloody fight,
> And Orlando Furioso
>   Was a very gallant knight.

That is not exactly of marble, in the manner of Racine or Alfieri; but it is classical. It comes out of a people living directly or indirectly on the classics. A rowdy and absurd patriotic song was devoted to the British Grenadiers; but in order to praise those island warriors, it began; "Some talk of Alexander and some of Hercules." In the loneliest inland hamlets, or the dreariest slums of the modern towns, English children can still be found playing a singing-game, with the chorus; "For we are the Romans". Thus, the great legend of Greece and Rome and the glory of antiquity has soaked through our society also, descending through poets to ballad-mongers and from ballad-mongers to gutter-boys; and even to me. I may be regarded for the purpose here as the dunce of the school; but it was, in the medieval phrase, a grammar-school; and began with the Latin grammar.

Perhaps, however, the greatest name will be the best illustration. It was often said that Shakespeare is the typical Englishman in the fact that he had "small Latin and less Greek"; but he had plenty of Plutarch, and he was stuffed to bursting with the classical spirit. Consider, for instance, that he was of the Tudor time, which worshipped monarchy and was always saying, "There's such divinity doth hedge a king." And then consider what a revolution the mere reading of Plutarch in a translation could effect, in making the same man write:

> There was a Brutus once that would have brook'd
> The eternal devil to keep his state in Rome,
> As easily as a king.

But in a much deeper sense, Shakespeare was classical, because he was civilized. Voltaire criticized him as a barbarian. But he was not a barbarian. The Germans have even admired him as a German; but by some strange accident of birth, he was not even a German. The point here, however, is that the classical spirit is no matter of names or allusion. I will take only one example to show what I mean by saying that Shakespeare was every bit as classical as Milton. Just before Othello kills his wife, he utters those words:

> If I quench thee, thou flaming minister,
> I can again thy former light restore,
> Should I repent me; but once put out thy light,

> Thou cunning'st pattern of excelling nature,
> I know not where is that Promethean heat
> That can thy light relume.

Let me explain why I find it convenient to my argument to take this phrase as a type of the classical. Every classical phrase means much more than it says; in contrast with the too vivid and violent modern phrase, which says much more than it means. Whether it be romanticism in the nineteenth century, or realism in the twentieth century, its weakness is that it says so much more than it means. The phrase of Shakespeare, like the phrase of Virgil, is always much greater than its occasion. The cry of Othello goes far beyond the death of Desdemona; it goes far beyond death itself; it is a cry for life and the secret of life. Where is the beginning of that bewildering splendour by which we are; why can we not make life as we can make death? It may be worth remarking in passing that even chemists who once claimed to manufacture everything, who could make synthetic leather or linen, have finally agreed that they cannot make synthetic life. They tell us that peculiar conditions must have existed once somewhere; though their laboratories should surely be capable of creating any conditions that could exist anywhere. "I know not where is that Promethean heat", nor do they. That cry still resounds unanswered in the universe. But the point for the present is that this profound resonance, striking such echoes out of such hollows and abysses, could not be thus achieved without a very deep understanding of classical diction. It could not be done without the word "Promethean"; without the legend of Prometheus; with those rolling polysyllables that are the power of Homer and Virgil. In one practical and prosaic sense, of course, a man might say what Othello says. He might say, "If I kill this woman, how the devil am I to bring her to life again"; but hardly with majesty; hardly with mystery; not precisely with all those meanings and echoes of meaning which belong to a great line of verse. But we need hardly condescend to deal with the realistic critic; the serious gentleman who points out the unquestionable fact that a man just about to smother his wife with a pillow does not talk about Prometheus or speculate on the spiritual origin of life. It is enough to tell him, to his bewilderment, that the soul never speaks until it speaks in poetry; and that in our daily conversation we do not speak; we only talk.

I have dwelt too long on that one example; but it happens to be essential to the end of my argument to insist that Shakespeare did possess a certain great quality that is sometimes denied to him, as well as many other great qualities, which are generally conceded to him. Shakespeare did not merely possess the things which Victor Hugo magnified and which Voltaire mocked; wild imagination, wonderful lyric outbursts and the power of varying tragedy and the fantastic and the grotesque. His work was more patchy than that of pure classicists like Virgil or Racine, largely owing to the accident of his own personal circumstances, mixed motives and practical necessities. But the patchwork did not consist only of purple patches. It did not consist only of passages that are vivid in the romantic or unrestrained manner. He was also capable of that structural dignity, and even of that structural simplicity, in which we feel that we could rest upon every word, as upon the stones of a stairway or a strong bridge. It is also important to realize, in relation to the rest of the thesis, that, after all, it was this classical part of Shakespeare, much more than the romantic part of Shakespeare, that was handed on as a heritage to the English poets immediately after him. His triumph was not

followed by a riot of fairies; but, on the contrary, by a return
of Hellenic gods or Hebraic archangels. But the soliloquies
of Satan and the choruses of *Samson Agonistes* Milton, in
his youth, exaggerated the youthful irresponsibility of
Shakespeare; describing him merely as Fancy's child, who
warbled his native wood-notes wild. But Milton did not continue the work, merely warbling wood-notes or behaving as
fancifully as a child of fancy. He set himself to do consistently and consciously what Shakespeare had only done
incidentally and unconsciously; to bring English literature
into the full inheritance of Latin literature and the classical
culture of the Continent.

Dryden, the next great name after Milton, was in some
ways even more classical and certainly much more
Continental. The whole tendency of his movement, which
culminated in Pope, was to make English poetry not only
rational enough to suit Boileau, but almost rational enough
to soothe Voltaire. The tendency had its deficiencies in
other ways; but that is not the point here. The point here is
that with the coming of the full eighteenth century, English
literature is entirely classical even in the merely scholarly
sense of a study of the classics. I summarize these things in
a series, because they illustrate the main truth of how long
that Latin tradition retained its continuity; how steady was
its progression; and, above all, how very late, how very odd,
and how very temporary, was its interruption.

English-Latin literature and English-French literature
are much older than English literature. The Middle Ages
were international; and England was completely Continental.
But even if we begin with Chaucer, who created English by
making it more than half French, the tradition of the classics
runs on steadily for fully five hundred years. The last point
at which it was undisputed might be represented by

Macaulay. And he is an excellent example of my whole thesis. Macaulay had not, perhaps, a first-class mind; but he was completely in contact with the common mind. He was not one of our best writers, but he was emphatically one of our best-sellers. He was, above all, a popular writer; and he was popular because he was classical, in the sense that he took a classical education for granted. He identified England with a classical education and in one place he quotes a line from one of Milton's Latin poems in threatening an attack on what he would call the new cranks in Germany; *"Frangere Saxonicos Brittanno Marte phalanges"*; "To break the Saxon ranks with British battle." That phrase is a landmark, because it shows that not only Milton, but also Macaulay, thought of himself simply as British, and Saxon simply as German. England had not yet been taught that Englishmen were all Saxons, but under the name of Anglo-Saxons.

But while Macaulay was girding himself to attack the German cranks, there had already arisen in his own time and country a German crank who was not a German. His name was Thomas Carlyle; and he threw himself enthusiastically into a new racial theory that had come to England from Germany. It must be most carefully understood that it was a theory of race and not of nationality. The nations of Europe are now all under conditions that are recognized. Politically, each is independent of all the others. Culturally, each is connected with all the others. For all inherit the civilization of antiquity and of ancient Christendom. Germany, considered as one of the great European States, would be no proper subject for criticism here; but then Germany, considered as a great European State, is just as much a growth of the old civilization as the other European States. Classic antiquity was stamped all over it, whether we like the symbols or no; its eagle was the Roman eagle; its Kaiser was only the German for Caesar; even its Iron Cross was said to be of Christian origin. Its great medieval men were in full touch with the common culture, from Albertus Magnus to Albert Dürer. And it was, if possible, even more true in modern times than in medieval times. Goethe was, perhaps, the most purely classical sort of classicist who ever lived, and his watch was much more on the Mediterranean than on the Rhine. And Schiller called back from Hades the gods of Olympus and not the gods of Asgard.

What appeared in the North in the nineteenth century was an entirely new notion about race, as distinct from nationality. The new figure that appeared was not the German, but rather Teuton. And a thing called the Teutonic race, afterwards called the Nordic race, and in moments of aberration, the Aryan race, was supposed to include the English as well as the Germans; at any rate by the Germans and by an increasing number of the English. The Nordic notion changed nineteenth-century England. All the educated English were taught something that none of the English had ever thought of in all their thousand years of history. It was an interpretation of history in general terms of race; it must not be confounded with the normal idea of nationality, or any sort of patriotism. No people were ever so passionately patriotic, not to say pigheadedly patriotic, as the English of the eighteenth century, whose effective classes wrote, spoke, and almost thought in Latin and Greek, and lived by the culture of the Continent. The English were most English in the time when Johnson wrote all his epitaphs in Latin and Gibbon nearly wrote his great history in French. But this new nineteenth-century theory of race altered everything, at least in the most cultured class. A nation defends its boundaries, or it may want to extend its boundaries. A race has no boundaries; or at least it is impossible to prove that it has any boundaries. Norway, Sweden, Denmark, Germany, Austria, England, are entirely distinct as nations. But the tribal theory, that arose in Germany and spread to England, invoked Scandinavian as Saxon gods and talked as if the Anglo-Saxon race lived in Saxony. If the Teutonic tribalists of that time had wanted to annex Norfolk and Suffolk instead of Alsace and Lorraine, they would have had a better case on their own theories of language and ethnology. The very names of the North Folk and the South Folk would have shown that they in the great Teutonic folk's kultur "included were."

This modern or recent English cult of the Barbarian was a bad thing; for it is chiefly responsible for the international impression that the Englishman can be and has now every intention of being a good European. And for that purpose, I have here insisted on three facts about this racial fad which reacted against the classic tradition of the Mediterranean. First, on how very late it was in our history; belonging to the time of my father, but not of my grandfather; and coming at the end of a thousand years of ever-accumulating classicism. Second, on how very superficial it was; even socially superficial, almost in the sense of snobbish. For, as I have already insisted, the Latin tradition is not a learned thing belonging to learned men; on the contrary, it is the common thing and the popular thing. In England, the classical past has penetrated into every cranny of common life, into the conversational speech and the very texture of society. Greek and Latin, as an influence, are not a luxury of any oligarchy. On the contrary, it was the reaction towards barbarism that was the mere affectation of an aristocracy. It was the tribal Teutonism that was a fashion for the fashionable. Professors who were academic and often aristocratic talked about Folklore; and duchesses organized Folk-Dances. But

anybody might talk about heroic conduct, about platonic
love, about a herculean effort, about a hectoring manner,
about working for somebody like a trojan or bearing a toothache like a stoic. Any modern Englishman might speak of a
forum for discussion or a quorum for an ordinary board-
meeting of a company. But not many modern Englishmen,
going to a committee, ever say to us gaily, "Let us go along
to the Folk-moot." Few Anglo-Saxons trouble about whether
the purest Anglo-Saxon requires them to talk about a wag-
gon or a wain. But they all talk Latin when they want an
omnibus.

   It is often said by the very young that the Victorian Age,
that is, the later nineteenth century in England, was a time
of conventional virtue, a time of sold and stolid respectability. It was exactly the opposite. It was the one and only occasion on which the English went mad in favour of Barbarism.
It was the one wild appearance of the Barbarian after a
thousand years. From the time when the real Anglo-Saxon
prayed in the Litany to be delivered *ab ira Normanorum*,
from the fury of the Northmen, to the time when Lord
Macaulay desired, as already noted, to break the Saxon
ranks with a British attack like that of King Arthur, there
had never been one single word said in all English literature
in favour of the Barbarians against the grandeur of Rome.
And the third thing about the barbaric interlude, on which
I would insist most of all, is that it was ephemeral. It
appeared in England very late and it disappeared from
England very soon. Wild as it was while it lasted in the
romances which were called the histories of Carlyle and
Freeman and Froude, it never lasted long enough to disturb
even the rather dismal externals of traditional life. . . . The
barbaric fancy has been shed so rapidly precisely because it
was not even a fancy of genuine barbarians but a fad of

sophisticated snobs. It has gone quickly out of fashion, for the reason I have emphasized; that it never was anything except a fashion of the few; and the common people are full of the common heritage of Europe. What was once common may often have become vulgar; but in this sense even when it is vulgar it is still classical. The imagery and terminology of it are still classical. The Regius Professor at the University of Oxford wrote letters to *The Times* to prove that his very remote ancestors were moved entirely by the tragedy of Baldur; but meanwhile the grocer's assistant and the errand-boy in the town of Oxford were still sending out vulgar Valentines covered with classical cupids; the last forlorn appearance of the little loves that lamented over the sparrow of Lesbia in the verses of Catullus. The nineteenth-century intellectuals went to the Wagner operas to watch Valkyrs and the Wotans of Nordic myth. But the cabman and the costermonger, who did not know a Valkyr from a Wagnerite, and to whom Götterdämmerung would only sound like a swear word, continued contentedly to go to the music-hall which is still named after the Muses.

I have, in a sense, made these suggestions pivot upon the name of Shakespeare, because he is, as I have said, in nothing more obviously the normal Englishman than in the fact that his whole culture was Greek and Latin, and yet he knew hardly any Latin or Greek. But he belonged to a time, and inherited a history in which it was never counted conceivable that England should really be separate from Europe. No man has suffered more than Shakespeare from being quoted; and nothing normally is less Shakespearian than a quotation from Shakespeare. Thus the world has been bored with poor Juliet's casual and emotional exclamation: "What's in a name?", as if the poet who used words like "Hercules" and "Hecuba" as he did was ever so silly as to suppose that there was nothing in a name. In the same way, an extraordinary impression has been created that Shakespeare was entirely insular, merely by quoting about a line and a half out of a long passage in which he takes a very natural poetical pleasure in the fact that England is an island. It would be quite enough to quote the rest of the passage, to show that though Shakespeare liked England to be an island, he did not in the least like it to be an insular island. Everyone will know the tag I mean, the first lines, "This precious stone set in the silver sea, Which serves it in the office of a wall." He goes on to praise this fortress, but what does he praise it for? In what warfare is that fortress shown as famous and triumphant? Because it was the seat of princes:

> Renowned for their deeds as far from home,
> (For Christian service and true chivalry,)
> As is the sepulchre in stubborn Jewry,
> Of the world's ransom, blessed Mary's Son.

Why did Shakespeare think the English had been glorious? Because they had gone on the Crusades. Because they had ridden with Tancred the Italian and with Godfrey the Frank to the defence of a common Christian civilization. We have cast in our lot with civilization; and we shall not again forget what was found by Caesar and refounded by Augustine.

(*The Fortnightly Review*, August, 1935. This is the text of a lecture Chesterton gave in Florence, Italy, in honor of Luigi Pirandello, on the occasion of his receiving the Nobel Prize for Literature.)

❖

The Mind of the Middle Ages v. The Renaissance

It is beginning to be realized that the English are the eccentrics of the earth. They have produced an unusually large proportion of what they used to call Humourists and would not perhaps rather call Characters. And nothing is more curious about them than the contradiction of their consciousness and the unconsciousness of their own merits. It is nonsense, I regret to say, to claim that they are incapable of boasting. Sometimes they boast most magnificently of their weaknesses and deficiencies. Sometimes they boast of the more striking and outstanding virtues they do not possess. Sometimes (I say it with groans and grovelings before the just wrath of heaven) they sink so low as to boast of not boasting. But it is perfectly true that they seem to be entirely unaware of the very existence of some of their most extraordinary claims to glory and distinction. One example among many is the fact that they have never realized the nature; let alone the scale, of the genius of Geoffrey Chaucer.

Most of the things that are hinted in depreciation of Chaucer could be said as easily in depreciation of Shakespeare. If Chaucer borrowed from Boccaccio and other writers, Shakespeare borrowed from anybody or anything, and often from the same French or Italian sources as his forerunner. The answer indeed is obvious and tremendous; that if Shakespeare borrowed, he jolly well paid back. . . . In the case of Shakespeare, as of Chaucer, his contemporaries and immediate successors seem to have been struck by something sweet or kindly about him, which they felt as too natural to be great in the grand style. He is chiefly praised, and occasionally rebuked, for freshness and spontaneity. Is it unfair to find a touch of that patronizing spirit even in the greatest among those who were less great?

> Or sweetest Shakespeare, fancy's child,
> Warble his native wood-notes wild.

I suspect Milton of meaning that his own organ-notes would be of a deeper and grander sort than wood-notes so innocently warbling. Yet somehow, as a summary of Shakespeare, the description does not strike one as comprehensive. Hung be the heavens with black . . . have lighted fools the way to dusty death . . . the multitudinous seas incarnadine . . . let the high gods, who keep this dreadful pother o'er our heads, find out their enemies now—these do not strike us exclusively as warblings. But neither, it may respectfully be submitted, are all the wood-notes of Chaucer to be regarded as warblings.

The greatest poets of the world have a certain serenity, because they have not bothered to invent a small philosophy, but have rather inherited a large philosophy. It is, nine times out of ten, a philosophy which very great men share with very ordinary men. It is therefore not a theory which attracts attention as a theory. In these days, when Mr. Bernard Shaw is becoming gradually, amid general applause, the Grand Old Man of English letters, it is perhaps ungracious to record that he did once say there was nobody, with the possible exception of Homer, whose intellect he despised so much as Shakespeare's. He has since said almost enough sensible things to outweigh even anything so silly as that. But I quote it because it exactly embodies the nineteenth-century notion of which I speak. Mr. Shaw had probably never read Homer; and there were passages in his Shakespearean criticism that might well raise a doubt about whether he ever read Shakespeare. But the point was that he could not, in all sincerity, see what the world saw in Homer and Shakespeare, because what the world saw was not what G.B.S. was then looking for. He was looking for that ghastly thing which Nonconformists call a Message, and continue to call a Message, even when they have become atheists and do not know who the Message is from. He was looking at a system; one of the very little systems that do very truly have their day. The system of Kant; the system of Hegel; the system of Schopenhauer and Nietzsche and Marx and all the rest. In each of these examples a man sprang up and pretended to have a thought that nobody had ever had. But the great poet only professes to express the thought that everybody has always had. The greatness of Homer does not consist in proving, by the death of Hector, that the Will to Live is a delusion and a snare. It does not consist in proving, by the victory of Achilles, that the Will to Power must express itself in a Superman; for Achilles is not a Superman, but, on the contrary, a hero. The greatness of Homer consists in the fact that he could make men feel, what they were already quite ready to think, that life is a strange mystery in which a hero may err and another hero may fail. The poet makes men realize how great are the great emotions which they, in a smaller way, have already experienced. Every man who has tried to keep any good thing going, though it were a little club or paper or political protest, sounds the depths of his own soul when he hears that rolling line, which can only be rendered so feebly: "For truly in my heart and soul I know that Troy will fall." Every man who looks back on old days, for himself and others, and realizes the changes that vex something within us that is unchangeable, realizes better the immensity of his own meaning in the mere sound of the Greek words, which only mean, "For, as we have heard, you too, old man, were at one time happy." These words are in poetry, and therefore they have never been translated. But there are perhaps some people to whom even the words of Shakespeare need to be translated. Anyhow, what a man learns from *Romeo and Juliet* is not a new theory of sex; it is the mystery of something much more than what sensualists call sex, and what cads call sex appeal. What he learns from *Romeo and Juliet* is not to call first love "calf-love"; not to call even fleeting love a flirtation; but to understand that these things which a million vulgarians have vulgarized, are not vulgar. The great poet exists to show the small man how great he is. A man does not learn from Hamlet a new method of Psychoanalysis, or the proper treatment of lunatics. What he learns is not to despise the soul as small; even when rather feminine critics say that the will is weak. As if the will were ever strong enough for the tasks that confront it in this world! The great poet is alone strong enough to measure that broken strength we call the weakness of man.

It has only been for a short time, a recent and disturbed time of transition, that each writer has been expected to write a new theory of all things, or draw a new wild map of the world. The old writers were content to write of the old world, but to write of it with an imaginative freshness which made it in each case look like a new world. Before the time of Shakespeare, men had grown used to the Ptolemaic astronomy, and since the time of Shakespeare men have grown used to the Copernican astronomy. But poets have never grown used to stars; and it is their business to prevent anybody else ever growing used to them. And any man who reads for the first time the words, 'Night's candles are burnt out,' catches his breath and almost curses himself for having neglected to look rightly, or sufficiently frequently, at the grand and mysterious revolutions of night and day. Theories soon grow stale; but things continue to be fresh. And, according to the ancient conception of his function, the poet was concerned with things; with the tears of things, as in the great lament of Virgil; with the delight in the number of things, as in the lighthearted rhyme of Stevenson; with thanks for things as in the Franciscan Canticle of the Sun or the *Benedicite Omnia Opera*. That behind these things there are certain great truths is true; and those so unhappy as not to believe in these truths may of course call them theories. But the old poets did not consider that they had to compete and bid against each other in the production of counter-theories. The coming of the Christian cosmic conception made a vast difference; the Christian poet had a more vivid hope than the Pagan poet. Even when he was sometimes more stern, he was always less sad. But, allowing for that more than human change, the poets taught in a continuous tradition, and were not in the least ashamed of being traditional. Each taught in an individual way; "with a perpetual slight novelty," as Aristotle said; but they were not a series of separate lunatics looking at separate worlds. One poet did not provide a pair of spectacles by which it appeared that the grass was blue, or another poet lecture on optics to teach people to say that the grass was orange; they both had the far harder and more heroic task of teaching people to feel that the grass is green. And because they continue their heroic task, the world, after every epoch of doubt and despair, always grows green again.

The life and death of Richard the Second constitute a tragedy which was perhaps the tragedy of English history, and was certainly the tragedy of English monarchy. It is seldom seen with any clearness; because of two prejudices that prevent men letting in on it the disinterested daylight of their minds. The first is the fact that, though it happened more than five hundred years ago, it is still dimly felt to be a Party Question. Shakespeare, in the time of the Tudors, saw it as an opportunity for exalting a sort of Divine Right; later writers, in the time of the Georges, have seen in it an opportunity for depreciating Divine Right. What is much more curious is the fact that neither ever noticed that the unfortunate Richard did not by any means merely stand for Divine Right; that in his earliest days he stood for what we are accustomed to consider much later rights, and for some which were, at least relatively speaking, the rights of democracy. The origin of this oblivion is in the second of the two modern prejudices. It is the extraordinary prejudice, sometimes identified with progress, to the effect that the world has always been growing more and more liberal, and that therefore there could be no popular ideals present in earlier times and forgotten in later times. The case of Richard the Second might have been specially staged in order to destroy this delusion. He was very far from being a faultless sovereign; he did various things which permit modern Parliamentarians to represent him as a despotic sovereign; but he was, by comparison with many contemporaries and most successors, a democratic sovereign. He did definitely attempt to help the democratic movement of his day, and he was definitely restrained from doing so. Shakespeare is full of sympathy for him, but Shakespeare was not full of sympathy for what most modern people would find sympathetic. He does not even mention the fact that the prince, whom he represents as bewailing the insult to his crown, and appealing to the sacred immunity of his chrism, had in his youth faced a rabble of roaring insurgent serfs, had declared that he himself would be their leader, the true demagogue of their new democracy, had promised to grant their demands, had disputed desperately with his nobles to get those demands granted, and had finally been overruled and forced to abandon the popular cause by that very baronial insolence which soon forced him to abandon the throne. If we ask why the greatest of dramatists was blind to the most dramatic of historic scenes, the young king claiming the leadership of the oppressed people, the explanation is perfectly simple. The explanation is that the whole theory, that "the thoughts of men are widen'd with the process of the suns", is all ignorant rubbish.

How could the suns widen anybody's thoughts? The explanation is that the men of Shakespeare's time understood far less of the democratic ideal than the men of Chaucer's time. The Tudors were occupied in their own time, as Shakespeare is occupied in his great play, with the sixteenth-century mystical worship of The Prince. There was much more chance in the fourteenth century of having a mystical feeling about The People. Shakespeare's Richard is religious, to the extent of always calling himself The Lord's Anointed. The real Richard would also, very probably, have referred to the people as God's Flock. Ideas were mixed and misused in both periods, as in all periods; but in the time of Chaucer and Langland there was much more vague and general moral pressure upon the mind of the presence of problems of mere wealth and poverty, of the status of a peasant or the standards of a Christian, than there was in the time of Shakespeare and Spenser; of the splendour of Gloriana and the Imperial Votaress in the West. Therefore Shakespeare, great and human as he was, sees in Richard only the insulted king; and seems to think almost as little about the subjects of Richard as about the subjects of Lear.

But Richard had thought about the subjects of Richard. He had, in his early days and in his own way, tried to be a popular king in the sense of a popular leader. And though the popular ideas failed, and in some cases were bound to fail, they would have been much more present to the mind of a great writer of that time, than they were to the mind of one of the Queen's Servants under the last of the Tudors. In other words, even when there really is progress, as there certainly is growth, the progress is not a progress in everything, perfectly simple and universal and all of a piece. Civilizations go forward in some things, while they go backward in others. Men had better looms and steam hammers in 1850 than in 1750, but not handsomer hats and breeches or more dignified manners and oratory. And in the same way a man in the position of Shakespeare had more subtle and many-coloured arts, but not more simple and popular sympathies, than a man in the position of Langland. The Renaissance exalted the Poet, but even more it exalted the Prince; it was not primarily thinking about the Peasant. Therefore the greatest of all the great sons of the Renaissance, rolling out thousands of thunderous and intoxicant lines upon the single subject of the reign of King Richard the Second, does not trouble himself about The Peasants' War.

There is a type of student who has a curious subconscious itch in the presence of poetry; an itch for explaining it, in the hope of explaining it away. But this sort of critic is in any case unreliable, because, in dealing with a poem, he cannot distinguish between its occasion and its origin. He is the sort of commentator who, listening to the enchanted voice of Oberon, telling of mermaids and meteors and the purple flower, is chiefly anxious to assure us that the imperial votaress was certainly Queen Elizabeth, and that there actually was a pageant at Nobbin Castle, for a wedding in the Fitznobbin family, in which a cupid and a mermaid figured in such a manner as completely to explain William

Shakespeare's remarks—and almost explain William Shakespeare. It is all quite probable; it is all quite true; by all means, let us be gravely grateful for the information. There were doubtless a good many pageants and a good many parades of Cupid and Dian; and I daresay a great many mermaids on a great many dolphins' backs. But, by an odd chance, only one of them ever, in the whole history of the world, uttered such dulcet and harmonious breath that the rude sea grew civil at her song, and certain stars shot madly from their spheres to hear the sea-maid's music. That is the kind of thing that has rather a way of only happening once. And if we really must find out where it came from, or why it came, we shall be wise to guess that it had a good deal less to do with the Mermaid at Nobbin Castle than with that other Mermaid at which Mr. William Shakespeare of Stratford sometimes took a little more wine than was good for him.

Chaucer was not an unsuccessful man. For the greater part of his life he was a successful man and a poet; and yet we cannot say exactly that he was a successful poet. That is, he was not successful as a poet in the way in which some of his contemporaries were successful as poets; praised and applauded as poets; crowned and enthroned as poets. In this respect there is a curious parallel between the mystery of Chaucer and the mystery of Shakespeare. They were neither of them failures or outcasts; they both seem to have had a good deal of solid success, though Shakespeare was wealthiest in later life and Chaucer in middle life. But they were more successful than famous; and more famous than glorious. The odd obscurity of Shakespeare, in some aspects, which has been the negative opportunity of so many cranks and quacks, is a real fact so far as it goes; and it can best be measured if we compare it, for instance, with the flamboyant fame of Ronsard a few years before in France. Some say that Shakespeare's death was disreputable; it is a far more creepy and uncanny fact that his life was respectable. He lived and died, not like a first-rate failure, but like a fourth-rate success. He lived and died a proper provincial burgess, a few years after Ronsard had gathered round his gorgeous death-bed that great assembly of nobles and princes in the robes of religion, and proclaimed to all Europe as with a trumpet that no man born had known so much glory as he, and that he was weary of it and thirsty for the glory of God. The obscure death of Shakespeare is almost as startling a contrast, whether it was disreputable or respectable.

I know that commentators, or those critics who chiefly shine as commentators, are often gravely anxious to clear great men of the charge of talking nonsense. They apply it to Shakespeare; who has whole passages in which he talks nothing but nonsense. When Hamlet says, "I am but mad north-north-west: when the wind is southerly, I know a hawk from a hand-saw," the remark strikes his critics as one eminently suitable for scientific and rationalizing treatment; some hastily amending it to, "I know a hawk from a heron-shaw," and the other, I think, inventing some new tool or utensil called a hawk. I know nothing of these things; they may be right. But seeing that the man was a fantastic humorist in any case, and pretending to be a lunatic at that, and seeing he starts the very same sentence by saying he is mad, it seems to me, as a humble fellow-habitant of Hanwell [an insane asylum], that he probably meant to say, "a hawk from a hand-saw", as he might have said, "a bishop from a blunderbuss" or, "a postman from a pickle-jar". Now this sort of wild fantasticality is Shakespearian but not Chaucerian. Chaucer has in the background too much of that logic which was the backbone of the Middle Ages. The Renaissance was, as much as anything, a revolt from the logic of the Middle Ages. We speak of the Renaissance as the birth of rationalism; it was in many ways the birth of irrationalism. It is true that the medieval School-men, who had produced the finest logic that the world has ever seen, had in later years produced more logic than the world can ever be expected to stand. They had loaded and lumbered up the world with libraries of mere logic; and some effort was bound to be made to free it from such endless chains of deduction. Therefore, there was in the Renaissance a wild touch of revolt, not against religion but against reason. . . . When all is said, there was in the very greatest of the sixteenth-century men of genius a slight slip or failure upon the point of common sense. That is what Voltaire meant when he called Shakespeare an inspired barbarian; and there is something to be said for Voltaire as well as for Shakespeare. Let it be agreed, on the one hand, that the Renaissance poets had in one sense obtained a wider as well as a wilder range. But though they juggled with worlds, they had less real sense of how to balance a world. I am sorry that Chaucer "left half-told the story of Cambuscan bold", and I can imagine that that flying horse might have carried the hero into very golden skies of Greek or Asiatic romance; but I am prepared to agree that he would never have beaten Ariosto in anything like a voyage to the moon. On the other hand, even in Ariosto there is something symbolic, if only accidentally symbolic, in the fact that his poem is less tragic but more frantic than *The Song of Roland*; and deals not with Roland Dead but with Roland Mad. Anyhow, what is here only accidental becomes in the Elizabethans rather anarchical. When all is said, there is something a little sinister in the number of mad people there are in Shakespeare. We say that he uses

his fools to brighten the dark background of tragedy; I think
he sometimes uses them to darken it. Somewhere on that
highest of all human towers there is a tile loose. There is
something that rattles rather crazily in the high wind of the
highest of mortal tragedies. What is felt faintly even in
Shakespeare is felt far more intensely in the other Elizabethan
and Jacobean dramatists; they seem to go in for dancing bal-
lets of lunatics and choruses of idiots, until sanity is the
exception rather than the rule. In some ways Chaucer's age
was even harsher than Shakespeare's; but even its ferocity
was rational. . . . In other words, the medieval mind did not
really believe that the truth was to be found by going to
extremes. And the Elizabethan mind had already had a sort
of hint that it might be found there; at the extreme edges of
existence and precipices of the human imagination.

Everything, even the great poetry of Elizabethan times,
was a little too much involved. In literature it was the age of
conceits. In politics it was the age of conspiracies. In those
conspiracies there is a curious absence of the fresh popular
spirit that often blew like a wind even through the heresies
and horrors of the Middle Ages. None of it was in the same
world with Peasants' Rising. The age of Richard the Second
was an age of revolutions. The age of Elizabeth was an age
of plots. And we all know that this was mirrored more or less
even in the mightiest minds of that epoch. It is almost in a
double sense that we talk about Shakespeare's 'plots'. In
almost every case, it is a plot about a plot. He has even a sort
of restlessness vaguely connected with the sixteenth-century
sense of the importance and the insecurity of princes.
'Uneasy lies the head that wears a crown'; and also the head
that has crowns on the brain.

That Shakespeare is the English giant, all but alone in his
stature among the sons of men, is a truth that does not really

diminish with distance. But it is a truth with two aspects; a shield with two sides; a sword with two edges. It is exactly because Shakespeare is an English giant that he blocks up the perspective of English history. He is as disproportionate to his own age as to every age; but he throws a misleading limelight on his own age and throws a gigantic shadow back on the other ages. For this reason many will not even know what I mean, when I talk about the greater spaciousness around the medieval poet. If the matter were pushed to a challenge, however, I could perhaps illustrate my meaning even better with another medieval poet. It is vaguely implied that Shakespeare was always jolly and Dante always gloomy. But, in a philosophical sense, it is almost the other way. It is notably so, if, so to speak, we actually bring Shakespeare to the test of Dante. Do we not know in our hearts that Shakespeare could have dealt with Dante's Hell but hardly with Dante's Heaven? In so far as it is possible to be greater than anything that is really great, the man who wrote of Romeo and Juliet might have made something even more poignant out of Paolo and Francesca. The man who uttered that pulverizing "He has no children," over the butchery in the house of Macduff, might have picked out yet more awful and telling words for the father's cry out of the Tower of Hunger. But the Tower of Hunger is not spacious. And when Dante is really dealing with the dance of the liberated virtues in the vasty heights of heaven, he is spacious. He is spacious when he talks of Liberty; he is spacious when he talks of Love. It is so in the famous words at the end about Love driving the sun and stars; it is the same in the far less famous and far finer passage, in which he hails the huge magnanimity of God in giving to the human spirit the one gift worth having; which is Liberty. Nobody but a fool will say that Shakespeare was a pessimist; but we may,

in this limited sense, say that he was a pagan; in so far that
he is at his greatest in describing great spirits in chains. In
that sense, his most serious plays are an Inferno. Anyhow,
they are certainly not a Paradiso.

(Extracts from *Chaucer*)

—— ❖ ——

The Origins of Elizabethan Drama

I have just been very much amused with a Nativity play of
the fourteenth century. . . . It was one of the Coventry
cycle of mediaeval plays, loosely called the Coventry
Mysteries . . . And in seeing this Bethlehem drama I felt that
good news might perhaps be as dramatic as bad news; and
that it was possibly as thrilling to hear that a child is born as
to hear that a man is murdered.

Doubtless there are some sentimental people who like
these old plays merely because they are old. My own sentiment could be more truly stated by saying that I like them
because they are new. They are new in the imaginative
sense, making us feel as if the first star were leading us to
the first child.

But they are also new in the historical sense, to most
people, owing to that break in our history which makes the
Elizabethans seem not merely to have discovered the new
world but invented the old one. Nobody could see this
mediaeval play without realizing that the Elizabethan was
rather the end than the beginning of a tradition; the crown
and not the cradle of the drama.

Many things that modern critics call peculiarly Elizabethan
are in fact peculiarly medieval. For instance, that the same
stage could be the place where meet the extremes of

tragedy and comedy, or rather farce. That daring mixture is always made a point of contrast between the Shakespearean play and the Greek play or the French classical play. But it is a point of similarity, or rather identity, between the Shakespearean play and the miracle play.

Nothing could be more bitterly tragic than the scene in this Nativity drama, in which the mothers sing a lullaby to the children they think they have brought into safety the moment before the soldiers of Herod rush in and butcher them screaming on the stage. Nothing could be more broadly farcical than the scene in which King Herod himself pretends that he has manufactured the thunderstorm.

In one sense, indeed, the old religious play was far bolder in its burlesque than the more modern play. Shakespeare did not express the unrest of King Claudius by making him fall over his own cloak. He did not convey his disdain for tyranny by letting Macbeth appear with his crown on one side. This was partly no doubt an improvement in dramatic art; but it was partly also, I think, a weakening of democratic satire.

Shakespeare's clowns are philosophers, geniuses, demi-gods; but Shakespeare's clowns are clowns. Shakespeare's kings may be usurpers, murderers, monsters; but Shakespeare's kings are kings. But in this old devotional drama the king is the clown. He is treated not so much with disdain as with derision; not so much with a bitter smile as with a broad grin. A cat may not only look at a king but laugh at a king; like the mythical Cheshire cat, an ancient cat as terrible as a tiger and grinning like a gargoyle.

("The Humour of King Herod," *The Uses of Diversity*)

The Renaissance Drama of Blood and Gold

If we look at the very great works of English literature, we see that each of them has something of that air of beginning big things; but in fact the big thing ends where it began. Shakespeare has all the Renaissance gesture of flinging open golden gates upon a new world of sunrise and song. He is full, as was the whole sixteenth century, of those radiant vistas of wealth, and treasure, which were sometimes worthy to be called, in an almost sublime sense, the dreams of avarice. He is full of all that glowing colour that belongs to the Venetian painting, as when with a touch he turns all the seas of the world to crimson. And when we compare all this breadth and glory with the stiff imitations of Seneca or the rude village plays of Quince and Bottom, we cannot but feel that Shakespeare is building a city, is making a world, is the beginning of something greater even than himself. But we have not had anything greater than himself. The Renaissance drama of blood and gold, of kings and usurpers, is not a beginning but an end; its gold and crimson are the colours of sunset and not of dawn.

(*Illustrated London News*, Dec. 22, 1928)

———— ❖ ————

This Sceptered Isle

Shakespeare looked on the sea round England as if it were the moat round a castle.

(*Illustrated London News*, Sept. 26, 1925)

———— ❖ ————

Shakespeare's London

(Review of *Shakespeare's London*.
By Henry Thew Stephenson)

Americans are celebrated, and justly celebrated, for a
certain freshness and poetic vivacity in their treatment
of the great monuments and great men of Europe.
Sometimes, perhaps, this freshness is if possible a little too
fresh; they are more enthusiastic about English celebrities
not only than an Englishman is, but than any man ought to
be. For the real fault of America is one for which she is very
little blamed, while she suffers slander in many other matters. It is not at all true to say that Americans worship
money; but perhaps it is true to say that they worship intellect. I do not say this as an apologia; for, as a matter of fact,
the worship of intellect is a meaner thing than the worship
of money. The worship of money, vile as it is, is at least a
crude symbol of the worship of life and of the whole of life;
money is not everything, but at least it is more than one
thing, it represents physical and mental and aesthetic parts
of man. Intellect represents only one part of man. Hence
many Americans tend to a certain starved intensity which is
more unhealthy than common vulgarity; they become
refined by refining away everything that is jolly. From these
dangers Professor Thew Stephenson is peculiarly free.
Something in his subject perhaps assists him; for it is difficult to retain any mere worship of intellect in the presence
of Shakespeare. But Professor Stephenson himself manages
to convey not only a great deal of Elizabethan information,
but something like a whiff from that larger world. The last
chapter on taverns and tavern life is especially typical and
atmospheric. Yet, although Professor Stephenson has been

more successful than most writers in trying to picture the
period, the mind is throughout all such books haunted with
a sense of mistake.

THE MODERN BIAS

The most difficult thing to realise about one's own time is
simply that it is a time. It is everyone's temptation to think
his own time is the day of judgment, the final test by which
everything is cleared up. The modern bias is a thing that
ought to be allowed for in all modern books, as much as a
Mohammedan bias in Mohammedan books or a Chinese
bias in Chinese books, but it is never allowed for. Men
observe the gaps in previous periods; but the corresponding
gaps in their own period are literally too large to see. There
is a good example in the first few pages of Professor Thew
Stephenson's book. "This people," he says of the Elizabethans, "in a sense was an ignorant people. Those of the
highest rank were well and laboriously educated according
to the contemporary standard; but the rank and file paid no
attention to learning." I am not sufficiently instructed to be
able to say whether this is a true description of Elizabethan
England; but I am quite sure that it is a precise and correct
description of modern England. Does Professor Stephenson
imagine that the highest rank is not now laboriously educated out of all proportion to the rest of the nation? Does he
suppose that the rank and file of navvies in Poplar pay any
extravagant attention to learning? Professor Stephenson
adds, "they neither read, wrote, nor thought." That they did
not read nor write is very probable; it was not the typical
accomplishment of their time, as can be seen by studying
their laboriously educated upper class in its spirited attempt
to spell. But as to whether the Elizabethan poor ever

thought I am very content to judge from the incomparable clowns of Shakespeare.

But Professor Thew Stephenson's mistake in this matter goes a great deal deeper. It is extraordinarily typical of the way the most learned men forget the framework of the past of Europe. Improving what he calls "the ignorance of the then common people concerning public affairs," he adds this illustration; "Compare a history like Holinshed's with a history like Froude's or Gardiner's. You find in the former no attempt to sift tradition from fact, no sense whatever of the dignity of a thousand page folio in black letter. On the other hand, we read in Holinshed of a terrible storm that killed a dog in Essex, or of a cow that gave birth to a five legged calf in Kent." Now, what is this comparison intended to suggest? It is meant to mean (or else it means nothing) that Holinshed did not introduce into his history an exposition of principles because either he or his audience were too barbarous or too stupid to care for such principles. The time of Bacon was too savage; the age of Montaigne was too imbecile. The generation which (unlike our own) could listen to Hamlet without cuts or scenery could not be interested in intellectual propositions. The people whose passions were making Puritanisms and the theological wars could not in any way be induced to interest themselves in any general principle. The company at the Mermaid could only just understand that a god had been killed in Essex. The Commons that shook Elizabeth and shattered Charles were just sufficiently intelligent to know that a normal calf had only four legs.

THE REAL REASON

The whole thing is incredible. And if Professor Stephenson has any memory of Europe in his blood he may very easily see why it really was that Holinshed put into his history five-legged calves but not general principles. He did it because living in an age unsettled indeed, but more settled than our own, he had a preference for minding his own business. General principles of life (that age thought) were the affair of religion and of the true Church—whichever it was! In our age we have no common philosophy to interpret all events; so every man has to put his own philosophy in everything he makes, even if it be a history of England. Holinshed thought himself a narrator of interesting facts (charming facts, I think, by the instances given). He did not give his view of them because he and his readers held the same view of them; there were only two or three views to hold. The whole Elizabethan world would have agreed on the grand philosophic truth that a calf with five legs was a funny calf. In a modern history it might be necessary to pause to explain that a calf with five legs was not necessarily the Super calf. Holinshed (in a word) did not leave philosophy out of his histories because he had no philosophy. He left it out for the same reason that Mr. Bradshaw leaves it out of his time tables.

(*Daily News*, April 20, 1906)

---------- ❖ ----------

Renaissance and Restoration

In history there is no Revolution that is not a Restoration. Among the many things that leave me doubtful about the modern habit of fixing eyes on the future, none is stronger than this: that all the men in history who have really done anything with the future have had their eyes fixed upon the past. I need not mention the Renaissance, the very word proves my case. The originality of Michael Angelo and

Shakespeare began with the digging up of old vases and manuscripts.

("The Fear of the Past," *What's Wrong with the World*)

———— ❖ ————

Enter Shakespeare

A Cockney [is] a man born within the immediate appeal of high civilisation and of eternal religion. Shakespeare, in the heart of his fantastic forest, turns with a splendid suddenness to the Cockney ideal as being the true one after all. For a jest, for a reaction, for an idle summer love or still idler summer hatred, it is well to wander away into the bewildering forest of Arden. It is well that those who are sick with love or sick with the absence of love, those who weary of the folly of courts or weary yet more of their wisdom, it is natural that these should trail away into the twinkling twilight of the woods. Yet it is here that Shakespeare makes one of his most arresting and startling assertions of the truth. Here is one of those rare and tremendous moments of which one may say that there is a stage direction, "Enter Shakespeare." He has admitted that for men weary of courts, for men sick of cities, the wood is the wisest place, and he has praised it with his purest lyric ecstasy. But when a man enters suddenly upon that celestial picnic, a man who is not sick of cities, but sick of hunger, a man who is not weary of courts, but weary of walking, then Shakespeare lets through his own voice with a shattering sincerity and cries the praise of practical human civilisation:

> If ever you have looked on better days,
> If ever you have sat at good men's feasts,

> If ever been where bells have knolled to church,
> If ever from your eyelids wiped a tear
> Or know what 't is to pity and be pitied.

There is nothing finer even in Shakespeare than that conception of the circle of rich men all pretending to rough it in the country, and the one really hungry man entering, sword in hand, and praising the city. "If ever been where bells have knolled to church."

(Introduction to *A Tale of Two Cities*)

II.
THE TRAGEDIES

The Difference Between Comedy and Tragedy

I have heard people protest against the profanity of burlesque Hamlets and burlesque Macbeths. But, indeed,
this is the strength of Macbeth, that he can be burlesqued.
Murder is a serious matter. You may make fifty glorious
jokes over the corpse of Duncan, and you must still come
back to the fact that a dead Duncan in your private house is
a serious matter. You can walk round the corpse; it is not
made of cardboard. You can make Macbeth comic—and you
still leave him tragic. You can burlesque a play of Shakespeare:
but you cannot burlesque a play of Maeterlinck.

(*Illustrated London News*, Dec. 25, 1909)

❖

The Moral Basis for Tragedy

The old writers knew exactly what they thought about
things, and then wrote about the things. They did not
write with a moral purpose, but with a moral assumption. The
author of *Macbeth* can sympathise with a murderer; but the
whole play would be meaningless if there were a moral doubt
about murder, like the modern doubt about marriage.

(*Illustrated London News*, June 24, 1922)

——— ❖ ———

The True Hamlet

(A Review of *The True Hamlet of William Shakespeare*
by Robert Gray)

Mr. Robert Gray enunciates a view of Hamlet which flies flat in the face of every accepted theory: he maintains that Hamlet was not irresolute, not over-intellectual, not procrastinating, not weak. The challenge, erroneous as it may be, is spirited, ingenious, and well-reasoned, and it can do nothing but good in the controversy and nothing but honour to Shakespeare. The more varied are the versions of friends and enemies, the more flatly irreconcilable are the opinions of various men about Hamlet, the more he resembles a real man. The characters of fiction, mysterious as they are, are far less mysterious than the figures of history. Men have agreed about Hamlet vastly more than they have agreed about Caesar or Mahomet or Cromwell or Mr. Gladstone or Cecil Rhodes. Nobody supposes that Mr. Gladstone was a solar myth; nobody has started the theory that Mr. Rhodes is only the hideous phantom of an idle dream. Yet hardly three men agree about either of them, hardly anyone knows that some new and suggestive view of them might not be started at any moment. If Hamlet can be thus surpassed, if he can thus be taken in the rear, it is a great tribute to the solidity of the figure. If from another standpoint he appears like another statue, it shows at least that the figure is made of marble and not of cardboard. Neither the man who thinks Lord Beaconsfield a hero nor the man who thinks a snob doubts his existence. It is a great tribute to literature if neither the man who thinks Hamlet a weakling nor the man who thinks him a hero ever thinks of doubting Hamlet's existence.

Personally, I think Mr. Gray absolutely right in denouncing the idea that Hamlet was a "witty weakling." There is a great difference between a weakness which is at liberty and a strength which is rusted and clogged. Hamlet was not a weak man fundamentally: Shakespeare never forgets to remind us that he had an elemental force and fire in him, liable to burst out and strike everyone with terror.

> "Yet have I something in me dangerous
> Which let thy wisdom fear."

But Hamlet was a man in whom the faculty of action had been clogged, not by the smallness of his moral nature, but by the greatness of his intellectual. Actions were really important to him, only they were not quite so dazzling and dramatic as thoughts. He belonged to a type of man which some men will never understand, the man for whom what happens inside his head does actually and literally happen; for whom ideas are adventures, for whom metaphors are living monsters, for whom all intellectual parallel has the irrevocable sanctity of a marriage ceremony. Hamlet failed, but through the greatness of his upper, not the weakness of his lower, storey. He was a giant, but he was top-heavy.

But while I warmly agree with Mr. Gray in holding that the moral greatness of Hamlet is enormously underrated, I cannot agree with him that Hamlet was a moral success. If this is true, indeed, the whole story loses its central meaning: if the hero was a success, the play is a failure. Surely no one who remembers Hamlet's tremendous speech, beginning:

> "O what a rogue and peasant slave am I,"

can share Mr. Gray's conclusion:

> "He is not here condemning himself for inaction, there is no cause
> for the reproach, he is using the resources of passion and elo-
> quence to spur himself to action."

It is difficult for me to imagine anyone reading that
appalling cry out of the very hell of inutility and think that
Hamlet is not condemning himself for inaction. Hamlet
may, of course, be only casually mentioning that he is a
moral coward: for the matter of that, the Ghost may be only
cracking a joke when he says he has been murdered. But if
ever there was sincerity in any human utterance, there is in
the remorse of Hamlet.

The truth is that Shakespeare's Hamlet is immeasurably
vaster than any mere ethical denunciation or ethical defence.
Figures like this, scribbled in a few pages of pen and ink,
can claim, like living human beings, to be judged by
Omniscience. To call Hamlet a 'witty weakling' is entirely to
miss the point, which is his greatness; to call him a triumphant hero is to miss a point quite as profound. It is the
business of art to seize these nameless points of greatness
and littleness: the truth is not so much that art is immoral as
that art has to single out sins that are not to be found in any
decalogue and virtues that cannot be named in any allegory.
But upon the whole it is always more indulgent than philan-
thropy. Falstaff was neither brave nor honest, nor chaste,
nor temperate, nor clean, but he had the eighth cardinal
virtue for which no name has ever been found. Hamlet was
not fitted for this world: but Shakespeare does not dare to
say whether he was too good or too bad for it.

(*The Speaker,* June 29, 1901)

———— ❖ ————

Hamlet and the Psycho-analyst

This morning, for a long stretch of hours before breakfast, and even as it were merging into breakfast, and
almost overlapping breakfast, I was engaged in scientific
researches in the great new department of psycho-analysis.
Every journalist knows by this time that psycho-analysis
largely depends on the study of dreams. But in order to
study our dreams it is necessary to dream; and in order to
dream it is necessary to sleep. So, while others threw away
the golden hours in lighter and less learned occupations,
while ignorant and superstitious peasants were already digging in their ignorant and superstitious kitchen-gardens, to
produce their ignorant and superstitious beans and potatoes, while priests were performing their pious mummeries
and poets composing lyrics on listening to the skylark—I
myself was pioneering hundreds of years ahead of this
benighted century; ruthlessly and progressively probing into
all the various horrible nightmares, from which a happier
future will take its oracles and its commandments. I will not
describe my dreams in detail; I am not quite so ruthless a
psychologist as all that. And indeed it strikes me as possible
that the new psychologist will be rather a bore at breakfast.
My dream was something about wandering in some sort of
catacombs under the Albert Hall, and it involved eating
jumbles (a brown flexible cake now almost gone from us,
like so many glories of England) and also arguing with a
Theosophist. I cannot fit this in very well with Freud and his
theory of suppressed impulses. For I swear I never in my
life suppressed the impulse to eat a jumble or to argue with

a Theosophist. And as for wandering about in the Albert Hall, nobody could ever have had an impulse to do that.

When I came down to breakfast I looked at the morning paper; not (as you humorously suggest) at the evening paper. I had not pursued my scientific studies quite so earnestly as that. I looked at the morning paper, as I say, and found it contained a good deal about Psycho-Analysis, indeed it explained almost everything about Psycho-Analysis except what it was. This was naturally a thing which newspapers would present in a rather fragmentary fashion; and I fitted the fragments together as best I could. Apparently the dreams were merely symbols; and apparently symbols of something very savage and horrible which remained a secret. This seems to me a highly unscientific use of the word symbol. A symbol is not a disguise but rather a display; the best expression of something that cannot otherwise be expressed. Eating a jumble may mean that I wished to bite off my father's nose (the mother-complex being strong on me); but it does not seem to show much symbolic talent. The Albert Hall may imply the murder of an uncle; but it hardly makes itself very clear. And we do not seem to be getting much nearer the truth by dreaming, if we hide things by night more completely than we repress them by day. Anyhow, the murdered uncle reminds me of Hamlet, of whom more anon; at the moment I am merely remarking that my newspaper was a little vague; and I was all the more relieved to open my *London Mercury* and find an article on the subject by so able and suggestive a writer as Mr. J. D. Beresford.

Mr. J. D. Beresford practically asked himself whether he should become a psycho-analyst or continue to be a novelist. It will readily be understood that he did not put it precisely in these words; he would probably put psycho-analysis higher, and very possibly his own fiction lower; for men of genius are often innocent enough of their own genuine originality. That is a form of the unconscious mind with which none of us will quarrel. But I have no desire to watch a man of genius tying himself in knots, and perhaps dying in agony, in the attempt to be conscious of his own unconsciousness. I have seen too many unfortunate sceptics thus committing suicide by self-contradiction. Haeckel and his Determinists, in my youth, bullied us all about the urgent necessity of choosing a philosophy which would prove the impossibility of choosing anything. No doubt the new psychology will somehow enable us to know what we are doing, about all that we do without knowing it. These things come and go, and pass through their phases in order, from the time when they are as experimental as Freudianism to the time when they are as exploded as Darwinism. But I never can understand men allowing things so visibly fugitive to hide things that are visibly permanent, like morals and religion and (what is in question here) the art of letters. *Ars longa, scientia brevis*. ["Art is long, science is short."]

Anyhow, as has been said, psycho-analysis depends in practice upon the interpretation of dreams. I do not know whether making masses of people, chiefly children, confess their dreams, would lead to a great output of literature; though it would certainly lead, if I know anything of human nature, to a glorious output of lies. There is something touching in the inhuman innocence of the psychologist, who is already talking of the scientific exactitude of results reached by the one particular sort of evidence that cannot conceivably be checked or tested in any way whatever. But, as Mr. Beresford truly says, the general notion of finding signs in dreams is as old as the world; but even the special theory of it is older than many seem to suppose.

Indeed, it is not only old, but obvious; and was never discovered, because it was always noticed. Long before the present fashion I myself (who, heaven knows, am no psychologist) remember saying that there is truth in all popular traditions, there is truth in the popular saying that dreams go by the rule of contraries. That is, that a man does often think at night about the very things he does not think by day. But the popular saying had in it a certain virtue never found in the anti-popular sciences of our day. Popular superstition has one enormous element of sanity; it is never serious. We talk of ages like the mediaeval as the ages of faith; but it would be quite as true a tribute to call them the ages of doubt; of a healthy doubt, and even a healthy derision. There was always something more or less consciously grotesque about an old ghost story. There was fun mixed with the fear; and the yokels knew too much about turnips not occasionally to think of turnip-ghosts. There is no fun about psycho-analysis. One yokel would say, "Ar, they do say dreams go by contraries." And then the others would say, "Ar," and they would all laugh in a deep internal fashion. But when Mr. J. D. Beresford says that Freud's theory is among scientific theories the most attractive for novelists, "it was the theory of sex, the all but universal theme of the novel," it is clear that our audience is slower and more solemn than the yokels. For nobody laughs at all.

People seem to have lost the power of reacting to the humorous stimulus. When one milkmaid dreamed of a funeral, the other milkmaid said, "That means a wedding," and then they would both giggle. But when Mr. J. D. Beresford says that the theory "adumbrated the suggestion of a freer morality, by dwelling upon the physical and spiritual necessity for the liberation of impulse," the point seems somehow to be missed. Not a single giggle is heard in the deep and disappointing silence. It seems truly strange that when a modern and brilliant artist actually provides jokes far more truly humorous than the rude jests of the yokels and the milkmaids, the finer effort should meet with the feebler response. It is but an example of the unnatural solemnity, like an artificial vacuum, in which all these modern experiments are conducted. But no doubt if Freud had enjoyed the opportunity of explaining his ideas in an ancient alehouse, they would have met with more spontaneous applause.

I hope I do not seem unsympathetic with Mr. Beresford; for I not only admire his talent, but I am at this moment acting in strict obedience to his theories. I am—I say it proudly—acting as a disciple of Freud, who apparently forbids me to conceal any impulse, presumably including the impulse to laugh. I mean no disrespect to Mr. Beresford; but my first duty, of course, is to my own psychological inside. And goodness knows what damage might not be done to the most delicate workings of my own mental apparatus (as Mr. Arnold Bennett called it) if I were to subject it to the sudden and violent strain of not smiling at the scientific theory which is attractive because it is sexual, or of forcing my features into a frightful composure when I hear of the spiritual necessity for the liberation of impulse. I am not quite sure how far the liberation of impulse is to be carried out in practice by its exponents in theory; I do not know whether it is better to liberate the impulse to throw somebody else out of an express train in order to have the carriage to oneself all the way; or what may be the penalties for repressing the native instinct to shoot Mr. Lloyd George. But obviously the greater includes the less; and it would be very illogical if we were allowed to chuck out our fellowtraveller but not to chaff him; or if I were permitted to shoot

at Mr. George but not to smile at Mr. Beresford. And
though I am not so serious as he is, I assure him that in this
I am quite as sincere as he is. In that sense I do seriously
regret his seriousness; I do seriously think such seriousness
a very serious evil. For some healthy human impulses are
really the better for the relief by words and gestures, and
one of them is the universal human sense that there is something comic about the relations of the sexes. The impulse to
laugh at the mention of morality as "free" or of sex science
as "attractive" is one of the impulses which is already grati-
fied by most people who have never heard of psycho-analysis and is only mortified by people like the psycho-analysts.

Mr. Beresford must therefore excuse me if, with a sincere desire to follow his serious argument seriously, I note
at the beginning a certain normal element of comedy of
which critics of his school seem to be rather unconscious.
When he asks whether this theory of the nemesis of suppression can serve the purposes of great literary work, it
would seem natural at first to test it by the example of the
greatest literary works. And, judged by this scientific test, it
must be admitted that our literary classics would appear to
fail. Lady Macbeth does not suffer as a sleep-walker because
she has resisted the impulse to murder Duncan, but rather
(by some curious trick of thought) because she has yielded
to it. Hamlet's uncle is in a morbid frame of mind, not, as
one would naturally expect, because he had thwarted his
own development by leaving his own brother alive and in
possession; but actually because he has triumphantly liberated himself from the morbid impulse to pour poison in his
brother's ear. On the theory of psycho-analysis, as expounded,
a man ought to be haunted by the ghosts of all the men he
has not murdered. Even if they were limited to those he has
felt a vague fancy for murdering, they might make a

respectable crowd to follow at his heels. Yet Shakespeare certainly seems to represent Macbeth as haunted by Banquo, whom he removed at one blow from the light of the sun and from his own subconsciousness. He ought to mean the regret for lost opportunities for crime; the insupportable thought of houses still standing unburned or unburgled, or of wealthy uncles still walking about alive with their projecting watch-chains. Yet Dante certainly seemed to represent it as concerned exclusively with things done and done with, and not as merely the morbidly congested imagination of a thief who had not thieved and a murderer who had not murdered. In short, it is only too apparent that the poets and sages of the past knew very little of psychoanalysis, and whether or no Mr. Beresford can achieve great literary effects with it, they managed to achieve their literary effects without it. This is but a preliminary point, and I shall touch the more serious problem in a few minutes, if the fashion has not changed before then. For the moment I only take the test of literary experience, and of how independent of such theories have been the real masterpieces of man. Men are still excited over the poetic parts of poets like Shakespeare and Dante; if they go to sleep it is over the scientific parts. It is over some system of the spheres which Dante thought the very latest astronomy, or some argument about the humours of the body which Shakespeare thought the very latest physiology. I appeal to Mr. Beresford's indestructible sense of humanity and his still undestroyed sense of humour. What would have become of the work of Dickens if it had been rewritten to illustrate the thesis of Darwin? What even of the work of Mr. Kipling if modified to meet the theories of Mr. Kidd? Believe me, the proportions are as I have said. Art is long, but science is fleeting; and Mr. Beresford's subconsciousness, though stout and

brave, is in danger of being not so much a muffled drum as
a drum which somebody silences for ever; by knocking a
hole in it, only to find nothing inside. But there is one incidental moral in the matter that seems to me topical and
rather arresting. It concerns the idea of punishment. The
psycho-analysts continue to buzz in a mysterious manner
round the problem of Hamlet. They are especially interested in the things of which Hamlet was unconscious, not
to mention the things of which Shakespeare was unconscious. It is in vain for old-fashioned rationalists like myself
to point out that this is like dissecting the brain of Puck or
revealing the real private life of Punch and Judy. The discussion no longer revolves round whether Hamlet is mad,
but whether everybody is mad, especially the experts inves-
tigating the madness. And the curious thing about this
process is that even when the critics are really subtle
enough to see subtle things, they are never simple enough
to see self-evident things. A really fine critic is reported as
arguing that in Hamlet the consciousness willed one thing
and the subconsciousness another. Apparently the conscious Hamlet had unreservedly embraced and even wel-
comed the obligation of vengeance, but the shock (we are
told) had rendered the whole subject painful, and started a
strange and secret aversion to the scheme. It did not seem
to occur to the writers that there might possibly be something slightly painful, at the best, in cutting the throat of
your own uncle and the husband of your own mother.
There might certainly be an aversion from the act; but I do
not quite see why it should be an unconscious aversion. It
seems just possible that a man might be quite conscious of
not liking such a job. Where he differed from the modern
morality was that he believed in the possibility of disliking
it and yet doing it.

But to follow the argument of these critics, one would think that murdering the head of one's family was a sort of family festivity or family joke; a gay and innocent indulgence into which the young prince would naturally have thrown himself with thoughtless exuberance, were it not for the dark and secretive thoughts that had given him an unaccountable distaste for it. Suppose it were borne in upon one of these modern middle-class critics, of my own rank and routine of life (possibly through his confidence in the messages at a Spiritualist séance) that it was his business to go home to Brompton or Surbiton and stick the carving-knife into Uncle William, who had poisoned somebody and was beyond the reach of the law. It is possible that the critic's first thought would be that it was a happy way of spending a half-holiday; and that only in the critic's subconsciousness the suspicion would stir that there was something unhappy about the whole business. But it seems also possible that the regret might not be confined to his subconsciousness, but might swim almost to the surface of his consciousness. In plain words, this sort of criticism has lost the last rags of common sense. Hamlet requires no such subconscious explanation, for he explains himself, and was perhaps rather too fond of doing so. He was a man to whom duty had come in a very dreadful and repulsive form, and to a man not fitted for that form of duty. There was a conflict, but he was conscious of it from beginning to end. He was not an unconscious person; but a far too conscious one.

Strangely enough, this theory of subconscious repulsion in the dramatic character is itself an example of subconscious repulsion in the modern critic. It is the critic who has a sort of subliminal prejudice which makes him avoid something that seems very simple to others. The thing which he secretly and obscurely avoids, from the start, is the very

simple fact of the morality in which Shakespeare did
believe, as distinct from all the crude psychology in which
he almost certainly did not believe. Shakespeare certainly
did believe in the struggle between duty and inclination.
The critic instinctively avoids the admission that Hamlet's
was a struggle between duty and inclination; and tries to
substitute a struggle between consciousness and subconsciousness. He gives Hamlet a complex to avoid giving him
a conscience. But he is actually forced to talk as if it was a
man's natural inclination to kill an uncle, because he does
not want to admit that it might be his duty to kill him. He is
really driven to talking as if some dark and secretive mono-
mania alone prevented us all from killing our uncles. He is
driven to this because he will not even take seriously the
simple and, if you will, primitive morality upon which the
tragedy is built. For that morality involves three moral
propositions, from which the whole of the morbid modern
subconsciousness does really recoil as from an ugly jar of
pain. These principles are: first, that it may be our main
business to do the right thing, even when we detest doing it;
second, that the right thing may involve punishing some
person, especially some powerful person; third, that the just
process of punishment may take the form of fighting and
killing. The modern critic is prejudiced against the first
principle and calls it asceticism; he is prejudiced against the
second principle and calls it vindictiveness; he is prejudiced
against the third and generally calls it militarism. That it
actually might be the duty of a young man to risk his own
life, much against his own inclination, by drawing a sword
and killing a tyrant, that is an idea instinctively avoided by
this particular mood of modern times. That is why tyrants
have such a good time in modern times. And in order to
avoid this plain and obvious meaning, of war as a duty and

peace as a temptation, the critic has to turn the whole play upside down, and seek its meaning in modern notions so remote as to be in this connexion meaningless. He has to make William Shakespeare of Stratford one of the pupils of Professor Freud. He has to make him a champion of psycho-analysis, which is like making him a champion of vaccination. He has to fit Hamlet's soul somehow into the classifications of Freud and Jung; which is just as if he had to fit Hamlet's father into the classifications of Sir Oliver Lodge and Sir Arthur Conan Doyle. He has to interpret the whole thing by a new morality that Shakespeare had never heard of, because he has an intense internal dislike of the old morality that Shakespeare could not help hearing of. And that morality, which some of us believe to be based on a much more realistic psychology, is that punishment as punishment is a perfectly healthy process, not merely because it is reform, but also because it is expiation. What the modern world means by proposing to substitute pity for punishment is really very simple. It is that the modern world dare not punish those who are punishable, but only those who are pitiable. It would never touch anyone so important as King Claudius—or Kaiser William.

Now this truth is highly topical just now. The point about Hamlet was that he wavered, very excusably, in something that had to be done; and this is the point quite apart from whether we ourselves would have done it. That was pointed out long ago by Browning in "The Statue and the Bust." He argued that even if the motive for acting was bad, the motive for not acting was worse. And an action or inaction is judged by its real motive, not by whether somebody else might have done the same thing from a better motive. Whether or no the tyrannicide of Hamlet was a duty, it was accepted as a duty and it was shirked as a duty. And that is precisely true of a

tyrannicide like that for which everybody clamoured at the
conclusion of the Great War. It may have been right or
wrong to punish the Kaiser; it was certainly even more right
to punish the German generals and admirals for their atroci-
ties. But even if it was wrong, it was not abandoned because
it was wrong. It was abandoned because it was troublesome.
It was abandoned for all those motives of weakness and
mutability of mood which we associate with the name of
Hamlet. It might be glory or ignominy to shed the blood of
imperial enemies, but it is certainly ignominy to shout for
what you dare not shed; "to fall a-cursing like a common
drab, a scullion." Granted that we had no better motives than
we had then or have now, it would certainly have been more
dignified if we had fatted all the region-kites with this slave's
offal. The motive is the only moral test. A saint might provide
us with a higher motive for forgiving the War-Lords who
butchered Fryatt and Edith Cavell. But we have not forgiven
the War-Lords. We have simply forgotten the War. We have
not pardoned like Christ; we have only procrastinated like
Hamlet. Our highest motive has been laziness; our common-
est motive has been money. In this respect indeed I must
apologize to the charming and chivalrous Prince of Denmark
for comparing him, even on a single point, with the princes
of finance and the professional politicians of our time. At
least Hamlet did not spare Claudius solely because he hoped
to get money out of him for the salaries of the Players, or
meant to do a deal with him about wine supplied to Elsinore
or debts contracted at Wittenberg. Still less was Hamlet acting entirely in the interests of Shylock, an inhabitant of the
distant city of Venice. Doubtless Hamlet was sent to England
in order that he might develop further these higher motives
for peace and pardon. "'Twill not be noticed in him there;
there the men are as mad as he."

It is therefore very natural that men should be trying to dissolve the moral problem of Hamlet into the unmoral elements of consciousness and unconsciousness. The sort of duty that Hamlet shirked is exactly the sort of duty that we are all shirking; that of dethroning injustice and vindicating truth. Many are now in a mood to deny that it is a duty because it is a danger. This applies, of course, not only to international but internal and especially industrial matters. Capitalism was allowed to grow into a towering tyranny in England because the English were always putting off their popular revolution, just as the Prince of Denmark put off his palace revolution. They lectured the French about their love of bloody revolutions, exactly as they are now lecturing the French about their love of bloody wars. But the patience which suffered England to be turned into a plutocracy was not the patience of the saints; it was that patience which paralysed the noble prince of the tragedy; *accidia* and the great refusal. In any case, the vital point is that by refusing to punish the powerful we soon lost the very idea of punishment; and turned our police into a mere persecution of the poor.

(From *Fancies vs. Fads*. Originally from *New Witness*, September 24, 1920; June 25, 1920; June 2, 1922)

❖

The Orthodoxy of Hamlet

I am sometimes tempted to think (like every other person who does think) that the people would always be right if only they were not educated. But this is, of course, quite the wrong way of putting it. The truth is that there is no such thing as education; there is only this education and that education. We are all ready to die in order to give the people this education, and (I hope sincerely) we are all ready to die to prevent the people having that education. Dr. Strong, in *David Copperfield*, educated little boys; but Mr. Fagin, in *Oliver Twist*, also educated little boys; they were both what we now call "educationalists".

But though the first mode of statement is certainly erroneous, one is driven back upon it sometimes in considering the case of the drama. I enjoy the drama far too much ever to be a dramatic critic; and I think that in this I am at one with that real people which never speaks. If anybody wants to know what political democracy is, the answer is simple; it is a desperate and partly hopeless attempt to get at the opinion of the best people—that is, of the people who do not trust themselves. A man can rise to any rank in an oligarchy. But an oligarchy is simply a prize for impudence. An oligarchy says that the victor may be any kind of man, so long as he is not a humble man.

A man in an oligarchical state (such as our own) may become famous by having money, or famous by having an eye for colour, or famous for having social or financial or military success. But he cannot become famous for having humility, like the great saints. Consequently all the simple and hesitating human people are kept entirely out of the running; and the cads stand for the common people, although as a matter of fact the cads are a minority of the common people. So it is quite especially with the drama. It is utterly untrue that the people do not like Shakespeare. That part of the people that does not like Shakespeare is simply that part of the people that is depopularised. If a certain crowd of Cockneys is bored with *Hamlet*, the Cockneys are not bored because they are too complex and ingenious for *Hamlet*. They feel that the excitement of the saloon bar, of the betting ring, of the halfpenny paper, of the topical music hall, is more complex and ingenious than *Hamlet*; and so it is.

In the absolutely strict sense of the word, the Cockneys are too aesthetic to enjoy *Hamlet*. They have goaded and jaded their artistic feelings too much to enjoy anything simply beautiful. They are aesthetes; and the definition of an aesthete is a man who is experienced enough to admire a good picture, but not inexperienced enough to see it. But if you really took simple people, honourable peasants, kind old servants, dreamy tramps, genial thieves, and brigands, to see *Hamlet*, they would simply be sorry for Hamlet. That is to say, they would simply appreciate the fact that it was a great tragedy.

Now I believe in the judgment of all uncultured people; but it is my misfortune that I am the only quite uncultured person in England who writes articles. My brethren are silent. They will not back me up; they have something better to do. But a few days ago when I saw Miss Julie Marlowe and Mr. Sothern give their very able representation of *Hamlet*, certain things came into my mind about that play which I feel sure that the other uncultured persons share with me. But they will not speak; with a strange modesty they hide their lack of cultivation under a bushel.

There is a threadbare joke which calls the gallery in a theatre "the gods". For my part I accept that joke quite seriously. The people in the gallery are the gods. They are the ultimate authority so far as anything human is the ultimate authority. I do not see anything unreasonable in the actor calling upon them with the same gesture with which he calls upon the mountain of Olympus. When the actor looks down, brooding in despair or calling up black Erebus or the evil spirits, then, in such moments, by all means let him bend his black brows and look down into the stalls. But if there be in any acted play anything to make him lift up his heart to heaven, then in God's name, when he looks up to heaven, let him see the poor.

There is one little point, for instance, upon which I think the public have mistaken Hamlet, not through themselves but through the critics. There is one point on which the uneducated would probably have gone right; only they have been perverted by the educated. I mean this: that everybody in the modern world has talked of Hamlet as a sceptic. The mere fact of seeing the play acted very finely and swiftly by Miss Marlowe and Mr. Sothern has simply swept the last rags of this heresy out of my head. The really interesting thing about Hamlet was that he was not a sceptic at all. He did not doubt at all, except in the sense that every sane man doubts, including popes and crusaders. The primary point is quite clear. If Hamlet had been a sceptic at all there would have been no tragedy of Hamlet. If he had had any scepticism to exercise, he could have exercised it at once upon the highly improbable ghost of his father. He could have called that eloquent person a hallucination, or some other unmeaning thing, have married Ophelia, and gone on eating bread and butter. This is the first evident point.

The tragedy of Hamlet is not that Hamlet is a sceptic. The tragedy of Hamlet is that he is very much too good a philosopher to be a sceptic. His intellect is so clear that it sees at once the rational possibility of ghosts. But the utter mistake of regarding Hamlet as a sceptic has many other instances. The whole theory arose out of quoting stilted passages out of their context, such as "To be or not to be", or (much worse) the passage in which he says with an almost obvious gesture of fatigue, "Why then, 'tis none to you; for there is nothing either bad or good, but thinking makes it so". Hamlet says this because he is getting sick of the society of two silly men; but if anyone wishes to see how entirely opposite is Hamlet's attitude he can see it in the same conversation. If anyone wishes to listen to the words of a man who in the most final sense is not a sceptic, here are his words:

> This goodly frame, the earth, seems to me a sterile promontory; this most excellent canopy the air, look you, this brave o'erhhanging firmament, this majestical roof fretted with golden fire, why it appears no other thing to me than a foul and pestilent congregation of vapours. What a piece of work is a man! how noble in reason! how infinite in faculty! in form and moving how express and admirable! in action how like an angel! in apprehension how like a god! the beauty of the world! the paragon of animals! And yet, to me, what is this quintessence of dust?

Oddly enough I have heard this passage quoted as a pessimistic passage. It is, perhaps, the most optimistic passage in all human literature. It is the absolute expression of the ultimate fact of the faith of Hamlet; his faith that, although he cannot see the world is good, yet certainly it is good; his faith that, though he cannot see man as the image of God, yet certainly he is the image of God. The modern, like the modern conception of Hamlet, believes only in mood. But the real Hamlet, like the Catholic Church, believes in reason. Many fine optimists have praised man when they felt like praising him. Only Hamlet has praised man when he felt like kicking him as a monkey of the mud. Many poets, like Shelley and Whitman, have been optimistic when they felt optimistic. Only Shakespeare has been optimistic when he felt pessimistic. This is the definition of a faith. A faith is that which is able to survive a mood. And Hamlet had this from first to last. Early he protests against a law that he recognises: "O that the Everlasting had not fixed his canon 'gainst self-slaughter." Before the end he declares that our clumsy management will be turned to something, "rough-hew it how we will".

If Hamlet had been a sceptic he would have had an easy life. He would not have known that his moods were moods. He would have called them Pessimism or Materialism, or some silly name. But Hamlet was a great soul, great enough to know that he was not the world. He knew that there was a truth beyond himself, therefore he believed readily in the things most unlike himself, in Horatio and his ghost. All through his story we can read his conviction that he is wrong. And that to a clear mind like his is only another way of stating that there is something that is right. The real sceptic never thinks he is wrong; for the real sceptic does not think that there is any wrong. He sinks through floor after floor of a bottomless universe. But Hamlet was the very reverse of a sceptic. He was a thinker.

(From *Lunacy and Letters*. Originally from *Daily News*, May 18, 1907)

——— ❖ ———

The Grave-digger

In looking over some medieval books in the beautiful Rylands Library at Manchester I was much struck by that perfection and precision in the decorative illumination which so many have praised and so few have realised in this industrious medieval art. But I was even more affected by a quality that belongs at once to the simplest and the soundest human feeling. Plato held this view, and so does every child. Plato held, and the child holds, that the most important thing about a ship (let us say) is that it is a ship. Thus, all these pictures are designed to express things in their quiddity. [The technical term of philosophy meaning the "whatness" of things] If these old artists draw a ship, everything is sacrificed to expressing the "shipishness" of the ship. If they draw a tower, its whole object is to be towering. If they draw a flower, its whole object is to be flowering. Their pencils often go wrong as to how the thing looks; their intellects never go wrong as to what the thing is.

These pictures are childish in the proper and complimentary sense of the word. They are childish in this sense, that they are Platonist. When we are very young and vigorous and human we believe in things; it is only when we are very old and dissolute and decaying that we believe in the aspects of things. To see a thing in aspects is to be crippled, to be defective. A full and healthy man realises a thing called a ship; he realises it simultaneously from all sides and with all senses. One of his senses tells him that the ship is tall or white, another that the ship is moving or standing still, another that it is battling with broken and noisy waves, another that it is surrounded and soaked with the smell of the sea. But a deaf man would only know that the ship was moving by the passing of objects. A blind man would only know that the ship was moving by the sound of the swirling water. A blind and deaf man would only know that a ship was moving by the fact that he was seasick. This is the thing called "impressionism", that typically modern thing.

Impressionism means shutting up all of one's nine million organs and avenues of appreciation except one. Impressionism means that, whereas Nature has made our senses and impressions support each other, we desire to suppress one part of perception and employ the other. Impressionism, in short, may be justly summarised as "winking the other eye". The

impressionist desires to treat mankind as a brood of the
Cyclops. It is not surprising that Whistler wore a monocle; his
philosophy was monocular. But the vice is not confined to the
pictorial impressionist who deals with visible powers. Just as
the painter of that type asks us to use only one of our eyes, so
the poet of that type asks us to use only one lobe of our brain.

The characteristic of the finest and most typical modern
plays is that they rule out altogether any element inconsistent with their subtle theme. I might almost say with their
secret theme. The laughter is excluded at the box-office. A
man may say of *Hamlet* or of *Romeo and Juliet* that the tragedy seems to him inadequate. But at least he must allow that
this tragedy has been at least adequate to admit and to over-
shadow comedy. Hamlet's dignity may be destroyed by the
German critic; but at least Hamlet's dignity is not destroyed
by the Grave-digger. Hamlet meets the Grave-digger, and
realises quite as well as any modern that serious things can
be laughed at even by those who are closest to them. The
hilarious song of the Grave-digger is the great heroic song
of all human democracy, and the first few notes of that cry
would have cracked from end to end, like the blast of cock-
crow, the whole world of Pelleas and Melisande.

There are some who say that Shakespeare was vitally anti-
democratic, because every now and then he curses the
rabble—as if every lover of the people had not often had
cause to curse the rabble. For this is the very definition of
the rabble—it is the people when the people are undemocratic. But if anyone fancies that Shakespeare did not, consciously or unconsciously, realise the rude veracity and
violent humour of the people, the complete answer is to be
found in the mere figure of the Grave-digger. "Has this fellow no feeling of his business, that he sings at grave-making?" In that Shakespeare has shown the utter inferiority of

Hamlet to the Grave-digger. Hamlet by himself might almost be a character in Maeterlinck. He wishes to make the play of *Hamlet* a Maeterlinck play—united, artistic, melancholy, in a monotone. He wishes the Grave-digger to be sad at his grave-digging; he wishes the Grave-digger to be in the picture. But the Grave-digger refused to be in the picture, and the grave-digger will always refuse. The common man, engaged in tragic occupation, has always refused and will always refuse, to be tragic.

If anybody really understands the London poor he will admit that there are two things that really strike him—first, the persistent tragedy of the poor; and, secondly, their persistent farce and their persistent frivolity. Fortunately for the world, these men have the power of raising a riotous carol of satire out of the deep pit in which they dig. Fortunately for the world, they have so little feeling of their business that they sing at grave-making. Shakespeare showed that he was not incapable of the ultimate comprehension of democracy when he made the hind happy and the prince a failure. Many have criticised the chaos of corpses that occurs at the end of *Hamlet*. But, after all, nobody professes to have found the corpse of the Grave-digger among the débris. If poets have made their tragedies out of kings it was partly not out of servility, but out of pity. The man who has dug and drained and ploughed and cut wood from the beginning of the world has lived under innumerable Governments, sometimes good and generally bad. But, as far as we have ever heard of him, he has always sung at his work. The grave-diggers, the poor men, always sang at their work when they were building the tombs of the Pharaohs. And in our civilized modern cities they are still singing at their work, although the graves that they are digging are their own.

My rambling meditations began among the Gothic illuminations of the Rylands Library, and they may very rightly end there. In all these pictured and painted medieval Bibles or missals there are traces of many fancies and fashions, but there is not even the trace of a trace of this one modern heresy of artistic monotone. There is not the trace of a trace of this idea of the keeping of comedy out of tragedy. The moderns who disbelieve in Christianity treat it much more reverently than these Christians who did believe in Christianity. The wildest joke in Voltaire is not wilder than some of the jokes coloured here by men, meek and humble, in their creed.

To mention one thing out of a thousand, take this. I have seen a picture in which the seven-headed beast of the Apocalypse was included among the animals in Noah's Ark, and duly provided with a seven-headed wife to assist him in propagating that important race to be in time for the Apocalypse. If Voltaire had thought of that, he would certainly have said it. But the restrictions of these men were restrictions of external discipline; they were not like ours, restrictions of mood. It might be a question how far people should be allowed to make jokes about Christianity; but there was no doubt that they should be allowed to feel jokes about it. There was no question of that merely impressional theory that we should look through only one peep-hole at a time. Their souls were at least stereoscopic. They had nothing to do with that pictorial impressionism which means closing one eye. They had nothing to do with that philosophical impressionism which means being half-witted.

(From *Lunacy and Letters*. Originally from *Daily News*, January 26, 1907)

❖

A Convincing Ghost

Personally, I have a profound distrust of things that are done on a large scale. Somebody said he would believe in ghosts if they would come into mixed company, instead of lurking in loneliness. My own feeling is quite the opposite. The mixed company is so very mixed. The loneliness is so much more suitable to a really confidential chat, in which we might put the rather delicate question to the ghost of whether he is a ghost. It is comparatively convincing when Hamlet's father, being a gentleman, beckons his son to a more removed spot in order to discuss painful family affairs. It would be much less convincing if Hamlet's father summoned a mob like Laertes, or insisted on making an exhibition of himself in a crowded lecture-theatre to all the students of Wittenberg. Somehow we should feel it was not what a ghost would do, or even what a king would do, least of all what a wounded husband and brother would do. I could much more easily believe in the individual dead revisiting the individual living, in some strange moment or some solitary place, than in some vast cosmic telephone exchange in which Hamlet could ring up all the Kings of Denmark whenever he felt inclined. In short, I am a partisan of the antiquated spectre with clanking chains in the churchyard. I am by this time perhaps the solitary friend of the solitary ghost. He may, of course, be a deception; but those who think that he must be a deception, or is more likely to be a deception than the other, are ignorant of the psychology of men, and especially of the psychology of crowds. They forget that light can blind as well as darkness. They forget that there are illusions of the theatre as well as of the hermitage; that there are deceptions of unanimity as well as of solitude; and that things can be too large as well as too small to be seen.

(*Illustrated London News*, Feb. 7, 1925)

❖

Hamlet and the Danes

I am all for going to fairyland, but I am also all for coming back. That is, I will admire, but I will not be magnetised, either by mysticism or militarism. I am all for German fantasy, but I will resist German earnestness till I die. I am all for Grimm's Fairy Tales; but if there is such a thing as Grimm's Law, I would break it, if I knew what it was. . . . The Germans cannot really be deep because they will not consent to be superficial. They are bewitched by art, and stare at it, and cannot see round it. They will not believe that art is a light and a slight thing—a feather, even if it be from angelic wing. . . . We see this in that very typical process, the Germanising of Shakespeare. I do not complain of the Germans forgetting that Shakespeare was an Englishman. I complain of their forgetting that Shakespeare was a man; that he had moods, that he made mistakes, and, above all, that he knew his art was an art and not an attribute of deity. That is what is the matter with the Germans; they cannot "ring fancy's knell"; their knells have no gaiety. The phrase of Hamlet about "holding the mirror up to nature" is always quoted by such earnest critics as meaning that art is nothing if not realistic. But it really means (or at least its author really thought) that art is nothing if not artificial. Realists, like other barbarians, really *believe* the mirror; and therefore break the mirror. Also they leave out the phrase "as 'twere," which must be read into every remark of

Shakespeare, and especially every remark of Hamlet. What I mean by believing the mirror, and breaking it, can be recorded in one case I remember; in which a realistic critic quoted German authorities to prove that Hamlet had a particular psycho-pathological abnormality, which is admittedly nowhere mentioned in the play. The critic was bewitched; he was thinking of Hamlet as a real man, with a background behind him three dimensions deep—which does not exist in a looking-glass. "The best in this kind are but shadows." No German commentator has ever made an adequate note on that. Nevertheless, Shakespeare was an Englishman; he was nowhere more English than in his blunders; but he was nowhere more successful than in the description of very English types of character. And if anything is to be said about Hamlet, beyond what Shakespeare has said about him, I should say that Hamlet was an Englishman too. He was as much an Englishman as he was a gentleman, and he had the very grave weaknesses of both characters.

The chief English fault, especially in the nineteenth century, has been lack of decision, not only lack of decision in action, but lack of the equally essential decision in thought— which some call dogma.

("Hamlet and the Danes," *The Crimes of England*)

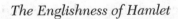

The Englishness of Hamlet

Hamlet always struck me as a particularly English character—which was, no doubt, the reason why he could not get on with the Danes, and had to be sent to England.
(*Illustrated London News*, Sept. 25, 1915)

——— ❖ ———

Hamlet's Education

It is very typical of the North Germans that they have turned *Hamlet* from a play into a puzzle, and make it merely mean that thought impedes action. Yet there is quite as good thought as Hamlet's, I will not say in Macbeth or Hotspur, but in Falstaff and Bottom the Weaver. Hamlet failed to act not because he thought, but because he thought in a particular way that does destroy the intellectual bases of action. In short, Hamlet failed to act because he had been taught to think at a German university. For him there was nothing, save to be Hamlet or else Fortinbras—a mere Force.

(*Illustrated London News*, Sept. 26, 1914)

——— ❖ ———

The Murderer as Maniac

I cannot understand why so many modern people like to be regarded as slaves. I mean the most dismal and degraded sort of slaves; moral and spiritual slaves. Popular preachers and fashionable novelists can safely repeat that men are only what their destiny makes them; and that there is no choice or challenge in the lot of man. Dean Inge declares, with a sort of gloomy glee, that some absurd American statistics or experiments show that heredity is an incurable disease and that education is no cure for it. Mr. Arnold Bennett says that many of his friends drink too much; but that it cannot be helped, because they cannot help it. I am not Puritanic about drink; I have drunk all sorts of things; and in my youth, often more than was good for me. But in any conceivable condition, drunk or sober, I should be furious at the suggestion that I could not help it. I should have wanted to punch the head of the consoling fatalist who told me so. Yet nobody seems to punch the heads of consoling fatalists. This, which seems to me the most elementary form of self-respect, seems to be the one thing about which even the sensitive are insensible. These modern persons are very sensitive about some things. They would be furious if somebody said they were not gentlemen; though there is really no more historical reason for pretending that every man is a gentleman than that every man is a marquis, or a man-at-arms. They are frightfully indignant if we say they are not Christians; though they hold themselves free to deny or doubt every conceivable idea of Christianity, even the historical existence of Christ. In the current cant of journalism and politics, they would almost prosecute us for slander if we said they were not Democrats; though any number of them actually prefer aristocracy or autocracy; and the real Democrats in English society are rather a select few. We might almost say that the true believers in democracy are themselves an aristocracy. About all these words men can be morbidly excitable and touchy. They must not be called pagans or plebeians or plain men or reactionaries or oligarchs. But they may be called slaves; they may be called monkeys; and, above all, they may be called machines. One could imagine that the really intolerable insult to human dignity would be to say that human life is not determined by human will. But so long as we do not say they are heathen, we may say they are not human. We may say that they develop as blindly as a plant or turn as automatically as a wheel.

There are all sorts of ways in which this humiliating heresy expresses itself. One is the perpetual itch to describe all crime as lunacy. Now, quite apart from virtue, I would much rather be thought a criminal than a criminal lunatic. As a point not of virtue but of vanity, I should be less insulted by the title of a murderer than by the title of a homicidal maniac. The murderer might be said, not unfairly, to have lost the first fragrance of his innocence, and all that keeps the child near to the cherubim. But the maniac has lost more than innocence; he has lost essence, the complete personality that makes him a man. Yet everybody is talking as if it would be quite natural, and even nice, to be excused for immorality on the ground of idiocy. The principle is applied, with every flourish of liberality and charity, to personalities whom one would imagine quite proud of being personal. It is applied not only to the trivial and transient villains of real life, but to the far more solid and convincing villains of romance.

I saw the other day that a distinguished doctor had written a book about the madmen of Shakespeare. By which he did not mean those few fantastic and manifest madmen, whom we might almost call professional madmen, who merely witnessed to the late Elizabethan craze for lurid and horrible grotesques. Ford or Webster, or some of their fellows, would hardly have hesitated to have a ballet or chorus of maniacs, like a chorus of fairies or fashionable beauties. But the medical gentleman seems to have said that any number of the serious characters were mad. Macbeth was mad; Hamlet was mad; Ophelia was congenitally mad; and so on. If Hamlet was really mad, there does not seem much point in his pretending to be mad. If Ophelia was always mad, there does not seem much point in her going mad. But anyhow, I think a saner criticism will always maintain that Hamlet was sane. He must be sane even in order to be sad; for when we get into a world of complete unreality, even tragedy is unreal. No lunatic ever had so good a sense of humour as Hamlet. A homicidal maniac does not say: "Your wisdom would show itself more richer to signify that to his doctor"; he is a little too sensitive on the subject of doctors. The whole point of Hamlet is that he is really saner than anybody else in the play; though I admit that being sane is not identical with what some call being sensible. Being outside the world, he sees all round it; where everybody else sees his own side of the world, his own worldly ambition, or hatred or love. But, after all, Hamlet pretended to be mad in order to deceive fools. We cannot complain if he has succeeded.

But, whatever we may say about Hamlet, we must not say this about Macbeth. Hamlet was only a mild sort of murderer; a more or less accidental and parenthetical murderer; an amateur. But Macbeth was a good, solid, serious, self-respecting murderer; and we must not have any nonsense about him. For the play of *Macbeth* is, in the supreme and special sense, the Christian Tragedy; to be set against the pagan Tragedy of Oedipus. It is the whole point about Oedipus that he does not know what he is doing. And it is the whole point about Macbeth that he does know what he is doing. It is not a tragedy of Fate but a tragedy of Freewill. He is tempted of a devil, but he is not driven by a destiny. If the actor pronounces the words properly, the whole audience ought to feel that the story may yet have an entirely new ending, when Macbeth says suddenly: "We will proceed no further in this business." The incredible confusion of modern thought is always suggesting that any indication that men have been influenced is an indication that they have been forced. All men are always being influenced; for every incident is an influence. The question is, which incident shall we allow to be most influential. Macbeth was influenced; but he consented to be influenced. He was not, like a blind tragic pagan, obeying; something he thought he ought to obey. He does not worship the Three Witches like the Three Fates. He is a good enlightened Christian, and sins against the light.

The fancy for reading fatalism into this play, where it is most absent, is probably due to the fallacy of a series; or three things in a row. It misleads Macbeth's critics just as it misleads Macbeth. Almost all our pseudo-science proceeds on the principle of saying that one thing follows on another thing, and then dogmatising about the third thing that is to follow. The whole argument about the Superman, for instance, as developed by Nietzsche and other sophists, depends entirely on this trick of the incomplete triad. First the scientist or sophist asserts that when there was a monkey, there was bound to be a man. Then he simply prophesies that something will follow the man, as the man followed the monkey. This is exactly the trick used by the Witches in Macbeth. They give him first a fact he knows already, that he is Thane of Glamis; then one fact really confirmed in the future, that he is Thane of Cawdor; and then something that is not a fact at all, and need never be a fact at all, unless he chooses to make it one out of his own murderous fancy. This false series, seeming to point at something, though the first term is trivial and the last untrue, does certainly mislead many with a fallacious sense of fate. It has been used by materialists in many ways to destroy the sense of moral liberty; and it has murdered many things besides Duncan.

("On a Humiliating Heresy," *Come to Think of It*. Originally from *Illustrated London News*, September 21, 1929)

❖

Ophelia's Madness

We do not sympathise with reckless imputations of universal power to Shakespeare—to be the greatest of earthly dramatists is enough for one son of Adam. We do not hold the theory that Shakespeare could have been Lord Chancellor; nor the alternative transatlantic theory that the Lord Chancellor succeeded in being Shakespeare. But we do seriously believe he might have been a great painter. Among the mazes of psychological interest, too little notice has been taken of his unique habit of symbolising his moral crises in singularly highly coloured and arresting pictorial groups. All other poets give a general sense of decorative unity—he alone is in love with contrasts, the contrasts of figure landscape and costume which make practical pictures. Touchstone and the Shepherd, Bottom and the Fairies, Lear and the Fool, Hamlet and the Gravediggers, are all scenes in which moral irony is expressed in definite diversities of colour and form. And in this he is qualified to unite the arts. He is a symbolist: he represents the mysterious mental connection between shapes and ideas, which must finally defeat any purely technical view of painting. A man can no more see certain clouds at evening without growing thoughtful than he can see a Bengal tiger without jumping. Both feelings are equally primal, fundamental, anthropological. Of all Shakespearian characters, that which has most perplexed actresses is Ophelia—probably, we think, because she was a pictorial rather than a psychological creation—and the bodily vision of weak, wild beauty, crowned with flowers and dancing to death, meant more to him than he could express in the character. . . . Ophelia's madness was little more than a slight improvement on her previous intelligence; she was never sane enough to go

vigorously mad. It was far different, for example, with Lear
... the wandering King against which no charges of mental
lucidity can be brought. Here we have the madness of a
strong man and a king, the madness which, rising into the
sublimity of Job, could welcome fire and hail, since they
were not his daughters.

(*The Bookman*, July, 1900)

❖

The Macbeths

In studying any eternal tragedy the first question necessarily is what part of tragedy is eternal. If there be any element in man's work which is in any sense permanent it must
have this characteristic, that it rebukes first one generation
and then another, but rebukes them always in opposite
directions and for opposite faults. The ideal world is always
sane. The real world is always mad. But it is mad about a
different thing every time; all the things that have been are
changing and inconstant. The only thing that is really reliable is the thing that has never been. All very great classics
of art are a rebuke to extravagance not in one direction but
in all directions. The figure of a Greek Venus is a rebuke to
the fat women of Rubens and also a rebuke to the thin
women of Aubrey Beardsley. In the same way, Christianity,
which in its early years fought the Manicheans because they
did not believe in anything but spirit, has now to fight the
Manicheans because they do not believe in anything but
matter. This is perhaps the test of a very great work of classic creation, that it can be attacked on inconsistent grounds,
and that it attacks its enemies on inconsistent grounds. Here
is a broad and simple test. If you hear a thing being accused

of being too tall and too short, too red and too green, too bad in one way and too bad also in the opposite way, then you may be sure that it is very good.

This preface is essential if we are to profit by the main meaning of *Macbeth*. For the play is so very great that it covers much more than it appears to cover; it will certainly survive our age as it has survived its own; it will certainly leave the twentieth century behind as calmly and completely as it has left the seventeenth century behind. Hence if we ask for the meaning of this classic we must necessarily ask the meaning for our own time. It might have another shade of meaning for another period of time. If, as is possible, there should be a barbaric return and if history is any kind of guide, it will destroy everything else before it destroys great literature. The high and civilized sadness of Virgil was enjoyed literally through the darkest instant of the Dark Ages. Long after a wealthier generation has destroyed Parliament they will retain Shakespeare. Men will enjoy the greatest tragedy of Shakespeare even in the thick of the greatest tragedy of Europe.

It is quite possible that Shakespeare may come to be enjoyed by men far simpler than the men for whom he wrote. Voltaire called him a great savage; we may come to the time far darker than the Dark Ages when he will really be enjoyed by savages. Then the story of Macbeth will be read by a man in the actual position of Macbeth. Then the Thane of Glamis may profit by the disastrous superstitions of the Thane of Cawdor. Then the Thane of Cawdor may really resist the impulse to be King of Scotland. There would be a very simple but a real moral if Macbeth could read *Macbeth*. "Do not listen to evil spirits; do not let your ambition run away with you; do not murder old gentlemen in bed; do not kill other people's wives and children as a part of diplomacy; for if you do these things it is highly probable that you will have a bad time." That is the lesson that Macbeth would have learnt from *Macbeth*; that is the lesson that some barbarians of the future may possibly learn from *Macbeth*. And it is a true lesson. Great work has something to say quite simply to the simple.

The barbarians would understand *Macbeth* as a solid warning against vague and violent ambition; and it is such a warning, and they would take along with it this lesson also, which is none the worse because perhaps only the barbarians could adequately understand it. "Distrust those malevolent spirits who speak flatteringly to you. They are not benevolent spirits; if they were they would be more likely to beat you about the head."

Before we talk then of the lesson of a great work of art, let us realize that it has a different lesson for different ages, because it is itself eternal. And let us realize that such a lesson will be in our own day not absolute but suited to the particular vices or particular misfortunes of that day. We are not in any danger at the moment of the positive and concrete actions which correspond to those of *Macbeth*. The good old habit of murdering kings (which was the salvation of so many commonwealths in the past) has fallen into desuetude. The idea of such a play must be for us (and for our sins) more subtle. The idea is more subtle but it is almost inexpressibly great. Let us before reading the play consider if only for a moment what is the main idea of *Macbeth* for modern men.

One great idea on which all tragedy builds is the idea of the continuity of human life. The one thing a man cannot do is exactly what all modern artists and free lovers are always trying to do. He cannot cut his life up into separate sections. The case of the modern claim for freedom in love is the first and most obvious that occurs to the mind; therefore I use it for this purpose of illustration. You cannot have an idyll with Maria and an episode with Jane; there is no such thing as an episode. There is no such thing as an idyll. It is idle to talk about abolishing the tragedy of marriage when you cannot abolish the tragedy of sex. Every flirtation is a marriage; it is a marriage in this frightful sense; that it is irrevocable. I have taken this case of sexual relations as one out of a hundred; but of any case in human life the thing is true. The basis of all tragedy is that man lives a coherent and continuous life. It is only a worm that you can cut in two and leave the severed parts still alive. You can cut a worm up into episodes and they are still living episodes. You can cut a worm up into idylls and they are quite brisk and lively idylls. You can do all this to him precisely because he is a worm. You cannot cut a man up and leave him kicking, precisely because he is a man. We know this because man even in his lowest and darkest manifestation has always this characteristic of physical and psychological unity. His identity continues long enough to see the end of many of his own acts; he cannot be cut off from his past with a hatchet; as he sows so shall he reap.

This then is the basis of all tragedy, this living and perilous continuity which does not exist in the lower creatures. This is the basis of all tragedy, and this is certainly the basis of *Macbeth*. The great ideas of *Macbeth*, uttered in the first few scenes with a tragic energy which has never been equalled perhaps in Shakespeare or out of him, is the idea of the enormous mistake a man makes if he supposes that one decisive act will clear his way. Macbeth's ambition, though selfish and someway sullen, is not in itself criminal or morbid. He wins the title of Glamis in honourable war; he deserves and gets the title of Cawdor; he is rising in the world and has a not ignoble exhilaration in doing so. Suddenly a new ambition is presented to him (of the agency and atmosphere which presents it I shall speak in a moment) and he realizes that nothing lies across his path to the Crown of Scotland except the sleeping body of Duncan. If he does that one cruel thing, he can be infinitely kind and happy.

Here, I say, is the first and most formidable of the great actualities of *Macbeth*. You cannot do a mad thing in order to reach sanity. Macbeth's mad resolve is not a cure even for his own irresolution. He was indecisive before his decision. He is, if possible, more indecisive after he has decided. The crime does not get rid of the problem. Its effect is so bewildering that one may say that the crime does not get rid of the temptation. Make a morbid decision and you will only become more morbid; do a lawlesss thing and you will only get into an atmosphere much more suffocating than that of law. Indeed, it is a mistake to speak of a man as "breaking out." The lawless man never breaks out; he breaks in. He smashes a door and finds himself in another room, he smashes a wall and finds himself in a yet smaller one. The more he shatters the more his habitation shrinks. Where he ends you may read in the end of *Macbeth*.

For us moderns, therefore, the first philosophical significance of the play is this; that our life is one thing and that our lawless acts limit us; every time we break a law we make a limitation. In some strange way hidden in the deeps of human psychology, if we build our palace on some unknown wrong it turns very slowly into our prison. Macbeth at the end of the play is not merely a wild beast; he is a caged wild beast. But if this is the thing to be put in a primary position there is something else that demands at least our second one. The second idea in the main story of *Macbeth* is, of course, that of the influence of evil suggestion upon the soul, particularly evil suggestion of a mystical and transcendental kind. In this connection the mystical character of the promptings is not more interesting than the mystical character of the man to whom they are especially sent. Mystical promptings are naturally sweet to a mystic. The character of Macbeth in this regard has been made the matter of a great deal of brilliant and futile discussion. Some critics have represented him as a burly silent soldier because he won battles for his country. Other critics have represented him as a feverish and futile decadent because he makes long practical speeches full of the most elaborate imagery. In the name of commonsense let it be remembered that Shakespeare lived before the time when unsuccessful poets thought it poetical to be decadent and unsuccessful soldiers thought it military to be silent. Men like Sidney and Raleigh and Essex could have fought as well as Macbeth and could have ranted as well as Macbeth. Why should Shakespeare shrink from making a great general talk poetry when half the great generals of his time actually wrote great poetry?

The whole legend, therefore, which some critics have based on the rich rhetoric of *Macbeth*: the legend that Macbeth was a febrile and egotistical coward because he liked the sound of his own voice, may be dismissed as a manifestation of the diseases of later days. Shakespeare meant Macbeth for a fine orator for he made fine speeches; he also meant him for a fine soldier because he made him not only win battles bravely but what is much more to the point, lose battles bravely; he made him, when overwhelmed by enemies in heaven and earth, die the death of a hero. But Macbeth is meant to be among other things an orator and a poet; and it is to Macbeth in this capacity that the evil supernatural appeal is made. If there be any such thing as evil influences coming from beyond the world, they have never been so suggestively indicated as they are here. They appeal, as evil always does, to the existence of a coherent and comprehensible scheme. It is the essence of a nightmare that it turns the whole cosmos against us. Two of their prophecies have been fulfilled; may it not be assumed then that the third will also be fulfilled?

Also they appeal, as evil always does (being slavish itself and believing all men slaves) to the inevitable. They put Macbeth's good fortune before him as if it were not so much a fortune as a fate. In the same way imperialists sought to salve the consciences of Englishmen by giving them the offer of gold and empire with all the gloom of predestination. When the devil, and the witches who are the servants of the devil, wish to make a weak man snatch a crown that does not belong to him, they are too cunning to come to him and say "Will you be King?" They say without further parley, "All hail, Macbeth, that shall be king hereafter". This weakness Macbeth really has; that he is easily attracted by that kind of spiritual fatalism which relieves the human creature of a great part of his responsibility. In this way there is a strange and sinister appropriateness in the way in which the promises of the evil spirits end in new fantasies; end, so to speak, as mere diabolical jokes. Macbeth accepts as a piece of unreasoning fate first his crime and then his crown. It is appropriate that this fate which he has accepted as external and irrational should end in incidents of mere extravagant bathos, in the walking forest and strange birth of Macduff. He has once surrendered himself with a kind of dark and evil faith, to a machinery of destiny that he can neither respect nor understand, and it is the proper sequel of this that the machinery should produce a situation which crushes him as something useless.

Shakespeare does not mean that Macbeth's emotionalism and rich rhetoric prove him to be unmanly in any ordinary sense. But Shakespeare does mean, I think, to suggest that the man, virile in his essential structure, has this weak spot in his artistic temperament; that fear of the mere strength of destiny and of unknown spirits, of their strength as apart from their virtue, which is the only proper significance of the word superstition. No man can be superstitious who loves his God, even if the god be Mumbo-Jumbo. Macbeth has something of this fear and fatalism; and fatalism is exactly the point at which rationalism passes silently into superstition. Macbeth, in short, has any amount of physical courage, he has even a great deal of moral courage. But he lacks what may be called spiritual courage; he lacks a certain freedom and dignity of the human soul in the universe, a freedom and dignity which one of the scriptural writers expresses as the difference between the servants and the sons of God.

But the man Macbeth and his marked but inadequate manliness, can only be expressed in connection with the character of his wife. And the question of Lady Macbeth immediately arouses again the controversies that have surrounded this play. Miss Ellen Terry and Sir Henry Irving acted *Macbeth* upon the theory that Macbeth was a feeble and treacherous man and that Lady Macbeth was a frail and clinging woman. A somewhat similar view of Lady Macbeth has been, I believe, consistently uttered by a distinguished American actress. The question as commonly stated, in short, is the question of whether Macbeth was really masculine, and second, of whether Lady Macbeth was not really feminine. The old critics assumed that because Lady Macbeth obviously ruled her husband she must have been a masculine woman. The whole inference of course is false.

Masculine women may rule the Borough Council, but they never rule their husbands. The women who rule their husbands are the feminine women and I am entirely in accord with those who think that Lady Macbeth must have been a very feminine woman. But while some critics rightly insist on the feminine character of Lady Macbeth they endeavour to deprive Macbeth of that masculine character which is obviously the corollary of the other. They think Lady Macbeth must be a man because she rules. And on the same idiotic principle they think that Macbeth must be a woman or a coward or a decadent or something odd because he is ruled. The most masculine kind of man always is ruled. As a friend of mine once said, very truly, physical cowards are the only men who are not afraid of women.

The real truth about Macbeth and his wife is somewhat strange but cannot be too strongly stated. Nowhere else in all his wonderful works did Shakespeare describe the real character of the relations of the sexes so sanely, or so satisfactorily as he describes it here. The man and the woman are never more normal than they are in this abnormal and horrible story. *Romeo and Juliet* does not better describe love than this describes marriage. The dispute that goes on between Macbeth and his wife about the murder of Duncan is almost word for word a dispute which goes on at any suburban breakfast-table about something else. It is merely a matter of changing "Infirm of purpose, give me the daggers", into "infirm of purpose, give me the postage stamps". And it is quite a mistake to suppose that the woman is to be called masculine or even in any exclusive sense strong. The strengths of the two partners differ in kind. The woman has more of that strength on the spot which is called industry. The man has more of that strength in reserve which is called laziness.

But the acute truth of this actual relation is much deeper even than that. Lady Macbeth exhibits one queer and astounding kind of magnanimity which is quite peculiar to women. That is, she will take something that her husband dares not do but which she knows he wants to do and she will become more fierce for it than he is. For her, as for all very feminine souls (that is, very strong ones) selfishness is the only thing which is acutely felt as sin; she will commit any crime if she is not committing it only for herself. Her husband thirsts for the crime egotistically and therefore vaguely, darkly, and subconsciously, as a man becomes conscious of the beginnings of physical thirst. But she thirsts for the crime altruistically and therefore clearly and sharply, as a man perceives a public duty to society. She puts the thing in plain words, with an acceptance of extremes. She has that perfect and splendid cynicism of women which is the most terrible thing God has made. I say it without irony and without any undue enjoyment of the slight element of humour.

If you want to know what are the permanent relations of the married man with the married woman you cannot read it anywhere more accurately than in the little domestic idyll of Mr. and Mrs. Macbeth. Of a man so male and a woman so female, I cannot believe anything except that they ultimately save their souls. Macbeth was strong in every masculine sense up to the very last moment; he killed himself in battle. Lady Macbeth was strong in the very female sense which is perhaps a more courageous sense; she killed herself, but not in battle. As I say, I cannot think that souls so strong and so elemental have not retained those permanent possibilities of humility and gratitude which ultimately place the soul in heaven. But wherever they are they are together.

For alone among so many of the figures of human fiction, they are actually married.

(From *The Spice of Life*. Originally from *John o'London's Weekly*, Jan. 5, 1951)

———— ❖ ————

The Moral Mystery in Tragedy

It is not easy to point to anything that is entirely Creative. In ultimate philosophy, as in ultimate theology, men are not capable of creation, but only of combination. But there is a workable meaning of the word, which I take to be this: some image evoked by the individual imagination which might never have been evoked by any other imagination, and adds something to the imagery of the world. I call it Creative to write "the multitudinous seas incarnadine." I call it Creative by three real and even practical tests: first, that nobody need ever have thought of such a thing if Mr. William Shakespeare had not happened to think of it; second, that while it is an apocalyptic, or titanic, it is not really an anarchic idea; it is gigantic, but it does not merely sprawl; it fits into the frame of thought exactly as the sea fits into all the fretted bays and creeks of the world. Also, in passing, with all its tragic occasion, it is a *jolly* image; it gives the mere imagination a positive and passionate joy of colour, like the joy of drinking a purple sea of wine. But, thirdly and most essentially, it does reveal the moral mystery that is the whole meaning of such a tragedy; expressed by the knocking without which startles the assassins within; the notion of the thin partition between the crime that is hidden in the house and the sin that fills the universe; what was meant by saying that things said in the inner chamber should be proclaimed from the housetops; the true idea of the Day of Judgment, in which the world is, really and truly, turned inside out. It may also be added that that astonishing phrase is not only a speech, but a gesture. It is dramatic, in the vital sense, to suppose that dipping a finger could suddenly turn all the seas of the world to scarlet. But this very drama is a morality, and it would mean nothing that the seas were scarlet unless the sins were scarlet. . . . It ought not to matter whether the spot on Lady Macbeth's finger was blood or red ink; or whether she turned the multitudinous seas the colour of carnage or tomato soup. It is evidently a very soothing and insulated condition of intellect, and avoids all the disturbing currents of ethical and theological criticism. There is nothing to be said against it; except that, if everybody were in that scientific state of mind, nobody could write *Macbeth*.

And there, as it seems to me, the whole theory of uncritical and uncriticised creative art breaks down. As a mere matter of fact, you cannot make any sense of *Macbeth* unless you not only recognise but share a decided horror of murder. And how you can be shocked by Murder and not moved by Morality I do not know. And if being Critical means the tracing of these electric wires or burglar-alarms, these live wires of the laws of life which do, in fact, give shocks when they are touched or transgressed, then it is not merely the classical critics who are critical. It is Shakespeare who is critical; nay, it is Lady Macbeth who is critical; she is extremely critical of Lady Macbeth. If the recognition of the real Ten Commandments of life and death is only being critical, then all the great creative artists are critical; and they would not be creative if they were not critical. Lady Macbeth would never see that blasting vision of a bloodshot world, except in the last agony of self-criticism.

(*Illustrated London News*, April 11, 1931)

———— ❖ ————

Free Will and the Drama

What fun it would be if good actors suddenly acted like real people! I do not mean anything about tone, manner, or gesture. The actor does not behave, even in public life, a scrap more artificially than does many a minister, parson or politician, even in private life. Every man has an accent; and no man knows he has it. Every man has an accent: and, to that extent, every man has an affectation. You and I are at least always clever enough to speak the speech of our class. Our limitation is, that though we can speak it, we cannot hear it. We cannot hear it as the other classes hear it. There is no convention of the theatre that may not tomorrow be the convention of the world. There is no conceivable drawl or bleat or bellow from one end of a Surrey melodrama to the other which might not easily become the admitted accent of the best society. Dropping the "h" might be as good English as it is French. Already the ladies on the stage are often less painted than the ladies in the stalls. Already the footlights are a faint and flickering barrier; *il n'y a plus de Pyrénées*. No; I mean nothing about natural or "quietly realistic" acting: that ideal is much too faint and far. When people have begun to act like life in a drawing-room, it will be time enough to ask them to act like life on a stage.

No, I mean something much funnier than that—as the man in Jerome's excellent tale said when he had told the dullest story ever endured by men. I mean the funniest of all earthly things: I mean what I say. I mean what fun it would be if actors suddenly acted as if they were in real life. Suppose they were to act *freely*; to change their minds. Suppose that when Joseph Surface told Lady Teazle to hide behind the screen, she said she wouldn't. Suppose she said there was no harm in visiting so virtuous a gentleman; and that she specially wanted to talk to Sir Peter on a point about the weekly washing. What *would* happen to the great Screen Scene? What would everybody do? Suppose Hamlet ended the soliloquy "To be or not to be" by suddenly deciding not to be. Suppose he really did his quietus make with a bare bodkin. What would the Gravedigger do? What would Osric do? It is awful to think of. Or, to take a far more terrible passage, suppose when Macbeth says, "We will proceed no further in this business"—suppose he stuck to his words! Suppose he declined to be henpecked. Suppose he raised on the stage the red banner of the revolted male against the eternal female tyranny. A gladiatorial show, with real men butchered, would be far less exciting.

We are always hearing about the limits of realism in art; that is, of this or that respect in which a written thing can never be quite like an acted thing. It seems odd to me that nobody ever mentions the chief chasm of cleavage between the thing written and the thing done. It turns on the old pivot of what theologians call Free Will. The difference is that all events in genuine art are decided: all events in genuine life (in anything worth calling life) are undecided. What is written is written [John 19:22] (to quote a Roman governor who showed his taste for epigram at a somewhat unlucky moment); what is written is written; but what is doing need not be done. Every artistic drama is named on the first page a tragedy or a comedy. That is because in every artistic drama the last page is written before the first. But it is not so in that terrific drama which Heaven has given us to play upon this earth, without any punctual cues, with a very invisible, and sometimes inaudible, prompter, and without the faintest notion about when the curtain will come down.

If the drama of real life is more dreadful, it has at least one agreeable quality; it is more uncertain. Every human life begins in tragedy, for it begins in travail. But every human life may end in comedy—even in divine comedy. It may end in a joy beyond all our jokes; in that cry across the chasm, "Fear not, I have conquered the world." [John 16:33] Real human life differs from all imitations of it in the fact that it can perpetually alter itself as it goes along. Art can hardly survive one such change. It could not possibly survive a series of such changes. The full cataract of Dickens's creative power was hardly strong enough to carry him round those two or three corners where the stream of his story really altered its course. Of a fictitious story we may say decisively that it should go as straight as possible to its end. Or, to put it another way, the sooner we have finished a novel the better. But of a real story, as distinct from a fictitious story, we may say that the more the stream straggles this way and that, the more likely it is to be a clean or even sacred stream. It proves its wish to go right by so often confessing that it has gone wrong.

I began to think of all these things in the last days of the late performances of Sir Herbert Tree's *Macbeth*. My meditation comes too late—like my copy. I am one of those who are doomed (an immoral expression) to be always late. I had a relative who came late for the Battle of Waterloo; and I sometimes almost hope that I myself may come late for the Day of Judgment. But though it was at Sir Herbert Tree's performance that I began thinking, I have only just finished thinking. And though I have not always agreed by any means with Sir Herbert's interpretation of great Shakespearean characters, I am bound to say that in this case he gave me, in the middle of a settled and hackneyed story, the electric shock of moral liberty. When he said, "We

will proceed no further in this business," for an instant I
thought he wouldn't—though I have read *Macbeth* a hundred times. In the midst of life we are in death: in that one
dead pageantry, in the midst of death I was in life. I thought
for a flash that the play might end differently. Alas! the play
was written more than three hundred years ago.

Calvinists objected to stage-plays. Yet all stage-plays are
forced to be Calvinistic. They are forced, by the very nature
of art, to damn or save a man from the beginning. That is
why the old Greek plays about fatality succeeded. Such
dramas were popular in spite of everything that could be
unpopular, and everything that could be undramatic—in
spite of masks and monologues and a shallow stage and an
absence of incident. They suited the drama because they
were full of destiny.

And yet I still think that the greatest drama of all is that
in which the throne of destiny is shaken for an instant. I
think the greatest drama in the world is *Macbeth*. I think
Macbeth the one supreme drama because it is the one
Christian drama; and I will accept the accusation of prejudice. But I mean by Christian (in this matter) the strong
sense of spiritual liberty and of sin; the idea that the best
man can be as bad as he chooses. You may call Othello a
victim of chance. You may call Hamlet a victim of temperament. You cannot call Macbeth anything but a victim of
Macbeth. The evil spirits tempt him, but they never force
him: they never even frighten him, for he is a very brave
man. I have often wondered that no one has made so obvious a parallel as that between the murders of Macbeth and
the marriages of Henry VIII. Both Henry and Macbeth
were originally brave, good-humoured men, better rather
than worse than their neighbours. Both Henry and Macbeth
hesitated over their first crime—the first stabbing and the

first divorce. Both found out the fate which is in evil—for Macbeth went on murdering and poor Henry went on marrying. There is only one fault in the parallel. Unfortunately for history, Henry VIII was not deposed.

(Also published under the title "Realism in Art". Originally from *Illustrated London News*, March 16, 1912)

❖

Out, Damned Spot!

I notice a curiously modern and sullen realism beginning to settle on some of the recognised tales of murder, once so gay, innocent, and refreshing. Once our detective art really was almost an unmoral art, and therefore the one which managed to remain almost a moral art. But shades of the prison-house—or, worse still, of the humane reformatory and the psychological clinic—begin to close upon the growing boy and the hopeful butcher of his kind. We are given detailed descriptions of depressing domestic interiors, as if being dumbly asked whether a wife so involved in the washing or the dusting or the spring-cleaning was not eventually bound to murder or be murdered in any case. It is all very well, but I would point out to the sanguinary sophist that the argument can be turned the other way. If it be true that a misguided wife may begin thoughtlessly by doing the washing, and find all sorts of vexatious consequences, possibly including death by violence, so it is equally true that she may begin by using murder as a minor gadget in the domestic machinery, taking death by violence in her stride as a plain, practical solution; and then, after all, find herself involved in a most inordinate amount of washing.

There could not be a grimmer example of this tragedy than poor Lady Macbeth. She had her faults, perhaps, but there is no ground for accusing her of any rooted or aboriginal taste for hygiene. When she was young and innocent, her imagination seems to have been quite unpolluted by the impure image of soap. I should even hesitate to accuse her of spring-cleaning in the serious, anti-social, and sinful sense of the term. Anyhow, a number of very different birds seem to have nested undisturbed over the main entrance to the reception-rooms; which looks as if she was once a human being, and more interested in spring-broods than in spring-cleaning. Unfortunately, like such a very large number of people living in dark, barbarous, ignorant, and ferocious times, she was full of modern ideas. She tended especially to maintain the two brightest and most philosophical of modern ideas: first, that it is often extremely convenient to do what is wrong; and second, that whenever it is convenient to do what is wrong, it immediately becomes what is right. Illuminated by these two scientific searchlights of the twentieth century in her groping among the stark trees and stone pillars of the Dark Ages, Lady Macbeth thought it quite simple and businesslike to kill an old gentleman of very little survival value, and offer her own talents to the world in the capacity of Queen. It seems natural enough; to most of us who are used to the morals of modern novels, it will seem almost humdrum and tiresomely obvious. And yet see what a snag there was in it after all!

On this one doomed and devoted woman, who had done nothing but a little bit of a murder which she thought little enough of at the time (as De Quincey says), there fell from heaven like the Deluge the deathly curse of Cleanliness. She, who seems never to have known such morbidities before, was tortured with horrid suggestions of washing her hands, and pursued by furies who seem to have taken the form of modern salesmen offering different brands of soap. Those ambitions of the housewife, which seem to the modern moralist so obvious a cause of murder, were, in fact, wildly exaggerated in her case as a consequence of murder. It was the worst doom of the murderess that she wanted to do the washing not on Monday, but at midnight; that she wanted to have a spring-cleaning not in the spring of the year, but in the middle of the night. Who shall say lightly that a murder or two does not matter, when it may lead to the murderess becoming as hygienic as all that?

Sinister minds may be clouded by dark and unworthy suspicions that the views here discussed are not wholly serious; but some of the modern moralists favouring murder, and other simple solutions of social difficulties, are serious with a dry-throated earnestness that no satire could simulate.

(*Illustrated London News*, Mar. 10, 1934)

———— ❖ ————

Eye of Newt and Toe of Frog

Whenever men really believe that they can get to the spiritual, they always employ the material. When the purpose is good, it is bread and wine; when the purpose is evil, it is eye of newt and toe of frog. In this particular matter the witch's charm included the hair of a black cat. But this is no more insane than the ingredients that have been immortalised by Shakespeare. And indeed it is beside the mark to call such ingredients insane. They are intended to be insane. They are chosen because they are insane. They are meant to put men into communication with the insane elements in the universe—with the lunatics of the spiritual world. How far they can succeed nobody can tell; but it is as reasonable to suppose that ugly actions (like tearing off a frog's toe) may dispose us towards bad influences as to suppose that beautiful actions (like kneeling or uncovering of the head) may dispose us towards good ones. How much is the act and how much the association we do not know; but neither do we know it in daily life. If you are braced with a sea bath you do not know how much of it is the chemistry of the salt and how much of it is the poetry of the sea. If you are warmed with a glass of wine you do not know how much of it is wine and how much of it is the idea of wine.

(*Illustrated London News*, Oct. 6, 1906)

——— ❖ ———

The Tragedy Of King Lear

The tragedy of King Lear, in some of its elements perhaps the very greatest of all the Shakespearian tragedies, is relatively seldom played. It is even possible to have a dark suspicion that it is not universally read; with the usual deplorable result; that it is universally quoted. Perhaps nothing has done so much to weaken the greatest of English achievements, and to leave it open to facile revolt or fatigued reaction, than the abominable habit of quoting Shakespeare without reading Shakespeare. It has encouraged all the pompous theatricality which first created an idolatry and then an iconoclasm; all that florid tradition in which old playgoers and after-dinner speakers talked about the Bard or the Swan of Avon, until it was comparatively easy, at the end of the Victorian era, for somebody like Bernard Shaw to propose an Edwardian massacre of Bards and almost to insinuate that the swan was a goose. Most of the trouble came from what are called "Familiar Quotations", which were hardly even representative or self-explanatory quotations. In almost all the well-known passages from Shakespeare, to quote the passage is to miss the point. It is almost needless to note what may be called the vulgar examples; as in the case of those who say that Shakespeare asks, "What is in a name?"; which is rather like saying that Shakespeare says murder must be done, and it were best if it were done quickly. The popular inference always is that Shakespeare thought that names do not matter; there being possibly no man on God's earth who was less likely to think so, than the man who made such magnificent mouthfuls out of mandragora and hurricanes, of the names of Hesperides or Hercules. The remark has no point, except in the purely personal circumstances in which it has poignancy, in the mouth of a girl commanded to hate a man she loves, because of a name that seems to her to have nothing to do with him. The play now under consideration is no exception to this disastrous rule. The old woman who complained that the tragedy of *Hamlet* was so full of quotations would have found almost as many in the tragedy of *King Lear*. And they would have had the same character as those from *Hamlet* or *Romeo and Juliet*: that those who leave out the context really leave out the conception. They have a mysterious power of making the world weary of a few fixed and disconnected words, and yet leaving the world entirely ignorant of the real meaning of those words.

Thus, in the play of *King Lear*, there are certain words which everybody has heard hundreds of times, in connections either intentionally or unintentionally absurd. We have all read or heard of somebody saying, "How sharper than a serpent's tooth it is to have a thankless child." Somehow the very words sound as if they were mouthed by some tipsy

actor or silly and senile person in a comic novel. I do not
know why these particular words, as words, should be
selected for citation. Shakespeare was a casual writer; he
was often especially careless about metaphors, careless
about making them and careless about mixing them. There
is nothing particularly notable about this particular metaphor of the tooth; it might just as well have been a wolf's
tooth or a tiger's tooth. The lines quoted only become
remarkable when we read them with the rest of the scene,
and with a very much more remarkable passage, which is
never quoted at all. The whole point of Lear's remark is
that, when buffeted by the first insult of Goneril, he breaks
forth into a blasting bodily curse upon the woman, praying
first that she may have no children, then that she may have
horrible and unnatural children, that she may give birth to a
monstrosity, *that she may feel how*, etc. Without that terrible implication, the serpent is entirely harmless and his
teeth are drawn. I cannot imagine why only the weakest
lines in the speech are everlastingly repeated, and the strongest lines in it are never mentioned at all.

A man might well harden into the horrid suspicion that
most people have hardly read the play at all, when he
remembers how many things there are in it that are not
repeated, and yet would certainly be remembered. There
are things in it that no man who has read them can ever
forget. Amid all the thunders of the storm, it comes like a
new clap of thunder, when the thought first crosses the mad
king's mind that he must not complain of wind and storm
and lightning, because they are not his daughters. "I never
gave you kingdoms, called you children." And I imagine that
the great imaginative invention of the English, the thing
called Nonsense, never rose to such a height and sublimity
of unreason and horror, as when the Fool juggles with time

and space and tomorrow and yesterday, as he says soberly at the end of his rant: "This prophecy Merlin shall make; for I live before his time." This is one of the Shakespearian shocks or blows that take the breath away. But in the same scene of the storm and the desolate wandering, there is another example of the sort of thing I mean in the matter of quotation. It is not so strong an example, because the words are very beautiful in themselves; and have often been applied beautifully to pathetic human circumstances not unworthy of them. Nevertheless, they are something not only superior, but quite startlingly different, in the circumstances in which they really stand. We have all of us heard a hundred times that some unlucky law-breaker, or more or less pardonable profligate, was "more sinned against than sinning". But the words thus used have not a hundredth part of the point and power of the words as used by Lear. The point of the passage is that he himself challenges the cosmic powers to a complete examination; that he finds in his despair a sort of dizzy detachment of the intellect, and strikes the balance to his own case with a kind of insane impartiality. Regarding the storm that rages round him as a universal rending and uprooting of everything, something that will pluck out the roots of all things, even the darkest and foulest roots of the heart of man deceitful above all things and desperately wicked, he affirms in the face of the most appalling self-knowledge, clear and blasting as the lightning, that his sufferings must still be greater than his sins. It is possibly the most tremendous thing a man ever said; whether or not any man had the right to say it. It would be hard to beat it even in the Book of Job. And it does weaken the particular strength of it that it should be used, however sympathetically, as a cheerful and charitable guess about the weaknesses of other people.

There are certain abstractions very strong in Shakespeare's mind, without which his plays are much misunderstood by modern people, who look to them for nothing whatever except realistic details about individuals. For instance, there runs through the whole play of *King Lear*, as there runs through the whole play of *Richard the Second*, an abstraction which was an actuality of awful vividness to the man of Shakespeare's time; the idea of the King. Under the name of Divine Right, a very unlucky name, it was mixed up with Parliamentary and sectarian quarrels which afterwards altogether dwarfed and diminished its dignity. But Divine Right was originally much more human than that. It resolved itself roughly into this; that there are three forms in which men can accept the idea of justice or the authority of the commonwealth; in the form of an assembly, in the form of a document, or in the form of a man. King Lear is a man; but he is or has been a sacramental or sacred man; and that is why he can be a desecrated man. Even those who prefer to be governed by the scroll of the law, or by the assembly of the tribe, must understand that men have wished, and may again wish, to be governed by a man; and that where this wish has existed the man does become, not indeed divine, but certainly different. It is not an accident that Lear is a king as well as a father, and that Goneril and Regan are not only daughters but traitors. Treason, or what is felt as treason, does break the heart of the world; and it has seldom been so nearly broken as here.

(From *The Spice of Life*. Originally published as an introduction in 1950)

❖

Madness in Lear

Nearly everybody in the play of King Lear is more or less mad.

(*G.K.'s Weekly*, Nov. 15, 1930)

———— ❖ ————

The Two Lears

Nobody has noticed, I suppose, the weird coincidence about the word Lear. Yet I could write a book called *The Two Lears* that should be (or ought to be) a complete history of our island literature. The Shakespearean Lear and the Victorian Lear [The painter and nonsense poet Edward Lear] are not generally classed together in the lectures of my fellow professors; of my dear colleagues, the other dons. Yet the Two Lears have clearly much in common. They are both English and both mad. One is melancholy and the other merry; but neither is methodical or consistent; and both depend upon intrinsic poetry rather than logical plan or classical design. Shakespeare's Cliff, from which the world is a map with men like beetles, is certainly not far from the precipices of the Chankley Bore; and when the fool says in the great tragedy, "This prophecy Merlin shall make; for I live before his time," there is sounded that note of madness that shall never wholly depart from the literature of England.

(*Week-End Review*, Dec. 20, 1930)

———— ❖ ————

Hope in the Face of Sorrow

In criticizing a play of Ibsen, the modern critic always assumes deduction is to be drawn from it about the rules of morals or the rules of marriage or education or socialism or free-love. Some people, for instance, think that *Ghosts* is an argument against certain forms of married life. Of them it can only be said that if *King Lear* were written in modern times by a Norwegian they would think it an excellent argument against parents bringing up their own children. It never occurred to anyone in the sixteenth or seventeenth centuries to regard *King Lear* as a controversial pamphlet against parents, or to regard *Hamlet* as a controversial pamphlet against a university education, or to regard *Othello* as a controversial pamphlet against mixed marriages between white people and black. In the times when these tragedies were written men accepted them as tragedies, that is to say, as simple stories of the ancient sadness of the world. The moral of *King Lear* was not and is not that a gentleman should hand over his daughters to be educated by Country Council experts; there is no moral to the story, except the monotonous "sunt lachrymae rerum." The curious thing is that man is hopeful in the face of sorrow, so long as that sorrow is hopeless. But in these days we are forced even against our will to judge everything, even plays, morally. A crowd of artists and aesthetes have declared in this age that art is immoral; but the fact plainly and obviously remains that there never was a time in the history of the world when art was so moral. If there be a fault in the popular criticism of the day, it is that it is far too much so.

(*Daily News*, Sept. 13, 1902)

——— ❖ ———

The Meaning of Mark Antony

I am very glad to see that Mr. Bernard Shaw has been throwing doubts on the anti-democracy attributed to Shakespeare; apparently by Mr. Frank Harris, and certainly by others. I am even more glad that he has pointed out that intensely valuable part of Mr. Harris's work for which I always thought he was poorly thanked: I mean the complete clearing of Shakespeare from all charge of perversion. For if we could believe him a pervert, it would be easier to believe him an oligarch: democracy is in the instincts.

The truth is that not only Shakespeare but most of the other great poets can only be convicted of anti-popular sentiment by the detestable habit of quoting tags. For instance, Carlyle solemnly quotes Horace about the duty of hating the profane vulgar. But Carlyle does not mention that, immediately after, Horace "proclaims silence" for all the world like Whiffin the Beadle at the Eatanswill Election, and announces, in the best manner of modern advertisement, that he has an entirely new *repertoire* of songs, especially suited to young people of both sexes. The atmosphere of the ode certainly is not that of the misanthropic artist. Or again, many imagine a faint oligarchic flavour about Gray's expression "far from the madding crowd's ignoble strife"; especially since it has been used as a title by the intensely anti-popular genius of the author of *Jude the Obscure*. A crowd more unmistakably madding than Mr. Hardy's suicidal rustics it would be hard to find in any slum. But the feeling in Gray's poem, the tone as distinct from the tag, is distinctly popular. He is praising the social strength and valve of hob-nailed louts; and his version involves a noble recognition of their roughness; though perhaps "the noiseless tenour of their way" is not the best description of their boots. In the same way, because somebody persuaded Shakespeare to write a rather dull play about Coriolanus, and he actually made Coriolanus talk like Coriolanus, critics have talked of poor Will from Stratford (who would often have written a play about the Man in the Moon for the sake of a job) as if he were a rigid Roman Patrician risen from the dead. But the general spirit of Shakespeare runs altogether the other way. It is founded on the popular Mediaeval feeling that Jack is as good as his master—and often better. Whenever Shakespeare's narrative brings Prince and clown together, the clown scores off the prince as systematically as Sam Weller scores off Pickwick, or Straker off Tanner. Hamlet and Laertes, leaping into the grave (and out again), seem, and I think are meant to seem, mere theatrical sentimentalists, compared with the workman who, being cheerful in the grave as in any other workshop, has some right to ask the grave where is its victory. Moreover, the gravedigger does utter the genuine democratic sentiment; and the only important political sentiment in the play. Mr. Shaw, by the way, truly points out that the man who makes the ultra-royalist speech about the divinity hedging a king, is a ruffian and is killed after all. But I think the case is even stronger than he says. It must surely have been a stroke of savage humour to put the dogma that kings cannot be murdered, into the mouth of the ambitious and successful gentleman who had the best possible private reasons for knowing that they could. The ghastly irony of the words in the mouth, not only of a usurper but a regicide, cannot be taken as a serious salute to monarchy. But the real philosophy of democracy, right or wrong, is excellently stated by the gravedigger, when he objects to great folk having countenance "to drown or hang themselves more than

their even Christian." One could write a whole history of
Europe on that phrase "even Christian." Note that broad
religious views are brought in to excuse narrow social sympathies; exactly as they are to-day by Dr. Inge and the model
employers. Laertes talks a lot of New Theology about
Churlish Priests; but the man with the spade knows the
truth. "If this had not been a gentlewoman . . ." This point is
very important; for nothing is commoner nowadays than to
make sentiment the excuse when snobbishness is the motive.
And when I watched the old problem plays; and when the
faithful old butler, bringing in the liqueurs, heard the young
genius shoot himself in the wings; or when the *femme
incomprise* wandered down by the exquisite azaleas and disappeared into the Maeterlinckian lake, something historic in
me hardened my heart. And I only murmured; "And the
more pity that great folk should have countenance in this
world to drown or hang themselves, more than their even
Christian." The man who wrote that was no anti-democrat.

Another difficulty is that geniuses who write unequally
and have a ringing talent for melodrama, like Shakespeare,
often do not get the credit of their subtlety when they really
are subtle. They are credited with performing some stale
mechanical trick; when the trick is really too quick and new
for the audience to follow it. A strong example is the other
great instance of the crowd in Shakespeare; the occasion of
Mark Antony's oration. The ordinary version, in our Victorian
youth, was that Brutus made a good speech against Caesar,
and the mob cheered him very much; then Antony made a
good speech for Caesar, and they cheered him even more;
and this was another example of Shakespeare's contempt for
the inconstant populace. Now this is very bad and careless
criticism. It is bad and careless, as it would be to treat
Robinson Crusoe as a tale of perils, and complain that the

hero had so long to fetch stores from the wreck. This would miss the point; that it is not Crusoe's insecurity, but his security, that puts a silence as of a divine punishment about his loneliness. It is bad and careless, as it is to say that Stevenson's *Jekyll and Hyde* shows that man has two natures, one good and the other evil; and that they can exist separately. This misses the point; that the interest of Jekyll is not in the success but the failure of his experiment. He sincerely tries to saw himself in half; but the spinal cord of conscience still connects the two parts. It is bad and careless, as it would be to say that Becky Sharp merely wanted Amelia to leave her on the Continent to capture Jos; and had no sort of respect for Dobbin and no sort of memory of old times; or as it would be to say that Lord Advocate Prestongrange *only* wanted David Balfour to save him from "the memorial," and had no respect for the fanaticism and the honour of the young. In other words, it is a vulgar simplification; like most modern religions. It is putting down everything in black and white; because you are colour-blind.

Antony's speech is not only sincere but passionate. I cannot prove it. Nor can you prove that Juliet was in love. That ornate blank verse is more likely to be used by a demagogue in a forum than by a girl in a balcony. There is no answer; except that there is a certain kind of blank verse that is by no means blank. It fills the heart of the reader, and unless we are all mad, it must have filled the heart of the writer.

Mark Antony roused the democracy because he was a democrat. He was addressing the members of a democracy suddenly cowed by a *coup d'etat* of the old aristocrats. He was expressing himself under restrictions; but so were they. He ran great risks in saying anything; but so did they. He did not want to die very much nor do the London poor. He had mostly to take refuge in irony: so do the London poor. But the man who can take such irony for artificial party speaking, ought to have boiling lava in his tea-cup for afternoon tea. His appeal throughout is to the plainest ideas of the people; death, friendship, tears, blood, money. Caesar cried at a story of suffering: Cato did not cry. Caesar had left the poor hard cash: Cassius probably would not have done so. Caesar's throat was cut; and after all Brutus's wasn't. Antony is the professional politician being as bold as he dares; but his appeal is to the ordinary man.

And now turn back to what I really think is almost the greatest thing in Shakespeare. Shakespeare's type of tragedy was the first tragedy of Free Will; the first Christian tragedy. "We will proceed no further in this business." If those words are properly spoken, the audience really feels that Duncan may have his porridge next morning in peace. It is something infinitely more living, original and spiritual than the flattening steam-roller of "fate": it is the villain tempted by virtue. Shakespeare has given us one tremendous picture, very much needed for these times. He has shown us the politician when he is suddenly tempted to be a man. When Antony actually finds the body of Caesar, he asks for death with startling and inspired impatience—knowing he will afterwards be a corpse or a "statesman."

> "There is no hour so fit
> As Caesar's death hour, nor no instrument
> Of half that worth as those your swords, made rich
> With the most noble blood of all this world."

Then he utters the rending phrase of revelation—

> "Live a thousand Years
> I shall not find myself so apt to die."

Most successful statesmen have passed through that heroic instant. And there are none who do not really regret that they have survived it.

(*New Witness*, June 4, 1914)

Richard II

("Professor Bradley on Shakespearian Tragedy")

Professor Bradley's critical work is nearly always of that rare and excellent kind that leaves the subject as inexhaustible as it found it. The only test that can be adequately suggested of a critic's work on a masterpiece is whether it freshens it or makes it stale, whether, like the inferior appreciation, it sends us to our hundredth reading of the work, or whether, like the higher appreciation, it sends us to our first reading of it. There is one kind of criticism which reminds us that we have read a book; there is another and better which convinces us that we have never read it. Mr. Bradley's comments can almost everywhere be praised for the supreme merit that they leave us not only interested, but what is almost the same thing, unsatisfied. Infinities of argument, of agreement, of violent disagreement, of qualification and exaggerative development, could be extracted from almost every sentence. He deals with each subject firmly, but yet in such a manner as to suggest indescribably that the subject is a subject for discussion. It may, perhaps, be wondered whether one could possibly say a worse thing of anybody than that he had said "the last word" on a subject. A man who says the last word on a subject ought to be killed. He is a murderer; he has slain a topic. The best kind of critic draws attention not to the finality of a thing, but to its infinity. Instead of closing a question, he opens a hundred; he creates enemies as much as admirers. If any of us should meet a man walking about and claiming to say the last word on tragedy let us also take tragic action and let it be his last word on anything.

Professor Bradley realizes to the full the depth and the delicacy and the darkness of his subject; and realizing this, he contrives to say some very admirable things about it. Nothing, for instance, could be better or sounder than this:

> "The tragic hero, with Shakespeare, then, need not be 'good', though generally he is 'good', and therefore at once wins sympathy in his error. But it is necessary that he should have so much of greatness in his error that we may be vividly conscious of the possibilities of human nature. Hence, in the first place, a Shakespearian tragedy is never, like some miscalled tragedies, depressing. No one ever closes the book with the feeling that man is a poor mean creature. He may be wretched and he may be awful, but he is not small. His lot may be heartrending and mysterious, but it is not contemptible. The most confirmed of cynics ceases to be a cynic while he reads these plays. . . . It forces the mystery upon us and it makes us realize so vividly the worth of that which is wasted that we cannot possibly seek comfort in the reflection that all is vanity."

That is both profound and simple and strong. I do not quite understand why the word "good" should be printed in inverted commas, as if it were some new and curious piece of slang . . . Nor can I agree for a moment with Professor Bradley in the view he takes of Richard II, in a note appended to the passage. He says that Richard II is, in his view, an exception to this general rule of dignity and value in character, that to him Richard is "scarcely a tragic figure, he is so only because his fall from prosperity to adversity is so great." Surely this is a very unfair and unappreciative view of the personality of Richard II. Richard may be what is called a weak man, but in that respect he is only in the spiritual position essential to the protagonist of tragedy. The whole meaning of tragedy is that every man is of necessity a weak man. A poet may lawfully take a particularly weak man and symbolize the general weakness of the human estate, just as he may lawfully take a particularly sad tale to symbolize the general sadness of the human lot. But if Richard II be weak in the sense that Hamlet is weak, he is also great in the sense that Hamlet is great—nay, he is strong in the sense that Hamlet is strong. Shakespeare has given him every quality that can set off and blazon misfortune, grace, eloquence, culture, and personal courage. He has not only given him the manners of a gentleman, he has in some sense given him the death of a hero. The hired brute who strikes him down, fighting against the odds, calls him as he dies "as full of valour as of noble blood". Above all, Shakespeare cannot surely have meant nothing when he poured out pages of his most superb poetry from the mouth of this man. The truth surely is that the tragedy of Richard II is the tragedy not of the King, but of the poet. Who would care how many times a dull fellow like Henry Bolingbroke won or lost his crown? The loss of a practical scheme is in its nature a trifle; it is only when it is idealized by the human imagination that it becomes a vision and hence a tragedy. The poet is a man who can value passionately the things about him, he is the man to whom the near things are not too near to be seen. He can focus them in some way; so that even the men who walk about in the room with him are seen, as it were, afar off from a peak and with a sudden cry.

Most poets, happily for them, are poor and live the life of common men. Thus the things which they make necessary to their imaginations are generally human or ordinary things. They see the poetry of the grass or of women or of bread or wine. But this unhappy man in Shakespeare was a man who was born in a crown, and his curse was that he saw the poetry of that. The trumpets blown before him were to him what the birds were to Keats or Tennyson.

The crimson canopy over his head was to him what the vault of heaven was to Shelley. Most kings are happy, because most kings are commonplace men, and being commonplace men they laugh at kingship as all commonplace men and all common sense men laugh at it. But Richard II in Shakespeare is so uncommon a King as actually to reverence his crown. His story, like that of Charles I, is simply the tragedy of Divine Right. It is safe enough (with reasonable precautions) to be a King; but it is very dangerous to be a King who is also a Royalist.

I have said above that Professor Bradley's book teems with suggestions and provocations in every sentence, and I have proved it by going off into an argument with him about a note. Properly understood, it is an excellent compliment, though it may not be an excellent advertisement. Of the four tragedies treated in the book, that which is handled in the most masterly manner is, I think, *King Lear*. The study of the character of Edgar, to take one example, with its religious faith and a kind of cheerfulness which seems almost inhuman, is one of those fine studies of normal psychology through which psychology almost becomes philosophy. Professor Bradley strikes a deep note in touching on Edgar's strange and innocent faith in "the clearest gods" amid all the monstrous darkness. It is an unconscious hypocrisy of the world and worldlings to say that they are angry with the gloom and asceticism of religious people. What they are and always have been angry with is their happiness.

(*Daily News*, December 22, 1904)

———— ❖ ————

Richard III and Nietzsche

Nietzsche, as everyone knows, preached a doctrine which he and his followers regard apparently as very revolutionary; he held that ordinary altruistic morality had been the invention of a slave class to prevent the emergence of superior types to fight and rule them. Now, modern people, whether they agree with this or not, always talk of it as a new and unheard-of idea. It is calmly and persistently supposed that the great writers of the past, say Shakespeare for instance, did not hold this view, because they had never imagined it; because it had never come into their heads.

Turn up the last act of Shakespeare's *Richard III* and you will find not only all that Nietzsche had to say put into two lines, but you will find it put in the very words of Nietzsche. Richard Crookback says to his nobles:

> Conscience is but a word that cowards use,
> Devised at first to keep the strong in awe.

As I have said, the fact is plain. Shakespeare had thought of Nietzsche and the Master Morality; but he weighed it at its proper value and put it in its proper place. Its proper place is the mouth of a half-insane hunchback on the eve of defeat. This rage against the weak is only possible in a man morbidly brave but fundamentally sick; a man like Richard, a man like Nietzsche. This case alone ought to destroy the absurd fancy that these modern philosophies are modern in the sense that the great men of the past did not think of them. They thought of them; only they did not think much of them. It was not that Shakespeare did not see the Nietzsche idea; he saw it, and he saw through it.

("On Reading," *The Common Man*)

III.
THE COMEDIES

The Other Difference Between Comedy and Tragedy

A few people have ventured to imitate Shakespeare's tragedy. But no audacious spirit has dreamed or dared to imitate Shakespeare's comedy. No one has made any real attempt to recover the loves and the laughter of Elizabethan England. The low dark arches, the low strong pillars upon which Shakespeare's temple rests we can all explore and handle. We can all get into his mere tragedy; we can all explore his dungeon and penetrate into his coal-cellar; but we stretch our hands and crane our necks in vain towards that height where the tall turrets of his levity are tossed towards the sky. Perhaps it is right that this should be so; properly understood, comedy is an even grander thing than tragedy.

(*Illustrated London News*, April 27, 1907)

———— ❖ ————

The Comedy of Love

Shakespeare's *Much Ado About Nothing* is a great comedy, because behind it is the whole pressure of that love of love which is the youth of the world, which is common to all the young, especially to those who swear they will die bachelors and old maids. *Love's Labour's Lost* is filled with the same energy, and there it falls even more definitely into the scope of our subject, since it is a comedy in rhyme in which all men speak lyrically as naturally as the birds sing in pairing time.

("Rostand," *Twelve Types*)

———— ❖ ————

Shakespeare and the Legal Lady

I wonder how long liberated woman will endure the invidious ban which excludes her from being a hangman. Or rather, to speak with more exactitude, a hangwoman. The very fact that there seems something vaguely unfamiliar and awkward about the word, is but a proof of the ages of sex oppression that have accustomed us to this sex privilege. The ambition would not perhaps have been understood by the prudish and sentimental heroines of Fanny Burney and Jane Austen. But it is now agreed that the farther we go beyond these faded proprieties the better; and I really do not see how we could go farther. There are always torturers of course, who will probably return under some scientific name. Obscurantists may use the old argument, that woman has never risen to the first rank in this or other arts; that Jack Ketch was not Jemima Ketch, and that the headsman was called Samson and not Delilah. And they will be overwhelmed with the old retort: that until we have hundreds of healthy women happily engaged in this healthful occupation, it will be impossible to judge whether they can rise above the average or no. Tearful sentimentalists may feel something unpleasing, something faintly repugnant, about the new feminine trade. But, as the indignant policewoman said the other day, when a magistrate excluded some of her sex and service from revolting revelations, "crime is a disease," and must be studied scientifically, however hideous it may be.

Death also is a disease; and frequently a fatal one. Experiments must be made in it; and it must be inflicted in any form, however hideous, in a cool and scientific manner.

It is not true, of course, that crime is a disease. It is criminology that is a disease. But the suggestion about the painful duties of a policewoman leads naturally to my deduction about the painful duties of a hangwoman. And I make it in the faint hope of waking up some of the feminists, that they may at least be moved to wonder what they are doing, and to attempt to find out. What they are not doing is obvious enough. They are not asking themselves two perfectly plain questions; first, whether they want anybody to be a hangman; and second, whether they want everybody to be a hangman. They simply assume, with panting impetuosity, that we want everybody to be everything, criminologists, constables, barristers, executioners, torturers. It never seems to occur to them that some of us doubt the beauty and blessedness of those things, and are rather glad to limit them like other necessary evils. And this applies especially to the doubtful though defensible case of the advocate.

There is one phrase perpetually repeated and now practically stereotyped, which to my mind concentrates and sums up all the very worst qualities in the very worst journalism, all its paralysis of thought, all its monotony of chatter, all its sham culture and shoddy picturesqueness, all its perpetual readiness to cover any vulgarity of the present with any sentimentalism about the past. There is one phrase that does measure to how low an ebb the mind of my unfortunate profession can sink. It is the habit of perpetually calling any of the new lady barristers "Portia."

First of all, of course, it is quite clear that the journalist does not know who Portia was. If he has ever heard of the story of the *Merchant of Venice*, he has managed to miss the

only point of the story. Suppose a man had been so
instructed in the story of *As You Like It* that he remained
under the impression that Rosalind really was a boy, and
was the brother of Celia. We should say that the plot of the
comedy had reached his mind in a rather confused form.
Suppose a man had seen a whole performance of the play of
Twelfth Night without discovering the fact that the page
called Cesario was really a girl called Viola. We should say
that he had succeeded in seeing the play without exactly
seeing the point. But there is exactly the same blind stupidity in calling a barrister Portia; or even in calling Portia a
barrister. It misses in exactly the same sense the whole
meaning of the scene. Portia is no more a barrister than
Rosalind is a boy. She is no more the learned jurist whom
Shylock congratulates than Viola is the adventurous page
whom Olivia loves. The whole point of her position is that
she is a heroic and magnanimous fraud. She has not taken
up the legal profession, or any profession; she has not
sought that public duty, or any public duty. Her action, from
first to last, is wholly and entirely private. Her motives are
not professional but private. Her ideal is not public but private. She acts as much on personal grounds in the Trial
Scene as she does in the Casket Scene. She acts in order to
save a friend, and especially a friend of the husband whom
she loves. Anything less like the attitude of an advocate, for
good or evil, could not be conceived. She seeks individually
to save an individual; and in order to do so is ready to *break*
all the existing laws of the profession and the public tribu-
nal; to assume lawlessly powers she has not got, to intrude
where she would never be legally admitted, to pretend to be
somebody else, to dress up as a man; to do what is actually
a crime against the law. This is not what is now called the
attitude of a public woman; it is certainly not the attitude of

a lady lawyer, any more than of any other kind of lawyer. But it is emphatically the attitude of a private woman; that much more ancient and much more powerful thing.

Suppose that Portia had really become an advocate, merely by advocating the cause of Antonio against Shylock. The first thing that follows is that, as like as not, she would be briefed in the next case to advocate the cause of Shylock against Antonio. She would, in the ordinary way of business, have to help Shylock to punish with ruin the private extravagances of Gratiano. She would have to assist Shylock to distrain on poor Launcelot Gobbo and sell up all his miserable sticks. She might well be employed by him to ruin the happiness of Lorenzo and Jessica, by urging some obsolete parental power or some technical flaw in the marriage service. Shylock evidently had a great admiration for her forensic talents; and indeed that sort of lucid and detached admission of the talents of a successful opponent is a very Jewish characteristic. There seems no reason why he should not have employed her regularly, whenever he wanted someone to recover ruthless interest, to ruin needy households, to drive towards theft or suicide the souls of desperate men. But there seems every reason to doubt whether the Portia whom Shakespeare describes for us is likely to have taken on the job.

Anyhow, that is the job; and I am not here arguing that it is not a necessary job; or that it is always an indefensible job. Many honourable men have made an arguable case for the advocate who has to support Shylock, and men much worse than Shylock. But that is the job; and to cover up its ugly realities with a loose literary quotation that really refers to the exact opposite, is one of those crawling and cowardly evasions and verbal fictions which make all this sort of servile journalism so useless for every worthy or working purpose. If we wish to consider whether a lady should be a barrister, we should consider sanely and clearly what a barrister is and what a lady is; and then come to our conclusion according to what we consider worthy or worthless in the traditions of the two things. But the spirit of advertisement, which tries to associate soap with sunlight or grape-nuts with grapes, calls to its rescue an old romance of Venice and tries to cover up a practical problem in the robes of a romantic heroine of the stage. This is the sort of confusion that really leads to corruption. In one sense it would matter very little that the legal profession was formally open to women, for it is only a very exceptional sort of woman who would see herself as a vision of beauty in the character of Mr. Sergeant Buzfuz. And most girls are more likely to be stage-struck, and want to be the real Portia on the stage, rather than law-struck and want to be the very reverse of Portia in a law court. For that matter, it would make relatively little difference if formal permission were given to a woman to be a hangman or a torturer. Very few women would have a taste for it; and very few men would have a taste for the women who had a taste for it. But advertisement, by its use of the vulgar picturesque, can hide the realities of this professional problem, as it can hide the realities of tinned meats and patent medicines. It can conceal the fact that the hangman exists to hang, and that the torturer exists to torture. Similarly it can conceal the fact that the Buzfuz barrister exists to bully. It can hide from the innocent female aspirants outside even the perils and potential abuses that would be admitted by the honest male advocate inside. And that is part of a very much larger problem, which extends beyond this particular profession to a great many other professions; and not least to the lowest and most lucrative of all modern professions; that of professional politics.

I wonder how many people are still duped by the story of the extension of the franchise. I wonder how many Radicals have been a little mystified, in remarking how many Tories and reactionaries have helped in the extension of the franchise. The truth is that caning in crowds of new voters will very often be to the interest, not only of Tories, but of really tyrannical Tories. It will often be in the interest of the guilty to appeal to the innocent; if they are innocent in the matter of other people's conduct as well as of their own. The tyrant calls in those he has not wronged, to defend him against those he has wronged. He is not afraid of the new and ignorant masses who know too little; he is afraid of the older and nearer nucleus of those who know too much. And there is nothing that would please the professional politician more than to flood the constituencies with innocent negroes or remote Chinamen, who might possibly admire him more, because they knew him less. I should not wonder if the Party System had been saved three or four times at the point of extinction, by the introduction of new voters who had never had time to discover why it deserved to be extinguished. The last of these rescues by an inrush of dupes was the enfranchisement of women.

What is true of the political is equally true of the professional ambition. Much of the mere imitation of masculine tricks and trades is indeed trivial enough; it is a mere masquerade. The greatest of Roman satirists noted that in his day the more fast of the fashionable ladies liked to fight as gladiators in the amphitheatre. In that one statement he pinned and killed, like moths on a cork, a host of women prophets and women pioneers and large-minded liberators of their sex in modern England and America. But besides these more showy she-gladiators there are also multitudes of worthy and sincere women who take the new (or rather old) professions seriously. The only disadvantage is that in many of those professions they can only continue to be serious by ceasing to be sincere. But the simplicity with which they first set out is an enormous support to old and complex and corrupt institutions. No modest person setting out to learn an elaborate science can be expected to start with the assumption that it is not worth learning. The young lady will naturally begin to learn Law as gravely as she begins to learn Greek. It is not in that mood that she will conceive independent doubts about the ultimate relations of Law and Justice. Just as the Suffragettes are already complaining that the realism of industrial revolution interferes with their new hobby of voting, so the lady lawyers are quite likely to complain that the realism of legal reformers interferes with their new hobby of legalism. We are suffering in every department from the same cross-purposes that can be seen in the case of any vulgar patent medicine. In Law and Medicine, we have the thing advertised in the public press instead of analysed by the public authority. What we want is not the journalistic Portia but the theatrical Portia; who is also the real Portia. We do not want the woman who will enter the law court with the solemn sense of a lasting vocation. We want a Portia; a woman who will enter it as lightly, and leave it as gladly as she did.

The same thing is true of a fact nobler than any fiction; the story, so often quoted, of the woman who won back mediaeval France. Joan of Arc was a soldier; but she was not a normal soldier. If she had been, she would have been vowed, not to the war for France, but to any war with Flanders, Spain or the Italian cities to which her feudal lord might lead her. If she were a modern conscript, she would be bound to obey orders not always coming from St. Michael. But the point is here that merely making all women soldiers, under either system, could do nothing at all except whitewash and ratify feudalism or conscription. And both feudalism and conscription are much more magnanimous things than our modern system of police and prisons.

In fact there are few sillier implications than that in the phrase that what is sauce for the goose is sauce for the gander. A cook who really rules a kitchen on that principle would wait patiently for milk from the bull, because he got it from the cow. It is neither a perceptible fact nor a first principle that the sexes must not specialize; and if one sex must specialize in adopting dubious occupations, we ought to be very glad that the other sex specializes in abstaining from them. That is how the balance of criticism in the commonwealth is maintained; as by a sort of government and opposition. In this, as in other things, the new regime is that everybody shall join the government. The government of the moment will be monstrously strengthened; for everybody will be a tyrant and everybody will be a slave. The detached criticism of official fashions win and none was ever so detached as the deadly criticism that came from women. When all women wear uniforms, all women will wear gags; for a gag is part of every uniform in the world.

(From *Fancies vs. Fads*. Originally from *New Witness*, December 1, 1922)

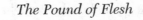

The Pound of Flesh

It is recognised that some of the greatest men in literature were plagiarists from much smaller men, and that they even more often borrowed from the stock of popular legends which were composed by nobody in particular. But we generally do less than justice to the value of this outline or framework of the tale that they borrowed. We think too exclusively of the work of the great man and far too little of the great story which was the work of many small men. Above all we omit to observe that the idea and philosophy of the story is generally present in the rude outline as well as in the finished product.

An instance will make the matter more clear. In Professor Raleigh's recent book on Shakespeare that shrewd and effective critic is concerned to explain (very truly on the whole) that it is possible to make too much fuss about the mysteries of Shakespeare, that many of them are accidents, many of them practical limitations of the playwright. But in the course of maintaining this he suggests, I think, that a certain brutality in the mere mechanism of *The Merchant of Venice* prevented Shakespeare from doing the most delicate spiritual justice to Shylock. He implies that the coarse old tale of the pound of flesh tied Shakespeare down, and prevented him from painting with full sympathy a noble Jew.

If I am right in my memory of Professor Raleigh's meaning, he thinks that Shylock would be finer without the story of Shylock; in that case he does a great injustice to the old story. It is at any rate an injustice that is often done to it. The truth is that the rude story of the pound of flesh is a very spiritual story. Moreover, it was exactly the spiritual story which Shakespeare wished to tell, out of which he wished to draw the full spirituality. No one but Shakespeare could have made the thought explicit; but the thought was implicit in the most jingling old ballad about the merchant and the Jew.

That idea was the profound philosophy of mercy or of charity, which Mr. Belloc has called somewhere "the appreciation of living things." In other words, there is a certain kind of sympathy or allowance which is due to organisms, and which cannot be given to the inorganic. There is a sense in which one can be just to a stone; but one could be merciful to a mushroom. When the thing has a life of its own, an interdependence of function, a circulation of power, then it becomes necessary to deal with it sympathetically and not literally, to remember that one thing goes with another, and that one cannot touch parts without injuring the whole.

If you chop a stone in two, you have two halves of a stone; but if you chop a horse in two you only have more horseflesh than you require for any domestic purpose.

Now the old tale of the Jew and the merchant of Venice was a satire on that commercial literalism which endeavours to apply hard contract and cruel exactitude to life and to living things. The Jew, as the great, mediaeval symbol of this unchivalrous calculation was represented as saying that he had a legal right to a pound of a man's flesh, and that he would take not a grain more or less. It was useless to point out to him that the pound was a part of an organic life, and that in taking that he was in fact taking more. So at last, when he had rejected all appeals to generosity and commonsense, he was at last routed by the reductio ad absurdum of justice. His own mad logic is pushed one step further, and it destroys his case. He may take flesh if he can manage to take flesh without blood.

The whole legend, even in its baldest and most brutal outline, has the clear voice of Christian morals and European sanity. It is a protest against that pedantry which always becomes inhumanity.

What Shakespeare did was to take this wild tale, to see the mother wit in it, and to develop that into an exalted spiritual wisdom. He was quite as sure that the Jew was wrong as any mediaeval could have been. But he emphasised the wrongness not by making him grotesquely wrong, but by making him splendidly and pathetically wrong. Instead of giving us the comic moneylender of mediaeval farce, he showed us a man mighty in error, whose morality had sublimely gone astray. Shylock, in his own eyes, is asking only for his rights; but he cannot be got to see that when dealing with life it is often possible to take rights and to leave wrongs instead. You not only deduct something, you also add something; you add a wound. Shylock's morality has not enough mysticism to make him see that in touching a living thing he is breaking into a sanctuary where unknown vengeances are hung over his head. And Shylock's philosophy has not enough of what always goes with mysticism, it has not enough *humour* to see that it is silly to talk about owning a part of another man.

Shylock's philosophy, the pedantic and inhuman philosophy, is held by many people in our own time, who are as dignified and sincere as Shylock. It is always marked by this inability to apprehend the interdependence between all the parts of a living thing.

When there has been question, for instance, of the suppression of some small nationality I have heard a quite good-natured young English guardsman or squire say "these people only had to give up their flag which was merely ornamental." To this I was impelled to reply, "My good sir, the only thing I ask of you is that you should cut off your head, which I am sure is merely ornamental. The rest of your attractive person will remain in full play; you can salute with your hand and waltz with your legs as before, without this sentimental emblem erected between your shoulders, of which, if you will permit me to say so, I have grown a little tired."

But, alas, that is the weakness of the Shylock philosophy, for, as the Guardsman lucidly and patiently explained to me, his head, however, useless for the higher purposes, was quite essential to his either drilling or dancing; in short, that I could not take his head without taking his life, which was a much more enjoyable thing. And then I told him that a Christian Commonwealth is an animal of a very funny shape, and it is often hard to say which is the head with the life in it; but, generally, the head is the flag. But I do not think that he quite followed my meaning.

But one may commit this anti-organic crime in many directions, and it concerns us more to realise that we can easily commit it in our arrangements for reforming human society. Do not let us be the dupe of lists and classifications in which Antonio"s flesh is put down to Shylock's banking account. Almost every book I find full of a righteous anger against the social evil slips into this bad habit of reckoning by tons or inches instead of by organisms. Like Shylock, it takes humanity by the pound instead of by the person.

Let me take but one case out of a hundred. All rational citizens have long had the thought that certain things ought to be run from the centre, and for all alike. The strongest case, I think, is transit. If a thousand people for a thousand reasons all want to go from Balham to Highgate it must be an advantage to take them all by one responsible system.

But from this certain modern writers, forgetting that they are dealing with living things, deduce the wildest things. They deduce, for instance, that in a better state of society we shall all dine together at a common restaurant. This is to forget all the vital element involved. Men take a tram for Highgate because they want to get to Highgate. But men do not dine because they want dinner. They dine because they want a certain human atmosphere, of repose, of domesticity, of hospitality, and of chosen friends, and they want dinner along with all this. They do not want their pound of flesh or their pound of beans and bacon. They want the spiritual sentiment of a good dinner. If you try to cut that out of humanity you will find (as Shylock did) that you cannot do it unless blood is shed.

(*Daily News*, February 15, 1908)

———— ❖ ————

The Character of Shylock

There was a controversy in the columns of an important daily paper, some time ago, on the subject of the character of Shylock in Shakespeare. Actors and authors of distinction, including some of the most brilliant of living Jews, argued the matter from the most varied points of view. Some said that Shakespeare was prevented by the prejudices of his time from having a complete sympathy with Shylock. Some said that Shakespeare was only restrained by fear of the powers of his time from expressing his complete sympathy with Shylock. Some wondered how or why Shakespeare had got hold of such a queer story as that of the pound of flesh, and what it could possibly have to do with so dignified and intellectual a character as Shylock. In short, some wondered why a man of genius should be so much of an Anti-Semite, and some stoutly declared that he must have been a Pro-Semite. But all of them in a sense admitted that they were puzzled as to what the play was about. The correspondence filled column after column and went on for weeks. And from one end of that correspondence to the other, no human being even so much as mentioned the word "usury." It is exactly as if twenty clever critics were set down to talk for a month about the play of Macbeth, and were all strictly forbidden to mention the word "murder."

The play called *The Merchant of Venice* happens to be
about usury, and its story is a medieval satire on usury. It is
the fashion to say that it is a clumsy and grotesque story; but
as a fact it is an exceedingly good story. It is a perfect and
pointed story for its purpose, which is to convey the moral
of the story. And the moral is that the logic of usury is in its
nature at war with life, and might logically end in breaking
into the bloody house of life. In other words, if a creditor
can always claim a man's tools or a man's home, he might
quite as justly claim one of his arms or legs. This principle
was not only embodied in medieval satires but in very sound
medieval laws, which set a limit on the usurer who was trying to take away a man's livelihood, as the usurer in the play
is trying to take away a man's life. And if anybody thinks that
usury can never go to lengths wicked enough to be worthy
of so wild an image, then that person either knows nothing
about it or knows too much. He is either one of the innocent
rich who have never been the victims of money-lenders, or
else one of the more powerful and influential rich who are
money-lenders themselves.

All this, I say, is a fact that must be faced, but there is
another side to the case, and it is this that the genius of
Shakespeare discovered. What he did do, and what the
medieval satirist did not do, was to attempt to understand
Shylock; in the true sense to sympathise with Shylock the
money-lender, as he sympathised with Macbeth the murderer. It was not to deny that the man was an usurer, but to
assert that the usurer was a man. And the Elizabethan
dramatist does make him a man, where the medieval satirist
made him a monster. Shakespeare not only makes him a
man but a perfectly sincere and self-respecting man. But
the point is this: that he is a sincere man who sincerely
believes in usury. He is a self-respecting man who does not

despise himself for being a usurer. In one word, he regards usury as normal. In that word is the whole problem of the popular impression of the Jews. What Shakespeare suggested about the Jew in a subtle and sympathetic way, millions of plain men everywhere would suggest about him in a rough and ready way.

("The Problem of Zionism," *The New Jersusalem*)

———— ❖ ————

The Merchant's Place

The old common sense of human communities . . . never allowed, as we have allowed, even the idea of merchandise to entirely outweigh and overwhelm the idea of agriculture. The merchant had his place, but it was not the supreme place, and it was not so near the very heart of the society as the place of the ploughman. The merchant might be congratulated on his courage rather than on his safety, but it was not allowed to usurp the place of the courage of the soldier. So one of the most famous merchants, called the Merchant of Venice, is encouraged to talk hopefully of his happiness when his ships come home; but he knows that ships sometimes do not come home. Since then we have further transferred the wealth of Antonio to things in some ways even less solid than ships; things often under influences more alien, remote and inhuman than the strangest storms on the most uncharted sea. And then, because we have taken the things out of the cupboard and put them in the coffers of foreign financiers, we calmly talk about something being "as safe as the bank." We are perfectly satisfied now, and have none of the hesitation of Shakespeare; because the wealth in the wandering ships has been transferred from Antonio to Shylock. This is a primary and preliminary fact of the problem, and has nothing to do with doubting any particular bank or denying that banks are useful; still less with merely destroying banks as useless. It merely gets the order and relation of the things stated right, in a world where they are always stated wildly wrong.

(*G.K.'s Weekly*, April 22, 1931)

❖

The Heroines of Shakespeare

It is an odd thing that the words hero and heroine have in their constant use in connection with literary fiction entirely lost their meaning. A hero now means merely a young man sufficiently decent and reliable to go through a few adventures without hanging himself or taking to drink. The modern realistic novelist introduces us to a weak-kneed young suburban gentleman who varies dull respectability with duller vice, and consumes three thick volumes before he has decided which woman he will marry. And by the strange, blasphemous perversion of words, he is called "The Hero." He might just as well, in reason, be called "The Saint", or "The Prophet", or "The Messiah". A hero means a man of heroic stature, a demigod, a man on whom rests something of the mystery which is beyond man. Now, the great and striking thing about heroines like Portia and Isabella and Rosalind is that they are heroines, that they do represent a certain dignity, a certain breadth, which is distinct from the mere homely vigour of the Shakespearian men. You could not slap Portia on the back as you could Bassanio. There may or may not be a divinity that cloth hedge a king, but there is certainly a divinity that cloth hedge a queen. To understand this heroic quality in the Shakespearian women it is necessary to grasp a little the whole Elizabethan, and especially the whole Shakespearian, view of this matter.

The great conception at the back of the oldest religions in the world is, of course, the conception that man is of divine origin, a sacred and splendid heir, the eldest son of the universe. But humanity could not in practice carry out this conception that everyone was divine. The practical imagination recoils from the idea of two gods swindling each other over a pound of cheese. The mind refuses to accept the idea of sixty bodies, each filled with a blazing divinity, elbowing each other to get into an omnibus. This mere external difficulty causes men in every age to fall back upon the conception that certain men preserved for other men the sanctity of man. Certain figures were more divine because they were more human. In primitive times of folklore, and in some feudal periods, this larger man was the conquering hero, the strong man who slew dragons and oppressors. To the old Hebrews this sacred being was the prophet: to the men of the Christian ages it was the saint. To the Elizabethans this sacred being was the pure woman.

The heroic conception of womanhood comes out most clearly in Shakespeare because of his astonishing psychological imagination, but it exists as an ideal in all Elizabethans. And the precise reason why the heroines of Shakespeare are so splendid is because they stand alone among all his characters as the embodiments of the primal ages of faith. They are the high and snowy peaks which catch the last rays of the belief in the actual divinity of man. We feel, as we read the plays, that the women are more large, more typical, belong more to an ideal and less to a realistic literature. They are the very reverse of abstractions; considered merely as women they are finished down to the finest detail. Yet there is something more in them that is not in the men. Portia is a good woman and Bassanio is a good man. But Portia is more than a woman: Portia is Woman and Bassanio is not Man. He is merely a very pleasant and respectable individual.

There are Elizabethan plays so dark and frightful that they read like the rubbish from the wastepaper basket of a madhouse. No one but a prophet possessed of devils, one might fancy, could produce incidents so abrupt and so sombre, could call up scenes so graphic and so unmeaning. In one play a man is forced to watch the murder of those he loves and cannot speak because his tongue is nailed to the floor with a dagger. In another a man is torn with red-hot pincers; in another a man is dropped through a broken floor into a cauldron. With horrible cries out of the lowest hell it is proclaimed that man cannot be continent, that man cannot be true, that he is only the filthiest and the funniest of monkeys. And yet the one belief that all these dark and brutal men admit, is the belief in the pure woman. In this one virtue, in this one sex, something heroic and holy, something, in the highest sense of that word, fabulous, was felt to reside. Man was natural, but woman was supernatural.

Now it is quite clear that this was the Elizabethan view of woman. Portia is not only the most splendid and magnanimous woman in literature. She is not only the heroine of the play, she is the play. She is the absolute heroic ideal upon which the play is built. Shakespeare had conceived, with extraordinary force, humour and sympathy, a man to express the ideal of technical justice, formal morality, and the claim of a man to his rights: the man was Shylock. Over against him he set a figure representing the larger conception of generosity and persuasion, the justice that is fused of a score of genial

passions, the compromise that is born of a hundred worthy
enthusiasms. Portia had to represent the ideal of magnanimity in law, morality, religion, art and politics. And Shakespeare
made this figure a good woman because, to the mind of his
day, to make it a good woman was to ring it with a halo and
arm it with a sword.

(*The Speaker*, October 26, 1901)

❖

Heroic Heroines

Shakespeare always made his heroines heroic as well as his
heroes.

(Introduction to *Nicholas Nickleby*)

❖

Beatrice

If Shakespeare really married a bad wife when he had
conceived the character of Beatrice he ought to have
been ashamed of himself: he had failed not only in his life,
he had failed in his art.

(*Daily News*, Dec. 9, 1902)

❖

The Repetition of Rosalind

In numberless modern novels and magazines stories, the
heroine is apparently complimented by being described
as "boyish." Doubtless there will soon be another fashion in

fiction, in which the hero will always be described as girlish. Fettered as we are with an antiquated Victorian prejudice of the equality of the sexes, we cannot quite understand why one should be a compliment any more than the other. But, anyhow, the present fashion offers a much deeper difficulty. For the girl is being complimented on her boyishness by people who obviously know nothing at all about boys. Nothing could possibly be more unlike a boy than the candid, confident, unconventional and somewhat shallow sylph who swaggers up to the unfortunate hero of the novel a la mode. So far from being unconventional and shallow, the boy is commonly conventional because he is secretive. He is much more sullen outside and much more morbid inside. Who then is this new Pantomime Boy, and where did she come from? In truth she comes out of a very old pantomime. About three hundred years ago William Shakespeare, not knowing what to do with his characters, turned them out to play in the woods, let a girl masquerade as a boy, and amused himself with speculating on the effect of feminine curiosity freed for an hour from feminine dignity. He did it very well, but he could do something else. And the popular romancers of to-day cannot do anything else. Shakespeare took care to explain in the play itself that he did not think that life should be one prolonged picnic. Nor would he have thought that feminine life should be one prolonged piece of private theatricals. But Rosalind, who was then unconventional for an hour, is now the convention of an epoch. She was then on a holiday; she is now very hard-worked indeed. She has to act in every play, novel, or short story, and always in the same old pert pose. Perhaps she is even afraid to be herself: certainly Celia is now afraid to be herself. We should think it rather a bore if all tragic youths wore black cloaks and carried skulls in imitation of

Hamlet, or all old men waved wands and clasped enormous books in imitation of Prospero. But we are almost as much tied to one type of girl in popular fiction to-day. And it is getting very tiresome. A huge human success is banking up for anybody bold enough to describe a quiet girl, a girl handicapped by good manners and a habit of minding her own business. Even a sulky girl would be a relief. The moral is one we often draw; that the family is the real field for personality. All the best Shakespearian dramas are domestic dramas; even when mainly concerned with domestic murders. So far from freedom following on the decay of the family, what follows is uniformity. The Rosalinds become a sort of regiment; if it is a regiment of vivandières. They wear uniform of shingled hair and short skirts; and they seem to stand in a row like chorus girls. Not till we have got back within the four walls of the home shall we have any great tragedy or great comedy. The attempts to describe life in a Utopia of the future are alone enough to prove that there is nothing dramatic about an everlasting picnic. Men and women must stand in some serious and lasting relation to each other for great passions and great problems to arise; and all this anarchy is as bad for art as it is for morals. Rosalind did not go into the wood to look for her freedom; she went into the wood to look for her father. And all the freedom—and even all the fun—of the adventure really arises from that fact. For even an adventure must have an aim. Anyhow, the modern aimlessless has produced a condition in which we are so bored with Rosalind that we almost long for Lady Macbeth.

(*G.K.'s Weekly*, September 3, 1927)

❖

A *Midsummer Night's Dream*

The greatest of Shakespeare's comedies is also, from a certain point of view, the greatest of his plays. No one would maintain that it occupied this position in the matter of psychological study if by psychological study we mean the study of individual characters in a play. No one would maintain that Puck was a character in the sense that Falstaff is a character, or that the critic stood awed before the psychology of Peaseblossom. But there is a sense in which the play is perhaps a greater triumph of psychology than *Hamlet* itself. It may well be questioned whether in any other literary work in the world is so vividly rendered a social and spiritual atmosphere. There is an atmosphere in *Hamlet*, for instance, a somewhat murky and even melodramatic one, but it is subordinate to the great character, and morally inferior to him; the darkness is only a background for the isolated star of intellect. But *A Midsummer Night's Dream* is a psychological study, not of a solitary man, but of a spirit that unites mankind. The six men may sit talking in an inn; they may not know each other's names or see each other's faces before or after, but night or wine or great stories, or some rich and branching discussion may make them all at one, if not absolutely with each other, at least with that invisible seventh man who is the harmony of all of them. That seventh man is the hero of *A Midsummer Night's Dream*.

A study of the play from a literary or philosophical point of view must therefore be founded upon some serious realisation of what this atmosphere is. In a lecture upon *As You Like It*, Mr. Bernard Shaw made a suggestion which is an admirable example of his amazing ingenuity and of his one most interesting limitation. In maintaining that the light sentiment and optimism of the comedy were regarded by Shakespeare merely as the characteristics of a more or less cynical pot-boiler, he actually suggested that the title "As You Like It" was a taunting address to the public in disparagement of their taste and the dramatist's own work. If Mr. Bernard Shaw had conceived of Shakespeare as insisting that Ben Jonson should wear Jaeger underclothing or join the Blue Ribbon Army, or distribute little pamphlets for the non-payment of rates, he could scarcely have conceived anything more violently opposed to the whole spirit of Elizabethan comedy than the spiteful and priggish modernism of such a taunt. Shakespeare might make the fastidious and cultivated Hamlet, moving in his own melancholy and purely mental world, warn players against an over-indulgence towards the rabble. But the very soul and meaning of the great comedies is that of an uproarious communion between the public and the play, a communion so chaotic that whole scenes of silliness and violence lead us almost to think that some of the "rowdies" from the pit have climbed over the footlights. The title "As you Like It", is, of course, an expression of utter carelessness, but it is not the bitter carelessness which Mr. Bernard Shaw fantastically reads into it; it is the god-like and inexhaustible carelessness of a happy man. And the simple proof of this is that there are scores of these genially taunting titles scattered through the whole of Elizabethan comedy. Is "As You Like It" a title demanding a dark and ironic explanation in a school of comedy which called its plays "What You Will", "A Mad World, My Masters", "If It Be Not Good, the Devil Is In It", "The Devil is an Ass", "An Humorous Day's Mirth", and "A Midsummer Night's Dream"? Every one of these titles is flung at the head of the public as a drunken lord might fling a purse at his footman. Would Mr. Shaw maintain that "If It Be Not Good, the Devil Is In It", was the opposite of "As You Like It", and was a solemn invocation of the supernatural powers to testify to the care and perfection of the literary workmanship? The one explanation is as Elizabethan as the other.

Now in the reason for this modern and pedantic error lies the whole secret and difficulty of such plays as *A Midsummer Night's Dream*. The sentiment of such a play, so far as it can be summed up at all, can be summed up in one sentence. It is the mysticism of happiness. That is to say, it is the conception that as man lives upon a borderland he may find himself in the spiritual or supernatural atmosphere, not only through being profoundly sad or meditative, but by being extravagantly happy. The soul might be rapt out of the body in an agony of sorrow, or a trance of ecstasy; but it might also be rapt out of the body in a paroxysm of laughter. Sorrow we know can go beyond itself; so, according to Shakespeare, can pleasure go beyond itself and become something dangerous and unknown. And the reason that the logical and destructive modern school, of which Mr. Bernard Shaw is an example, does not grasp this purely exuberant nature of the comedies is simply that their logical and destructive attitude have rendered impossible the very experience of this preternatural exuberance. We cannot realise *As You Like It* if we are always considering it as we understand it. We cannot have *A Midsummer's Night Dream* if our one object in life is to keep ourselves awake with the black coffee of criticism. The whole question which is balanced, and balanced nobly and fairly, in *A Midsummer Night's Dream*, is whether the life of waking, or the life of the vision, is the real life, the *sine qua non* of man. But it is difficult to see what superiority for the purpose of judging is possessed by people whose pride it is not to live the life of vision at all. At least it is questionable whether the

Elizabethan did not know more about both worlds than the modern intellectual; it is not altogether improbable that Shakespeare would not only have had a clearer vision of the fairies, but would have shot very much straighter at a deer and netted much more money for his performances than a member of the Stage Society.

In pure poetry and the intoxication of words, Shakespeare never rose higher than he rises in this play. But in spite of this fact, the supreme literary merit of *A Midsummer Night's Dream* is a merit of design. The amazing symmetry, the amazing artistic and moral beauty of that design, can be stated very briefly. The story opens in the sane and common world with the pleasant seriousness of very young lovers and very young friends. Then, as the figures advance into the tangled wood of young troubles and stolen happiness, a change and bewilderment begins to fall on them. They lose their way and their wits for they are in the heart of fairyland. Their words, their hungers, their very figures grow more and more dim and fantastic, like dreams within dreams, in the supernatural mist of Puck. Then the dream-fumes begin to clear, and characters and spectators begin to awaken together to the noise of horns and dogs and the clean and bracing morning. Theseus, the incarnation of a happy and generous rationalism, expounds in hackneyed and superb lines the sane view of such psychic experiences, pointing out with a reverent and sympathetic scepticism that all these fairies and spells are themselves but the emanations, the unconscious masterpieces, of man himself. The whole company falls back into a splendid human laughter. There is a rush for banqueting and private theatricals, and over all these things ripples one of those frivolous and inspired conversations in which every good saying seems to die in giving birth to another. If ever the son of a man in his wanderings

was at home and drinking by the fireside, he is at home in
the house of Theseus. All the dreams have been forgotten,
as a melancholy dream remembered throughout the morning might be forgotten in the human certainty of any other
triumphant evening party; and so the play seems naturally
ended. It began on the earth and it ends on the earth. Thus
to round off the whole midsummer night's dream in an
eclipse of daylight is an effect of genius. But of this comedy,
as I have said, the mark is that genius goes beyond itself; and
one touch is added which makes the play colossal. Theseus
and his train retire with a crashing finale, full of humour and
wisdom and things set right, and silence falls on the house.
Then there comes a faint sound of little feet, and for a
moment, as it were, the elves look into the house, asking
which is the reality. "Suppose we are the realities and they
the shadows." If that ending were acted properly any modern man would feel shaken to his marrow if he had to walk
home from the theatre through a country lane.

It is a trite matter, of course, though in a general criticism
a more or less indispensable one to comment upon another
point of artistic perfection, the extraordinarily human and
accurate manner in which the play catches the atmosphere
of a dream. The chase and tangle and frustration of the incidents and personalities are well known to everyone who has
dreamt of perpetually falling over precipices or perpetually
missing trains. While following out clearly and legally the
necessary narrative of the drama, the author contrives to
include every one of the main peculiarities of the exasperating dream. Here is the pursuit of the man we cannot catch,
the flight from the man we cannot see; here is the perpetual
returning to the same place, here is the crazy alteration in
the very objects of our desire, the substitution of one face
for another face, the putting of the wrong souls in the wrong

bodies, the fantastic disloyalties of the night, all this is as
obvious as it is important. It is perhaps somewhat more
worth remarking that there is about this confusion of comedy yet another essential characteristic of dreams. A dream
can commonly be described as possessing an utter discor-
dance of incident combined with a curious unity of mood;
everything changes but the dreamer. It may begin with
anything and end with anything, but if the dreamer is sad at
the end he will be sad as if by prescience at the beginning;
if he is cheerful at the beginning he will be cheerful if the
stars fall. *A Midsummer Night's Dream* has in a most singular degree effected this difficult, this almost desperate subtlety. The events in the wandering wood are in themselves,
and regarded as in broad daylight, not merely melancholy
but bitterly cruel and ignominious. But yet by the spreading
of an atmosphere as magic as the fog of Puck, Shakespeare
contrives to make the whole matter mysteriously hilarious
while it is palpably tragic, and mysteriously charitable, while
it is in itself cynical. He contrives somehow to rob tragedy
and treachery of their full sharpness, just as a toothache or
a deadly danger from a tiger, or a precipice, is robbed of its
sharpness in a pleasant dream. The creation of a brooding
sentiment like this, a sentiment not merely independent of
but actually opposed to the events, is a much greater triumph of art than the creation of the character of Othello.

It is difficult to approach critically so great a figure as that
of Bottom the Weaver. He is greater and more mysterious
than Hamlet, because the interest of such men as Bottom
consists of a rich subconsciousness, and that of Hamlet in
the comparatively superficial matter of a rich consciousness.
And it is especially difficult in the present age which has
become hag-ridden with the mere intellect. We are the victims of a curious confusion whereby being great is supposed

to have something to do with being clever, as if there were
the smallest reason to suppose that Achilles was clever, as if
there were not on the contrary a great deal of internal evidence to indicate that he was next door to a fool. Greatness
is a certain indescribable but perfectly familiar and palpable
quality of size in the personality, of steadfastness, of strong
flavour, of easy and natural self-expression. Such a man is as
firm as a tree and as unique as a rhinoceros, and he might
quite easily be as stupid as either of them. Fully as much as
the great poet towers above the small poet the great fool
towers above the small fool. We have all of us known rustics
like Bottom the Weaver, men whose faces would be blank
with idiocy if we tried for ten days to explain the meaning of
the National Debt, but who are yet great men, akin to
Sigurd and Hercules, heroes of the morning of the earth,
because their words were their own words, their memories
their own memories, and their vanity as large and simple as
a great hill. We have all of us known friends in our own
circle, men whom the intellectuals might justly describe as
brainless, but whose presence in a room was like a fire roaring in the grate changing everything, lights and shadows and
the air, whose entrances and exits were in some strange
fashion events, whose point of view once expressed haunts
and persuades the mind and almost intimidates it, whose
manifest absurdity clings to the fancy like the beauty of first-
love, and whose follies are recounted like the legends of a
paladin. These are great men, there are millions of them in
the world, though very few perhaps in the House of
Commons. It is not in the cold halls of cleverness where
celebrities seem to be important that we should look for the
great. An intellectual salon is merely a training-ground for
one faculty, and is akin to a fencing class or a rifle corps. It
is in our own homes and environments, from Croydon to St.

John's Wood, in old nurses, and gentlemen with hobbies, and talkative spinsters and vast incomparable butlers, that we may feel the presence of that blood of the gods. And this creature so hard to describe, so easy to remember, the august and memorable fool, has never been so sumptuously painted as in the Bottom of *A Midsummer Night's Dream*.

Bottom has the supreme mark of this real greatness in that like the true saint or the true hero he only differs from humanity in being as it were more human than humanity. It is not true, as the idle materialists of today suggest, that compared to the majority of men the hero appears cold and dehumanised; it is the majority who appear cold and dehumanised in the presence of greatness. Bottom, like Don Quixote and Uncle Toby and Mr. Richard Swiveller and the rest of the Titans, has a huge and unfathomable weakness, his silliness is on a great scale, and when he blows his own trumpet it is like the trumpet of the Resurrection. The other rustics in the play accept his leadership not merely naturally but exuberantly; they have to the full that primary and savage unselfishness, that uproarious abnegation which makes simple men take pleasure in falling short of a hero, that unquestionable element of basic human nature which has never been expressed, outside this play, so perfectly as in the incomparable chapter at the beginning of *Evan Harrington* in which the praises of The Great Mel are sung with a lyric energy by the tradesmen whom he has cheated. Twopenny sceptics write of the egoism of primal human nature; it is reserved for great men like Shakespeare and Meredith to detect and make vivid this rude and subconscious unselfishness which is older than self. They alone with their insatiable tolerance can perceive all the spiritual devotion in the soul of a snob. And it is this natural play between the rich simplicity of Bottom and the

simple simplicity of his comrades which constitutes the
unapproachable excellence of the farcical scenes in this
play. Bottom's sensibility to literature is perfectly fiery and
genuine, a great deal more genuine than that of a great
many cultivated critics of literature—"the raging rocks, and
shivering shocks shall break the locks of prison gates, and
Phibbus' car shall shine from far, and make and mar the
foolish fates", is exceedingly good poetical diction with a
real throb and swell in it, and if it is slightly and almost
imperceptibly deficient in the matter of sense, it is certainly
every bit as sensible as a good many other rhetorical
speeches in Shakespeare put into the mouths of kings and
lovers and even the spirits of the dead. If Bottom liked cant
for its own sake the fact only constitutes another point of
sympathy between him and his literary creator. But the style
of the thing, though deliberately bombastic and ludicrous, is
quite literary, the alliteration falls like wave upon wave, and
the whole verse, like a billow mounts higher and higher
before it crashes. There is nothing mean about this folly; nor
is there in the whole realm of literature a figure so free from
vulgarity. The man vitally base and foolish sings "The
Honeysuckle and the Bee", he does not rant about "raging
rocks" and "the car of Phibbus". Dickens, who more perhaps than any modern man had the mental hospitality and
the thoughtless wisdom of Shakespeare, perceived and
expressed admirably the same truth. He perceived, that is to
say, that quite indefensible idiots have very often a real
sense of, and enthusiasm for letters. Mr. Micawber loved
eloquence and poetry with his whole immortal soul; words
and visionary pictures kept him alive in the absence of food
and money, as they might have kept a saint fasting in a desert. Dick Swiveller did not make his inimitable quotations
from Moore and Byron merely as flippant digressions. He

made them because he loved a great school of poetry. The
sincere love of books has nothing to do with cleverness or
stupidity any more than any other sincere love. It is a quality
of character, a freshness, a power of pleasure, a power of
faith. A silly person may delight in reading masterpieces just
as a silly person may delight in picking flowers. A fool may
be in love with a poet as he may be in love with a woman.
And the triumph of Bottom is that he loves rhetoric and his
own taste in the arts, and this is all that can be achieved by
Theseus, or for the matter of that by Cosimo di Medici. It is
worth remarking as an extremely fine touch in the picture of
Bottom that his literary taste is almost everywhere concerned with sound rather than sense. He begins the
rehearsal with a boisterous readiness, "Thisby, the flowers
of odious savours sweete." "Odours, odours," says Quince,
in remonstrance, and the word is accepted in accordance
with the cold and heavy rules which require an element of
meaning in a poetical passage. But "Thisby, the flowers of
odious savours sweete", Bottom's version, is an immeasurably finer and more resonant line. The "i" which he inserts
is an inspiration of metricism.

There is another aspect of this great play which ought to
be kept familiarly in the mind. Extravagant as is the masquerade of the story, it is a very perfect aesthetic harmony
down to such *coup-de-maître* as the name of Bottom, or the
flower called Love in Idleness. In the whole matter it may
be said that there is one accidental discord; that is in the
name of Theseus, and the whole city of Athens in which the
events take place. Shakespeare's description of Athens in *A
Midsummer Night's Dream* is the best description of
England that he or anyone else ever wrote. Theseus is quite
obviously only an English squire, fond of hunting, kindly to
his tenants, hospitable with a certain flamboyant vanity.

The mechanics are English mechanics, talking to each other with the queer formality of the poor. Above all, the fairies are English; to compare them with the beautiful patrician spirits of Irish legend, for instance, is suddenly to discover that we have, after all, a folk-lore and a mythology, or had it at least in Shakespeare's day. Robin Goodfellow, upsetting the old women's ale, or pulling the stool from under them, has nothing of the poignant Celtic beauty; his is the horse-play of the invisible world. Perhaps it is some debased inheritance of English life which makes American ghosts so fond of quite undignified practical jokes. But this union of mystery with farce is a note of the medieval English. The play is the last glimpse of Merrie England, that distant but shining and quite indubitable country. It would be difficult indeed to define wherein lay the peculiar truth of the phrase "merrie England", though some conception of it is quite necessary to the comprehension of *A Midsummer Night's Dream*. In some cases at least, it may be said to lie in this, that the English of the Middle Ages and the Renaissance, unlike the England of today, could conceive of the idea of a merry supernaturalism. Amid all the great work of Puritanism the damning indictment of it consists in one fact, that there was one only of the fables of Christendom that it retained and renewed, and that was the belief in witchcraft. It cast away the generous and wholesome superstition, it approved only of the morbid and the dangerous. In their treatment of the great national fairy-tale of good and evil, the Puritans killed St. George but carefully preserved the Dragon. And this seventeenth-century tradition of dealing with the psychic life still lies like a great shadow over England and America, so that if we glance at a novel about occultism we may be perfectly certain that it deals with sad or evil destiny. Whatever else we expect we certainly should never expect to find in it spirits such as those in *Aylwin* as inspirers of a tale of tomfoolery like the *Wrong Box* or *The Londoners*. That impossibility is the disappearance of "merrie England" and Robin Goodfellow. It was a land to us incredible, the land of a jolly occultism where the peasant cracked jokes with his patron saint, and only cursed the fairies good-humouredly, as he might curse a lazy servant. Shakespeare is English in everything, above all in his weaknesses. Just as London, one of the greatest cities in the world, shows more slums and hides more beauties than any other, so Shakespeare alone among the four giants of poetry is a careless writer, and lets us come upon his splendours by accident, as we come upon an old City church in the twist of a city street. He is English in nothing so much as in that noble cosmopolitan unconsciousness which makes him look eastward with the eyes of a child towards Athens or Verona. He loved to talk of the glory of foreign lands, but he talked of them with the tongue and unquenchable spirit of England. It is too much the custom of a later patriotism to reverse this method and talk of England from morning till night, but to talk of her in a manner totally un-English. Casualness, incongruities, and a certain fine absence of mind are in the temper of England; the unconscious man with the ass's head is no bad type of the people. Materialistic philosophers and mechanical politicians have certainly succeeded in some cases in giving him a greater unity. The only question is, to which animal has he been thus successfully conformed?

(From *The Common Man*. Originally from *Good Words*, September–October, 1904)

The Man with the Ass's Head

Bottom, Shakespeare's true hero, is the type of the art enthusiast of that time, omnivorous, inconsistent, extravagant, the man with the ass's head. The modern Ibsenite and Student of Drama has got rid of the hybrid character, though we are not quite sure to which of the two animals he has been finally assimilated.

(*The Bookman*, July, 1900)

———— ❖ ————

A Hundred Heads

The vague modern hedonist . . . is not satisfied with saying that he must live his life. He seems to mean that he must live everybody else's life. He is consumed with a sort of envy of everybody else for being everybody else. He is not, like the old decadent of the days of my childhood, rendered more or less dependable by the very limitations of his pose. He is not satisfied with saying that he has a right to be what he is; he seems rather to think he has a right to be whatever he might have been. He does not say he is entitled to drink absinthe because he is an artist; he rather implies that he is entitled to eat hashish because he might have been an assassin, or possibly entitled to eat human flesh because he might have been a cannibal. He is not content with wasting his substance, or even other people's substance, in riotous living. He does not wish to be a rioter but to be a riot—that is, to be a crowd. He thinks he could fulfil everybody else's destinies. Like the decadent, he has his toadies; there are many to tell us that the hedonist must have his head, because it is such a highly intellectual head. Unfortunately, as I say,

he wants to have a hundred heads, like the hydra. There are
many to praise this new universality; but I am haunted with
the memory of somebody else who thought that he could
play all the parts at once. I cannot help recalling who it was
who said "Let me play the lion too," and what sort of a head
it was that they gave him in the end.

(*Illustrated London News*, May 16, 1925)

❖

Buffoonery

To cut the buffoonery out of Shakespeare is as hopeless
as to cut it out of Rabelais—or, for the matter of that, to
cut the name of God out of the Bible.

(*Illustrated London News*, Oct. 31, 1914)

❖

Love's Labour's Lost

Love's Labour's Lost is chronologically as well as philosophically the youngest of Shakespeare's plays. It is
chiefly to be understood as a study of the spirit and the
nature of youth, and it is so true in this respect that it must
offend almost all critics who judge of things by what they
logically should be, by what they inevitably must be, rather
than by what they are. The world of life, and equally and
even more decisively the world of literature, is always out-
witting the philosophers; things do not accord themselves to
our great critical syntheses, even to the latest and largest
and most sympathetic. According to our modern ethics and
ethnology, the emergence from barbarism to civilization

ought to be the gradual subordination of grotesque and obscene passions to a calmer moral selection; yet when we come to the facts of literature, we find the modern arts full of sensuality and a savage tribal epic like the *Iliad*—in all essentials a Zulu war song—as pure as Sir Galahad. Savage peoples ought to exhibit a muddy materialism, a mere interest in meat and blood and animals, and civilized people an interest in the abstract and the ideal; yet when we come to the facts of literature we find that all the discoveries about blood and animals, about food and the seasons, have been made by civilized men, and all the discoveries about the abstract, about mystery and hope, about justice and brotherhood, have been made by savages; we find that barbarians sitting in mud huts have been unable to study the mud they lived in, but have been able to write the Book of Job. Thus upon every side of literature we have to be on our guard against a facile literalism; we have to be ready to receive, with infantile credulity, a paradox. And in nothing is this so striking as in the Shakespearean drama; in nothing so striking especially as in that cycle of early comedies, celebrating the mystery of youth, of which *As You Like It*, *A Midsummer Night's Dream*, and *Twelfth Night* are examples, but of which *Love's Labour's Lost* is the earliest and infinitely the most typical example. The account of youth given in these appears like the sculptures of a lunatic asylum; it is fantastic, solemn, full of preposterous observances, of fanciful limits. The only answer is that youth is an experience, like Freemasonry, and no one who does not remember it can recognize its signs.

There are certain matters of human psychology in which Shakespeare is so singularly and strangely right that his rightness will only with great difficulty be appreciated by those few persons who happen intensely to remember the experience. Thus, for instance, it would occur to most people, it does occur to the realistic and hysterical moderns, to represent the hour of deadly peril as an hour which leads to frenzied assertions of authority, to selection, to decimation, to a fierce and merciless inequality. The short-story writer of to-day who has never been in danger of anything (except perhaps of delirium tremens) represents the leader of a small army hemmed in by the enemy as asserting himself with a splendid brutality, as domineering, as sneering, as striking men when they murmur and shooting them when they disobey. But Shakespeare in that splendid scene in *Henry V* perceived the spiritual truth that danger reveals democracy:

> We few, we happy few, we band of brothers—
> For who this day shall shed his blood with me
> Shall be my brother; be he ne'er so vile
> This day shall gentle his condition.

Ten men cast on a desert island might have ten different social ranks, for the time they would be only men. So in Shakespeare these Englishmen, islanded as it were in a sea of enemies, are only Englishmen. Instances of the same kinds of truth, too true to impress the outsider, abound in Shakespeare. Thus when he glorifies his native land in that incomparable and hackneyed passage in *Richard II*, he does not dwell, like a windy journalist, upon the largeness of his country; he dwells, like a lover, on its smallness—he calls it a jewel and a little fort; he feels the real love and therefore tends, like the amatory poet, to diminutives, or like the collector, to a careful and almost compassionate manner of hovering over something infinitesimal. These are merely random examples of the general psychological truth that the place where most modern men, careless of actuality or ignorant of passionate experience would go wrong, is precisely the place where Shakespeare goes right. It is so supremely in this matter of the nature of youth as revealed in *Love's Labour's Lost*. Sullen and Byronic poets depict youth as extravagant in enjoyment and demand, as splendidly sensual and mingled of the animal and the God. This is the universal habit of literary Puritans and of those hackneyed epicureans and hedonists who are more gloomy than any Puritans. But any one who can really recall the nature of youth, will perceive that the Elizabethans had hold of precisely the accurate and precisely the opposite view. Shakespeare in *Love's Labour's Lost* perceives first of all the one great mark of a generous boyhood—the vow of celibacy. Youth with its sense of a reserve force, of an unexplored strength, with its delight in trifles, with its readiness for a crusade, has always been favourable to the frenzy of virginity. It has the power of extracting from comradeship (as Plato and Walt Whitman did) almost all the romance of first love: it has the power of trusting itself. There is about the celibate and scholarly brotherhood in *Love's Labour's Lost* something of the radiant childishness which marks, to those who can read history rightly, the inception of the greater monastic orders, such as that of St. Francis, inceptions which make us feel, as we read of them, that in their gay austerity was the very April of the soul, and that no revelers will ever be so light-hearted as those ascetics. Shakespeare, at one with the early Middle Ages in their sympathy with an ecstatic bachelorhood, is separated from the Middle Ages in that he thinks that bachelorhood is not a final vocation but a splendid vigil. His three celibate heroes in *Love's Labour's Lost* are quite passionately and sincerely attached to their celibacy, but they succeed

afterwards in becoming equally passionately and equally
sincerely attached to three young ladies. Although this is
almost the very earliest of the great Shakespearean love-
stories, the love poetry in it rises here and there to a height
which he seldom afterwards touched even in his greatest
moments. There are lines that have the one essential of
great song, that of seeming, the reader knows not how, to
be fragments of some more prehistoric and gigantic poem,
glimpses of a far-off beauty:

> For valour, is not love a Hercules
> Still climbing trees in the Hesperides.

But though the victory is in this play, as in all Shakespeare's
comedies, given to the higher power of sex, the critics make
a great mistake who treat their early theories of virginity as
a mere folly to be exploded by the story. Many writers have
spoken of this play as if it were an attack on mediaeval celibacy, as if it were meant merely to satirise a resistance to
nature. This is profoundly to misinterpret the levity and
purity of the story, the pure gold and the clear silver of that
Elizabethan dawn. The love would be quite as much spoilt
without the celibacy as the celibacy without the love. The
note of severity struck at the beginning of the story is simply
the note struck at the beginning of all honest youth and pas-
sion. For Shakespeare wrote, as we say, from the inside of
youth: he was a young man beginning a young literature. He
uttered true things that seem fantastic, as the true things of
war seem to the civilian. And he uttered above all the central truth that the right and primary attitude of happy youth
towards sex is an attitude of consuming fear.

(*Good Words*, January, 1904)

———— ❖ ————

Falstaff

There has been a new literary competition, touching the question of our favorite character in fiction; and this cannot be made an international issue, for it seems to have started in London; indeed, with *John o'London*, who must surely represent that city. Afterwards it seems to have gone on a lecturing tour in America, like so many Johns of London, and turned up in the *New York Times*, after which it has returned to London and to me.

Like most of these selections, it suffers from some ambiguity in the terms of reference. Our favorite character might mean the most psychologically credible character, as in so much of Balzac or Trollope or Jane Austen; or the most gloriously and divinely incredible character, as in so much of Dickens; or the character for whom we should have the most affection in real life; which is something entirely different.

Thus, when Mr. H. E. Bates chooses Uncle Toby and Mr. T. G. Powys chooses Parson Adams, they may well love these persons as persons, and not only admire them as *personae*. But when Mr. Arthur Symons chooses Père Goriot he means the most vivid or pathetic person, not the person he would like to live with; and when Mr. L. A. G. Strong gives the second place to Mrs. Gamp it is rather to a conversationalist to whom he would like to listen than to a nurse whom he would trust with his life.

In this sense there are a throng of Dickens characters competing for my favor, some of the most insignificant being the most important. I am not sure I would not award the laurel to Trabb's Boy, in *Great Expectations*. He is

Democracy in daemonic power, when he blasts the snobbishness of Pip.

But as Mr. Strong gives Falstaff as his first choice, I am
moved to support him and say a word about that great original among the comic characters of our literature. I do so
because Falstaff has always been a puzzle to moralists, and
it was by a sort of accident that I found the key.

I was deep in controversy with a very learned Cambridge
don on the subject of Pride, a point perhaps a little too personal to Cambridge dons. Anyhow, this professor was grumbling that Pride is not so bad after all, since swaggerers are
admired and we all like Falstaff. And then I suddenly saw
the truth, as I have often seen it, in a blaze of light revealed
by the black falsehood and folly of professors. The scholar is
often a guide to truth because he states clearly the exact
contrary of the truth.

Falstaff is a coward, a thief, an old man encouraging the
young in vice; he has not, in our ethical definition, one ordinary virtue to his name. And yet all Christian people love
him; and they are right. They love him because, in his welter
of vices, there is not one drop of Pride. He knows what he
is; he jeers at himself for being what he is.

But because our evolutionary ethics have forgotten
Humility we cannot understand even our own affections.
We love Falstaff because he is everything else except a
Pharisee. And so his admirers have been driven to pretend
they are cynics or anarchists when the dreadful secret is that
they are still Christians.

(*New York American*, December 29, 1934)

❖

Falstaff Was Real

Smaller characters give us the impression that the author has told the whole truth about them, greater characters give the impression that the author has given of them, not the truth, but merely a few hints and samples. In some mysterious way we seem to feel that even if Shakespeare was wrong about Falstaff, Falstaff existed and was real; that even if Dickens was wrong about Micawber, Micawber existed and was real.

("Bret Harte," *Varied Types*)

IV.
THE PLAY'S THE THING

Everything is Dramatic

Shakespeare, being interested in everything, put every-thing into a play. If he had lately been thinking about the irony and even contradiction confronting us in self-preser-vation and suicide, he put it all into *Hamlet*. If he was annoyed by some passing boom in theatrical babies he put that into *Hamlet* too. He would put anything into *Hamlet* which he really thought was true, from his favourite nursery ballads to his personal (and perhaps unfashionable) convic-tion of the Catholic purgatory. There is no fact that strikes one, I think, about Shakespeare, except the fact of how dramatic he could be, so much as the fact of how undra-matic he could be . . . Shakespeare (in a weak moment, I think) said that all the world is a stage. But Shakespeare acted on the finer principle that a stage is all the world.

("The Philosopher," *George Bernard Shaw*)

———— ❖ ————

The Fun of the Drama

To amuse oneself is a mark of gaiety, vitality and love of life. To be amused is a mark of melancholy, surrender and a potentiality of suicide.

The former means that a man's own thoughts are attrac-tive, artistic and satisfying; the latter means that his own thoughts are ugly, unfruitful and stale. And the happiness of a people is not to be judged by the amount of fun provided for them. For fun can be provided as food can be provided; by a few big stores or shops. The happiness of the people is to be judged by the fun that the people provide. In healthier ages any amount of fun was really provided by the people and not merely for the people. It was so in a vast multitude of songs, fairly tales and dances; but it was so even in the more ornate and official business of the drama.

The men of the mediaeval guilds enacted in person the miracle plays, with all their highly-coloured symbolism of the mysteries of heaven and hell. I have the fullest political sympathy with the modern Trades Unions; but I confess I cannot easily imagine a railway-porter feeling quite comfortable in the costume of the Archangel Gabriel; or even a plumber getting the full delight out of being the Devil. Yet it must have been a very pure delight to be the Devil. There was any amount of gagging and grotesque impromptu in such a part; for the mediaeval men were quite without the modern reverence. That is, they were quite without the modern reverence for the Devil. The carpenter or cobbler who had the happiness of acting Caiphas used to borrow a cope or a chasuble from the parish church; and I earnestly hope that the Archbishop of Canterbury would now lend his apron and gaiters to a dustman for such a purpose.

But the only point here is that numbers of ordinary poor people acted; and there was nothing to prevent it being done in every town and even every village. I daresay they acted as badly as Bottom the Weaver; but I am not talking about art, but about amusement. Above all, I am talking about people amusing themselves; and not only being amused. None will dare deny that Bottom the Weaver amused himself, even more than he amused his audience. Certainly that great man did not stoop merely to be amused; indeed, to amuse

Bottom would be a bold and almost blasphemous undertaking; in which all the frolics of the fairies failed.

Shakespeare was probably thinking of the "hard-handed men" whom he may have seen thus acting the last of the mediaeval plays; as he was almost certainly thinking of the traditional figure of Herod in the Bethlehem plays, when he makes Bottom talk of playing a tyrant. A hundred years before he might have found such things in a hundred hamlets.

(*Vanity Fair*, February, 1920)

———— ❖ ————

The Silver Goblets

It was reported that at the sumptuous performance of *Henry VIII* at His Majesty's Theatre, the urns and goblets of the banquet were specially wrought in real and solid silver and in the style of the sixteenth century. This bombastic literalism is at least very much the fashion in our modern theatricals. Mr. Vincent Crummles considered it a splendid piece of thoroughness on the part of an actor that he should black himself all over to perform Othello. But Mr. Crummles's ideal falls far short of the theoretic thoroughness of the late Sir Herbert Tree; who would consider blacking oneself all over as comparatively a mere sham, compromise, and veneer. Sir Herbert Tree would, I suppose, send for a real negro to act Othello; and perhaps for a real Jew to act Shylock—though that, in the present condition of the English stage, might possibly be easier. The strict principle of the silver goblets might be a little more arduous and unpleasant if applied, let us say, to *The Arabian Nights*, if the manager of His Majesty's Theatre presented *Aladdin*, and had to produce not one real negro but a hundred real

negroes, carrying a hundred baskets of gigantic and genuine
jewels. In the presence of this proposal even Sir Herbert
might fall back on a simpler philosophy of the drama. For
the principle in itself admits of no limit. If once it be allowed
that what looks like silver behind the footlights is better also
for really being silver, there seems no reason why the wildest developments should not ensue. The priests in *Henry
VIII* might be specially ordained in the green-room before
they come on. Nay, if it comes to that, the head of
Buckingham might really be cut off; as in the glad old days
lamented by Swinburne, before the coming or an emascu-
late mysticism removed real death from the arena. We
might re-establish the goriness as well as the gorgeousness
of the amphitheatre. If real wine-cups, why not real wine?
If real wine, why not real blood ?

Nor is this an illegitimate or irrelevant deduction. This
and a hundred other fantasies might follow if once we admit
the first principle that we need to realize on the stage not
merely the beauty of silver, but the value of silver.
Shakespeare's famous phrase that art should hold the mirror
up to nature is always taken as wholly realistic; but it is really
idealistic and symbolic—at least, compared with the realism
of His Majesty's. Art is a mirror not because it is the same
as the object, but because it is different. A mirror selects as
much as art selects; it gives the light of flames, but not their
heat; the colour of flowers, but not their fragrance; the faces
of women, but not their voices; the proportions of stockbro-
kers, but not their solidity. A mirror is a vision of things, not
a working model of them. And the silver seen in a mirror is
not for sale.

But the results of the thing in practice are worse than its
wildest results in theory. This Arabian extravagance in the
furniture and decoration of a play has one very practical

disadvantage—that it narrows the number of experiments, confines them to a small and wealthy class, and makes those which are made exceptional, erratic, and unrepresentative of any general dramatic activity. One or two insanely expensive works prove nothing about the general state of art in a country. To take the parallel of a performance somewhat less dignified, perhaps, than Sir Herbert Tree's, there has lately been in America an exhibition not unanalogous to a conflict in the arena, and one for which a real negro actually was procured by the management. The negro happened to beat the white man, and both before and after this event people went about wildly talking of "the White Man's champion" and "the representative of the Black Race." All black men were supposed to have triumphed over all white men in a sort of mysterious Armageddon because one specialist met another specialist and tapped his claret or punched him in the bread-basket. Now the fact is, of course, that these two prize-fighters were so specially picked and trained—the business of producing such men is so elaborate, artificial, and expensive—that the result proves nothing whatever about the general condition of white men or black. If you go in for heroes or monsters it is obvious that they may be born anywhere. If you took the two tallest men on earth one might be born in Corea and the other in Camberwell, but this would not make Camberwell a land of giants inheriting the blood of Anak. If you took the two thinnest men in the world, one might be a Parisian and the other a Red Indian. And if you take the two most scientifically developed pugilists, it is not surprising that one of them should happen to be white and the other black. Experiments of so special and profuse a kind have the character of monstrosities, like black tulips or blue roses. It is absurd to make them representative of races and causes that they do not represent. You

might as well say that the Bearded Lady at a fair represents
the masculine advance of modern woman; or that all Europe
was shaking under the banded armies of Asia, because of
the co-operation of the Siamese Twins.

So the plutocratic tendency of such performances as
Henry VIII is to prevent rather than to embody any movement of historical or theatrical imagination. If the standard
of expenditure is set so high by custom, the number of com-
petitors must necessarily be small, and will probably be of a
restricted and unsatisfactory type. Instead of English history
and English literature being as cheap as silver paper, they
will be as dear as silver plate. The national culture, instead
of being spread out everywhere like gold leaf, will be hardened into a few costly lumps of gold—and kept in very few
pockets. The modern world is full of things that are theo-
retically open and popular, but practically private and even
corrupt. In theory any tinker can be chosen to speak for his
fellow-citizens among the English Commons. In practice he
may have to spend a thousand pounds on getting elected—a
sum which many tinkers do not happen to have to spare. In
theory it ought to be possible for any moderately successful
actor with a sincere and interesting conception of Wolsey to
put that conception on the stage. In practice it looks as if he
would have to ask himself, not whether he was as clever as
Wolsey, but whether he was as rich. He has to reflect, not
whether he can enter into Wolsey's soul, but whether he can
pay Wolsey's servants, purchase Wolsey's plate, and own
Wolsey's palaces.

Now people with Wolsey's money and people with Wolsey's
mind are both rare; and even with him the mind came before
the money. The chance of their being combined a second time
is manifestly small and decreasing. The result will obviously be
that thousands and millions may be spent on a theatrical misfit,

and inappropriate and unconvincing impersonation; and all the time there may be a man outside who could have put on a red dressing-gown and made us feel in the presence of the most terrible of the Tudor statesmen. The modern method is to sell Shakespeare for thirty pieces of silver.

(also published under the title "Realism in the Theatre", *Illustrated London News*, October 8, 1910)

—— ❖ ——

On Stage Costume

While watching the other evening a very well managed reproduction of *A Midsummer Night's Dream*, I had the sudden conviction that the play would be much better if it were acted in modern costume, or, at any rate, in English costume. We all remember hearing in our boyhood about the absurd conventionality of Garrick and Mrs. Siddons, when he acted Macbeth in a tie-wig and a tail-coat, and she acted Lady Macbeth in a crinoline as big and stiff as a cartwheel. This has always been talked of as a piece of comic ignorance or impudent modernity; as if Rosalind appeared in rational dress with a bicycle; as if Portia appeared with a horsehair wig and side-whiskers. But I am not so sure that the great men and women who founded the English stage in the eighteenth century were quite such fools as they looked; especially as they looked to the romantic historians and eager archaeologists of the nineteenth century. I have a queer suspicion that Garrick and Siddons knew nearly as much about dressing as they did about acting.

One distinction can at least be called obvious. Garrick did not care much for the historical costume of Macbeth; but he cared as much as Shakespeare did. He did not know

much about that prehistoric and partly mythical Celtic
chief; but he knew more than Shakespeare; and he could
not conceivably have cared less. Now the Victorian age was
honestly interested in the dark and epic origins of Europe;
was honestly interested in Picts and Scots, in Celts and
Saxons; in the blind drift of the races and the blind drive of
the religions. Ossian and the Arthurian revival had interested people in distant dark-headed men who probably
never existed. Freeman, Carlyle, and the other Teutonists
had interested them in distant fairheaded men who almost
certainly never existed. Pusey and Pugin and the first High
Churchmen had interested them in shaven-headed men,
dark or fair, men who did undoubtedly exist, but whose real
merits and defects would have startled their modern admirers very considerably. Under these circumstances it is not
strange that our age should have felt a curiosity about the
solid but mysterious Macbeth of the Dark Ages. But all this
does not alter the ultimate fact: that the only Macbeth that
mankind will ever care about is the Macbeth of Shakespeare,
and not the Macbeth of history. When England was romantic it was interested in Macbeth's kilt and claymore. In the
same way, if England becomes a Republic, it will be specially interested in the Republicans in *Julius Caesar*. If
England becomes Roman Catholic, it will be specially interested in the theory of chastity in *Measure for Measure*. But
being interested in these things will never be the same as
being interested in Shakespeare. And for a man interested
in Shakespeare, a man merely concerned about what
Shakespeare meant, a Macbeth in powdered hair and knee-
breeches is perfectly satisfactory. For Macbeth, as Shakespeare shows him, is much more like a man in knee-breeches
than a man in a kilt. His subtle hesitations and his suicidal
impenitence belong to the bottomless speculations of a

highly civilized society. The "Out, out, brief candle" is far more appropriate to the last wax taper after a ball of powder and patches than to the smoky but sustained fires in iron baskets which probably flared and smouldered over the swift crimes of the eleventh century. The real Macbeth probably killed Duncan with the nearest weapon, and then confessed it to the nearest priest. Certainly, he may never have had any such doubts about the normal satisfaction of being alive. However regrettably negligent of the importance of Duncan's life, he had, I fancy, few philosophical troubles about the importance of his own. The men of the Dark Ages were all optimists, as all children and all animals are. The madness of Shakespeare's Macbeth goes along with candles and silk stockings. That madness only appears in the age of reason.

So far, then, from Garrick's anachronism being despised, I should like to see it imitated. Shakespeare got the tale of Theseus from Athens, as he got the tale of Macbeth from Scotland; and having reluctantly seen the names of those two countries in the record, I am convinced that he never gave them another thought. Macbeth is not a Scotchman; he is a man. But Theseus is not only not an Athenian; he is actually and unmistakably an Englishman. He is the Super-Squire; the best version of the English country gentleman; better than Wardle in *Pickwick*. The Duke of Athens is a duke (that is, a cook), but not of Athens. That free city is thousands of miles away.

If Theseus came on the stage in gaiters or a shooting-jacket, if Bottom the Weaver wore a smock-frock, if Hermia and Helena were dressed as two modern English school-girls, we should not be departing from Shakespeare, but rather returning to him. The cold, classical draperies (of which he probably never dreamed, but with which we drape

Aegisthus or Hippolyta) are not only a nuisance, but a false-hood. They misrepresent the whole meaning of the play. For the meaning of the play is that the little things of life as well as the great things stray on the borderland of the unknown. That as a man may fall among devils for a morbid crime, or fall among angels for a small piece of piety or pity, so also he may fall among fairies through an amiable flirta-tion or a fanciful jealousy. The fact that a back door opens into elfland is all the more reason for keeping the fore-ground familiar, and even prosaic. For even the fairies are very neighbourly and fire-light fairies; therefore the human beings ought to be very human in order to effect the fantas-tic contrast. And in Shakespeare they are very human. Hermia the vixen and Helena the may-pole are obviously only two excitable and quite modern girls. Hippolyta has never been an Amazon; she may perhaps have once been a Suffragette. Theseus is a gentleman, a thing entirely differ-ent from a Greek oligarch. That golden good-nature which employs culture itself to excuse the clumsiness of the uncul-tured is a thing quite peculiar to those lazier Christian coun-tries where the Christian gentleman has been evolved:

> For nothing in this world can be amiss
> When simpleness and duty tender it.

Or, again, in that noble scrap of sceptical magnanimity which was unaccountably cut out in the last performance:

> The best in this kind are but shadows; and the worst are no
> worse if imagination amend them.

These are obviously the easy and reconciling comments of some kindly but cultivated squire, who will not pretend to his guests that the play is good, but who will not let the actors see that he thinks it bad. But this is certainly not the way in which an Athenian Tory like Aristophanes would have talked about a bad play.

But as the play is dressed and acted at present, the whole idea is inverted. We do not seem to creep out of a human house into a natural wood and there find the superhuman and supernatural. The mortals, in their tunics and togas, seem more distant from us than the fairies in their hoods and peaked caps. It is an anticlimax to meet the English elves when we have already encountered the Greek gods. The same mistake, oddly enough, was made in the only modern play worth mentioning in the same street with *A Midsummer Night's Dream*, *Peter Pan*. Sir James Barrie ought to have left out the fairy dog who puts the children to bed. If children had such dogs as that they would never wish to go to fairyland.

This fault or falsity in *Peter Pan* is, of course, repeated in the strange and ungainly incident of the father being chained up in the dog's kennel. Here, indeed, it is much worse: for the manlike dog was pretty and touching; the doglike man was ignominious and repulsive. But the fallacy is the same; it is the fallacy that weakens the otherwise triumphant poetry and wit of Sir James Barrie's play; and weakens all our treatment of fairy plays at present. Fairyland is a place of positive realities, plain laws, and a decisive story. The actors of *A Midsummer Night's Dream* seemed to think that the play was meant to be chaotic. The clowns thought they must be always clowning. But in reality it is the solemnity—nay, the conscientiousness—of the yokels that is akin to the mystery of the landscape and the tale.

(*Illustrated London News*, June 24, 1911)

——— ❖ ———

Shakespeare in Modern Dress

The Drury Lane performance of *A Midsummer Night's Dream*, which almost avowedly turned it into a Christmas pantomime, did not, in my opinion, fail thereby in respect for its great traditional and almost religious beauty; for there can be nothing more Christian than Christmas and nothing more ancient than pantomime. Especially do I rejoice in the fact that the clowns really were clowns, in the sense of clowns and pantaloons. It seems to me quite as bad art to play Bottom in a quiet realistic way as to play Hamlet in a vulgar theatrical way. I know not if any dramatic critic has expressed the joy which one spectator at least felt in the impersonation of the Wall, certainly the wittiest partition that ever I heard discourse; though the discourse consisted almost entirely of a laugh. But I have no intention of trespassing on the province of any such dramatic critics. I refer to this particular performance for the moment because it raises, as do all such performances, one particular question of historical and artistic setting. The bridal of Theseus and Hippolyta was set in the stiff but strongly coloured framework of archaic Greek art, with the red clay and black profiles of Greek vases; and for the spectacular and pantomimic purpose the effect was very fine. But we all know in reading the play that Theseus is no more an archaic Achaean chief than Hamlet is a barbaric Danish Viking. If Theseus, like Snug the Joiner, could be induced to name his name and tell them plainly who he is, it would be soon apparent that he, Theseus, is not Theseus but Southampton, or Essex, or some genial gentleman of Elizabethan culture and exceedingly English good-nature. His making the best of a bad play is something I recognize as more unmistakable than St. George's Cross. I do not think that national virtue the one thing needful, but I think it very national. There may or may not have been a Greek Theseus; but I cannot imagine a French Theseus—still less an Irish one.

But I mention the matter here for another reason. There is a certain maxim that nearly everybody now repeats and I am disposed to dispute. It is of the sort not very easy to dispute; because it is not yet a proverb, though it is rapidly becoming a platitude. It is at that precise stage at which everybody says it, yet everybody thinks he is alone in saying it. It is said for the thousandth time with an irritating freshness, as if it were said for the first time. It is to this effect: that we only think our own age vulgar and past ages romantic because people in past ages did the same. They also thought their own clothes comic or commonplace, and the clothes of their grandfathers dignified and distinguished. Old clothes are only beautiful as distant hills are blue—with distance. Thus Mr. Kipling describes the prehistoric men as saying that Romance went with bone and flint and could not survive metals and fire. Thus many have said that my praise of the Guilds is only the recurrent retrospective romance of a past Golden Age. It is suggested that men always think the present prosaic and only the past poetical.

I venture to doubt it. And I will test it by this plain and practical test of theatrical costume. Suppose I suggested that *Hamlet*, let us say, should be acted seriously in modern costume. It might be quite interesting—if occasionally rather amusing. It would begin, I suppose, with a sentinel in a busby, like the sentinel in *Iolanthe*. Then Horatio would come out in evening dress, smoking a cigarette. And so on throughout, up to the last catastrophic scene when the

Queen takes the tabloid and the King is shot with the automatic. Hamlet was in many ways very modern; and many of his sceptical meditations would sound very suitable to evening dress and a cigarette. Nevertheless, it would be impossible to prevent it seeming like a burlesque. Yet Garrick acted Macbeth in powdered hair and a coat and breeches of his own period; and it did not seem like a burlesque. Why? The simple reason is, I believe, that men in former ages did *not* have the contempt for their own costume that we have to-day. They did *not* think knee-breeches absurd, as we think trousers absurd. They did *not* think a triangular hat a joke, as we think a top-hat a joke. It is a modern custom to despise modern costume.

It is clear, I think, that Shakespeare thought of his most dignified figures in Elizabethan or Jacobean fashions. He saw Hamlet with a beard; I suspect he saw him with a ruff. The mortal combat is not the less heroic because Osric can gush over the new pattern of the swords. From the innumerable incidental allusions to sixteenth-century custom and costume in the Shakespearean plays, I am convinced that the poet thought in terms of his own time, even if it was, so to speak, when he was thinking without thinking. And nothing is so great in Shakespeare as those abrupt and unexpected bursts of thoughtless thought. But at least he cannot have felt the details altogether incongruous with the design. I take it that for various reasons such details of daily life were really not felt as ignominious or farcical. Of course, there really is in all cases, and was in his case, a certain moderate and normal tendency to regard the remote past as something mystical and imaginative. But it is one thing to do that and another to regard your own hat as merely a bad joke or a blot on the Forest of Arden.

(*Illustrated London News*, January 10, 1925)

———— ❖ ————

Shakespeare in Modern Dress (Again)

I suggested a long time ago . . . somewhere in the appalling stacks of journalistic stuff that I have contributed to this page . . . that Hamlet is so modern that he might well appear in evening dress with a cigarette. But I meant it to be a foolish passage. I meant it merely as a passing fancy; and I was much amused when I discovered that this also had been carried out by more serious persons in a more solid manner. I remember saying about the same time something that is not irrelevant to the issue. I pointed out that, as a matter of fact, this is the only period of human history when it would have seemed particularly incongruous or inconceivable to act a heroic scene in the costume of the period. People use this argument and say, "Shakespeare thought of Hamlet as a sixteenth-century gentleman; Garrick acted Hamlet as an eighteenth-century gentleman; why cannot we present him as a twentieth-century gentleman?" The obvious answer is: "Why indeed?" Why do we feel the costume of our period to be unsuitable? The very question proves that we *do* feel it to be unsuitable. There must be some reason for our feeling, so different from the feeling of our fathers. Is it conceivable that there may be something a little unsuitable to the soul of man about the costume? Or about the period?

I think the answer is that to dress Hamlet up in the secondhand clothes of the Manchester merchant of the nineteenth century is not to free him, but to restrain him. And what we call modern costume is simply the last patchwork compromise of the hideous black commercial uniform that the Victorians thought correct and conventional. A man is much freer in an inky cloak than he is in an inky coat. And when the Victorian merchants wore customary suits of solemn black, they were not confined to one individual, to one tragic prince rather ostentatiously in mourning. They really were customary suits; and no bank clerk was allowed to go to business in anything else. What we call modern costume is simply the remains of that queer Puritanical convention; and to make Hamlet modern is not in the least to make him more unconventional. It is to make him more conventional. But I feel this to be even more true in the case of the King, the villain of the story. A dramatic critic for whose judgment I have a very high regard indeed declares that King Claudius becomes much more vivid and human in modern costume. In one sense this may be true, but not in the sense in which I have always understood the character of that agreeable gentleman. The point interests me a little, because (to reveal a dark episode in my life), I did once, in one sense, act King Claudius in modern costume. It was, indeed, in a very mild private reading of *Hamlet*; but even there I felt that the modern setting made the reading far too mild. It was in my own house; and I became painfully conscious of all the respects in which that lowly cot differs from the Castle of Elsinore.

Whatever else King Claudius was, it struck me at the time that he was a very noisy gentleman. He was very fond of noise; apparently, like a true artist, of noise for noise's sake. Again and again there is mention of his taste for having his smallest domestic actions saluted with a blare of trumpets and a roar of guns. He himself declares it in glorious blank verse that thunders like the guns and trumpets. Hamlet mentions it, in a passage of imperfect sympathy, which has sometimes given me a horrible feeling that Hamlet had a hankering after temperance. Anyhow the King's toasts at table and similar things were always saluted in this stupendous and crashing style. And I felt considerable sympathy, and even envy. I wish that, whenever I happen to drink a glass of wine, a small park of artillery in the back garden could be timed to explode and the echoes roll back bespeaking earthly thunder. I wish there were a brass band, with cannons in the orchestra in the Russian manner, to punctuate any little social observation I might have to make, such as "Shall we join the ladies?" or "Take another cigar." That was the way King Claudius went through life; and I do seriously think it throws, and was meant to throw, a great deal of light on his character.

I think Claudius is a very fine and true study of the Usurper; because he is the man who really wants to be King. A man must take the monarchy very seriously to be a Usurper. In a certain somewhat irregular sense, he must be an extreme Royalist, or even an extreme Loyalist. And in the sixteenth century especially the Crown was really a sort of dizzy and divine glory; like having stolen the sun out of the sky. That I think is the meaning of all the towering pomp of trumpet and cannon with which this Usurper surrounds himself; he is enjoying what he has stolen. He has not stolen mere money; he is not enjoying mere land; what he is enjoying is being *Dominus Rex*. And *that* explains, what nobody else ever really explains, why Shakespeare has put into the mouth of this low impostor and assassin the most stately declaration of the doctrine of the Divine Right of Kings. That is why he says, "There's such divinity doth hedge a king." That is why in facing the fury of Laertes he can play the man, because he can play the king. The liar fights bravely for his lie. The dream of royalty he has raised around him has become a sort of reality. It is for this that he lives; and for this, in the queer inversion of human virtue, he will almost die. Perhaps it was something hypnotic and overpowering in his haughty pose that drove Hamlet to such raging recriminations about his pettiness and baseness, comparing him to a pickpocket and a slave.

Now my conception of Claudius may be right or wrong, but, anyhow, it is a character Shakespeare might well have drawn. But it is a character that no man in modern clothes could really represent. We do not fire off cannons when we drink a glass of claret any more than we wear crowns when we are kings, or swords when we are gentlemen. The whole of that superb self-expression of the Usurper in pomp and noise becomes impossible. The fulfilment of the false king's dream cannot even be suggested in modern scenery. It may have many morals; but the moral that strikes me is that of the extreme narrowness of the modern world.

(also published as "King Claudius: Dominus Rex", *Illustrated London News*, September 12, 1925)

— ❖ —

On Eyebrows

I know very little about fashions; I seldom move in what are called fashionable circles. At this moment I do not want to move at all, and certainly not to move in circles. I become conscious, or half-conscious, of some change in dress or deportment when it has already become general. In this manner, for instance, it was lately borne in upon me that another change had taken place in the human countenance.

It is already a commonplace, I suppose, that the ideal and immortal Lover, as conceived by Shakespeare, "sighing like furnace, with a woeful ballad made to his mistress' eyebrow," must now go away and sigh about something else. His mistress has no eyebrows; and it might be inferred that he would produce no ballads. Anyhow, it suggests a sort of metaphysical duel between the Lover and the Poet, rather attractive to the metaphysical poets of that period. Would the balladist still cling to his ballad, pursuing the abstract and archetypal image of an Eyebrow, even when it was entirely detached from a face? Would he prefer the lady's eyebrow to the lady, leaving the rest of the lady behind like so much lumber, and pursuing only that peculiar vision of vanished hair? Or would he make the supreme sacrifice of tearing up the ballad and taking up with the lady, however strangely disfigured, resolving henceforward to write ballads only about her nose, her ears, or some portion of her which it seemed improbable that she would be in any immediate hurry to cut off? Even about those, of course, he could never be quite safe, if amputation were really the fashion.

In fact, touching that famous phrase, I have often wondered why modern poets do not amuse themselves by reproducing the imaginary Ballad to an Eyebrow. Shakespeare is full of hints that could be used as the basis of all sorts of games and experiments; Browning accepted such a challenge in expanding the suggestive like of "Childe Roland to the Dark Tower came"; and my own father, who was a man of many crafts and hobbies he had no ambition to exploit, made a table ornament modelled in every detail on the Three Caskets of Portia. Surely some of us might have a shot at a really Elizabethan address to the supercilious feature. Surely any modern writer, after sighing like a furnace for a few minutes, might be able to attempt something appropriate in the sixteenth-century manner—

> As seven-dyed Iris doth o'erarch the spheres,
> Love made that bridge that doth o'erarch thine eyne
> Bright as that bonded bow enskied; a sign

> Against the crystal Deluge of thy tears
> As line on line, so brow to brow appears . . .

At this point the poet looks up at the lady's eyebrow and
finds that it disappears. The pen drops from his fingers, and
this immortal fragment (if I may so modestly describe it)
remains for ever fragmentary. Shakespeare, especially the
Shakespeare of the Sonnets, knew more than most people
about the law of change and dissolution spread over all
earthly things, even those that seem the most natural—

> Since brass, not stone, nor earth, nor boundless sea,
> But sad mortality o'ersways their power,
> How with this rage shall Beauty hold a plea,
> Whose action is no stronger than a flower.

I quote from memory. Anyhow, even this argument does
not force us to a premature plucking of the flower or plucking out of the eyebrow. But, in spite of Shakespeare's somewhat excessive preoccupation, at one period, with the
images of mutability and mortality, I very gravely doubt
whether he ever did expect that sonnets or ballads to eyes,
eyebrows, ears, noses, and the rest would ever become
impossible by a general obliteration of these features. But
what is stranger still, and what would have struck Shakespeare
as very strange indeed, is the fact that this negative and
destructive operation should take place in a society devoted
to pleasure, and in an age commonly supposed to be even
more pagan than his own.

(*Illustrated London News*, September 17, 1932)

❖

Modern Drama and Old Conventions

It is obvious that a thing can always be new if it is sufficiently old; that is, that it may seem to be fresh so long as
it is stale enough to be forgotten. In several modern experiments in art, especially in dramatic art, I have noticed this
fact of late—the fact that what we call novelties might be
called rather neglected antiquities. There were rumours of
a new kind of drama, in Russia and elsewhere, in which the
whole scene was conceived as taking place inside a man's
mind; a theatre for thoughts, rather than things. The characters were ideas, such as will or memory or what not. Some
scoffed at it as mad; and of course it is only too easy to scoff
at anything as mad. Some admired it as new; and it is only
too easy to admire anything as new. But nobody seemed to
notice that, good or bad, it is a return to an older and more
religious kind of drama, and a reaction against a more recent
and realistic kind. It is the sort of mediaeval play that was
called a Morality. It is full of that passionate appetite for
abstractions that marked the Middle Ages. They would put
two deadly sins like Pride and Jealousy on one side of the
stage, and two virtues like Love and Pity on the other side,
and let them contend, to represent the war in the soul of
man. Then when mediaevalism gave way to the realism and
rationalism of the Renaissance, people said, "We are tired of
these allegories; we wish to see pride and jealousy fighting
with love and pity in a real live complex organism called
Othello." In other words, they first took Othello to pieces
and exhibited his qualities separate; then they put Othello
together again and represented him as a real man; and now
they have taken him to pieces again and represent him as a
series of separate qualities. It makes no difference that the
modern Morality has not the same moral. It makes no

difference that it has, in some cases, a much more obscure and inconclusive moral. It makes no difference that we think that the Morality should rather be called an Immorality. Precisely what these people profess to offer is an entirely new technique; and it is the technique that is five hundred years old.

I heard of a much queerer case the other day. The case is queerer because the convention that is revived was much more recently rejected; that is, the old thing seems really hardly old enough to be new just yet. Somebody told me that a new psychological drama was being produced at the Stage Society, in which the dialogue represented not merely the spoken words, but the unspoken thoughts of the characters. They poured out all that really passed in their minds, as if the others were not present, or as if they were in the Palace of Truth. I understand that somebody called it the Expressionist School of Drama. This amuses me, because I should have called it the very stalest tradition of the very stalest school of melodrama. It involves the very things that the realists in my youth were sweeping from the stage as the last tawdry rags and tinsel of the old artificial theatre. It means simply a return to the soliloquy and to the aside. The realists of my youth jeered at the hero for making a long and florid speech about the heroine, which was addressed only to heaven, himself, or the audience. They jeered at the villain for saying, "A time will come," in an aside that was inaudible to the people on the stage, but heard distinctly by the people in the gallery. They objected because people do not really say such things, and a realistic drama ought only to represent what they really say. But it would seem that the Adelphi hero and the transpontine villain were the forerunners of futurist and advanced art. Yet they were derided as old-fashioned for going only a few steps along the path of progress. The most courageous hero had not the moral courage to soliloquise all the time. The most hardened villain did not venture to tell us all his thoughts and feelings. But he began the great innovation; he told us some of his thoughts; and it would seem that the world soon thought it had had enough of them.

But of course this business of the soliloquy goes far beyond mere melodrama; it involves some of the greatest dramas the world has known. Yet the same objections were raised against the Shakespearean soliloquy in the days of the Shavian criticism. It is obvious that there has been another reversal and reversion; that the drama has first become more realistic, and then become less realistic. And in the clash of these two contradictory innovations, it would seem possible that we might return to the rudiments of commonsense. It seems clear that the critics were quite wrong in their attack on the Elizabethan drama; and chose the wrong ground even for their attack on the modern melodrama. If there was any objection to the villain saying, "A time will come," it was not in the least that a man would not say it; it was either that the villain did not think it or, more probably, that the dramatist did not think it. The dramatist did not think what he was saying, or what he was making the villain say. But, as a matter of fact, the critic was quite as thoughtless as the dramatist. He repeated the tag about realism exactly as the villain repeated the tag about revenge. Indeed, the realistic critic of the Ibsen period really was very like the villain of the Adelphi melodrama. The Ibsenite also was always saying, "A time will come." Most of Mr. Bernard Shaw's earlier plays and prefaces have a continual chorus of "A time will come." They were always saying that a time will come which will produce a real realistic drama, that shall be like our daily life, with men speaking as they do speak, and acting as they do act. The time has come; and it has produced the very opposite.

A convention is a form of freedom. That is the reality that the realists cannot get into their heads. A dramatic convention is not a constraint on the dramatist; it is a permission to the dramatist. It is a permit allowing him to depart from the routine of external reality, in order to express a more internal and intimate reality. Just as a legal fiction has often been the defence of political liberty, so a dramatic fiction is the defence of imaginative liberty. For instance, it is by a convention that the hero of a tragedy talks in blank verse. But the convention does not consist in saying to Mr. William Shakespeare, "You must and shall write a decasyllabic line properly scanned; and we will count the syllables to see you do." It consists in saying to Mr. William Shakespeare, "You are hereby allowed to make the speeches of Macbeth move to a certain measure and music, which they would not have in real life, if that will give you a greater scope to express the real emotions." If Shakespeare were under the limitations of realism, he would be forced to make Macbeth express his depressions or despair by saying, "Blast it all!" or "What a bore!" And these ejaculations do not express it; that is part of the bore. But as Shakespeare had the liberty of a literary convention, he can make Macbeth say something that nobody in real life would say, but something that does express what somebody in real life would feel. It expresses such things as music expresses them; though nobody in those circumstances would recite that particular poem, any more than he would begin suddenly to play on the violin. But what the audience wants is the emotion expressed; and poetry can express it and commonplace conversation cannot. Nothing but the convention of blank verse will leave you at liberty to say: "Told by an idiot, full of sound and fury, signifying nothing"; or "All our yesterdays have lighted fools the way to dusty death." It is only an artificial metre that can give the soul so much liberty as that. The realist is reduced to inarticulate grunts and half-apologetic oaths, like an apoplectic major in a club.

It is another matter, of course, whether the new unconventional conventions express as much truth as the old poetical conventions. But at least it is quite obvious that the unconventional have come back to conventions. It is a theatrical fiction of the most glaring and even ghastly kind to suppose that one of the characters is speaking, and none of the others are listening. It is a far more fictitious fiction than that of allowing his voice to move in a more or less natural rhythm of verse. It is more startling than the stalest jokes of the theatre of Mr. Crummles; than the old provincial drama in which a man was completely hidden behind a post or completely disguised in a hat. But, anyhow, the reign of realism is over; even if we have to pass through unreality to get back to the real.

(*Illustrated London News*, March 29, 1924)

———— ❖ ————

The Ideal Detective Story

There has been some renewal of debate on the problem of the problem story; sometimes called the police novel, or the detective story, but there is one aspect of the detective story which is almost inevitably left out in considering the detective stories. That tales of this type are generally slight, sensational, and in some ways superficial, I know better than most people, for I have written them myself. If I say there is in the abstract something quite different,

which may be called the Ideal Detective Story, I do not
mean that I can write it. I call it the Ideal Detective Story
because I cannot write it. Anyhow, I do think that such a
story, while it must be sensational, need not be superficial.
In theory, though not commonly in practice, it is possible to
write a subtle and creative novel, of deep philosophy and
delicate psychology, and yet cast it in the form of a sensational shocker.

The detective story differs from every other story in this:
that the reader is only happy if he feels a fool. At the end of
more philosophic works he may wish to feel a philosopher.
But the former view of himself may be more wholesome—
and more correct. The sharp transition from ignorance may
be good for humility. It is very largely a matter of the order
in which things are mentioned, rather than of the nature of
the things themselves. The essence of a mystery tale is that
we are suddenly confronted with a truth which we have
never suspected and yet can see to be true. There is no reason, in logic, why this truth should not be a profound and
convincing one as much as a shallow and conventional one.
There is no reason why the hero who turns out to be a villain, or the villain who turns out to be a hero, should not be
a study in the living subtleties and complexities of human
character, on a level with the first figures in human fiction.
It is only an accident of the actual origin of these police
novels that the interest of the inconsistency commonly goes
no further than that of a demure governess being a poi-
soner, or a dull and colourless clerk painting the town red
by cutting throats. There are inconsistencies in human
nature of a much higher and more mysterious order, and
there is really no reason why they should not be presented
in the particular way that causes the shock of a detective
tale. There is electric light as well as electric shocks, and

even the shock may be the bolt of Jove. It is, as I have said, very largely a matter of the mere order of events. The side of the character that cannot be connected with the crime has to be presented first; the crime has to be presented next as something in complete contrast with it; and the psychological reconciliation of the two must come after that, in the place where the common or garden detective explains that he was led to the truth by the stump of a cigar left on the lawn or the spot of red ink on the blotting-pad in the boudoir. But there is nothing in the nature of things to prevent the explanation, when it does come, being as convincing to a psychologist as the other is to a policeman.

There is Shakespeare, for instance: he has created two or three extremely amiable and sympathetic murderers. Only we can watch their amiability slowly and gently merging into murder. Othello is an affectionate husband who assassinates his wife out of sheer affection, so to speak. But as we know the story from the first, we can see the connection and accept the contradiction. But suppose the story opened with Desdemona found dead, Iago or Cassio suspected, and Othello the very last person likely to be suspected. In that case, *Othello* would be a detective story. But it might be a true detective story; that is, one consistent with the true character of the hero when he finally tells the truth. Hamlet, again, is a most lovable and even peaceable person as a rule, and we pardon the nervous and slightly irritable gesture which happens to have the result of sticking an old fool like a pig behind a curtain. But suppose the curtain rises on the corpse of Polonius, and Rosencrantz and Guildenstern discuss the suspicion that has immediately fallen on the First Player, an immoral actor accustomed to killing people on the stage; while Horatio or some shrewd character suspects another crime of Claudius or the reckless and unscrupulous Laertes. Then *Hamlet* would be a shocker, and the guilt of Hamlet would be a shock. But it might be a shock of truth, and it is not only sex novels that are shocking. These Shakespearean characters would be none the less coherent and all of a piece because we brought the opposite ends of the character together and tied them into a knot. The story of Othello might be published with a lurid wrapper as "The Pillow Murder Case." But it might still be the same case; a serious case and a convincing case. The death of Polonius might appear on the bookstalls as "The Vanishing Rat Mystery," and be in form like an ordinary detective story. Yet it might be The Ideal Detective Story.

Nor need there be anything vulgar in the violent and abrupt transition that is the essential of such a tale. The inconsistencies of human nature are indeed terrible and heart-shaking things, to be named with the same note of crisis as the hour of death and the Day of Judgment. They are not all fine shades, but some of them very fearful shadows, made by the primal contrast of darkness and light. Both the crimes and the confessions can be as catastrophic as lightning. Indeed, The Ideal Detective Story might do some good if it brought men back to understand that the world is not all curves, but that there are some things that are as jagged as the lightning-flash or as straight as the sword.

(*Illustrated London News*, October 25, 1930)

—— ❖ ——

On Shakespeare's Method of Opening His Plays

I once read a paper about Lord Macaulay, which I believe started in my mind the string of notions that afterwards resolved themselves into the nonsense I am now going to inflict on you. Lord Macaulay once said to a famous literary contemporary, "Thackeray, if you want to read *Clarissa* you should begin at the third volume and skip all letters to Italians, from Italians, or about Italians, and you will find it most interesting" . . . The real point I wished to introduce to you by the anecdote I have quoted is that in the works of most authors, as well as those of Richardson, the first chapter, book, canto, scene, or whatever it may be, is the most difficult to write and the most tedious to read. Before entering, therefore, into Shakespeare's way of overcoming the difficulty, I propose to glance at the differing treatments of it at the hands of the minor English story-tellers. Foremost among the novelists popularly appreciated at the present day is Sir Walter Scott, who, in spite of his long-winded prolixity, I must mention with the deepest reverence and gratitude. The Scott method is simple enough. You have a string of prefaces and a baker's dozen of introductions. You then devote the two first chapters to an account of the time, the description of the country, and the history of the noble house, and then you start the third chapter with a couple of servants talking about their master's affairs. But this method, which I uphold, as it gets the worst over and then launches you fairly into the story, has been found somewhat too long-winded for readers of this degenerate age, and has given prominence to a school of novelists writing on an entirely different principle.

The logician who founded this sect argued in this way.

The most uninteresting part of a story is the beginning. The best romancer cannot begin it attractively. The natural inference is, don't begin at the beginning, begin in the middle. Struck by this reasoning, the novelist of the new school begins thus:

CHAPTER I.

"No; they weren't mine," or some such remark, and continues a mysterious conversation straggling down three pages in short lines, at the end of which he informs you that the speaker was a tall dark man, or some other kind of man of whom we are thoroughly tired.

Among the many talented authors of the present day who have embraced this startling form of opening the most prominent is Mrs. Hodgson Burnett, whose beautiful story of *Little Lord Fauntleroy*, you will remember, begins "Cedric himself knew nothing whatever about it." What's "it"? I remember reading down in the country one of the most clever and amusing of her books, which began with the explanatory sentence, "By Jove! How she rides." Such is the new style to all appearance most rapid and interesting. My friends, one word is as good as a thousand. It is a fraud.

The guileless victim reads on in his simplicity through the first or jerky conversational chapter, exultant in the absence of dates, reflections, and hard names, little dreaming that the same old history and geography, the same philosophy and genealogy, that he dreamt he had escaped, do but lie in wait for him in the second chapter. You must have them sooner or later, as Serjeant Buzfuz said, and the thin disguise of conversation is a deception and a snare.

But the case is different, and the difficulty overcome, when we turn to the system of Shakespeare.

It is well worth while to notice with what wonderful skill and ingenuity the great dramatist overcomes the difficulty by introducing into a casual conversation, which is at once natural and interesting, all that is necessary to communicate to the reader as to the personal and historical situations.

Look, for instance, at the first scene of *Richard III*, which opens with the soliloquy of Gloucester, beginning "Now is the winter of our discontent made glorious summer by this son of York." In it are introduced, with all the naturalness of an actual train of thought, the chaos left by the Wars of the Roses, the peaceful time following, the pleasures of Edward IV, the intrigues of his court, all, as it were, brooded over and seen through by the dark spirit of the speaker, which is fully and yet naturally laid bare in the speech. This, then, is the secret. The intriguing and ambitious soul of Gloucester is the pervading idea of the story, and this being introduced into the first scene makes that scene interesting. The long-winded descriptions of the older school have no real dependence on the spirit of the story, and are therefore tedious.

The servants' conversation dodge is dull for the same reason. The spasmodic colloquial chapter of the new school has seldom any bearing on the point of the story, being generally merely a pretext for mentioning the heroine's beautiful eyes and the villain's easy laugh. It is a curious thing to notice, by the way, that in novels villains always have easy laughs. This facility of merriment seems somehow incompatible with honesty. I cannot say that I have ever noticed it in real life, but the truth is that I am not at all sure that I know what an easy laugh is like. However, it sounds well. But to return to Richard III.

It is the grim misshapen figure of Richard of Gloucester that first occupies the stage, and it is that figure that walks through the entire play, the spirit of the whole, the conception of the highest courage and genius, linked with the darkest falsehood and cruelty. It is this introducing into the opening scene the central thought of the play that shows itself in almost all of Shakespeare's dramas, and gives them their interest. In *Macbeth*, for instance, the first scene on the blasted heath introduces the witches, the three unearthly beings by whose deep evil influence is swayed the whole dark tale of blood and crime. In *The Merchant of Venice*, again, although the circumstances of the plot forbid any direct reference to the actual catastrophe, it is suggested both by Antonio's general presentiments of the calamity and the mention of the actual cause of it, in the danger of merchant vessels at sea. *Antony and Cleopatra* opens with the Roman soldier, statesman, and orator courting ruin. There are many more instances which I will not delay to cite, but . . . I think . . . my rule, though liable to exceptions like other rules, yet does on the whole apply to the works of the great dramatist.

(*The Debater*, September, 1891)

❖

The Merits of Shakespeare's Plots

I see that Mr. John M. Robertson has written a book about the problem of *Hamlet*, round which the critics still revolve with all the irresolution of which they accuse the hero. I have not read Mr. Robertson's book, and am thus inhibited by a fine fantastic scruple from reviewing it. But I gather from one of the shrewdest and sanest of critics, Mr. J. C. Squire, that it explains the inconsistencies of the play as mainly the rugged remains of the old romances or chronicles. It may be suggested that in truth a hero is made human when he is made inconsistent. This is true; but the explanation is at least a great improvement on the insane seriousness of the German psychologists. They talked of Hamlet not merely as a human character, but as a historical character. They talked as if he had secrets, not only hidden from Shakespeare's readers, but hidden from Shakespeare.

This is madness; it is merely staring at a portrait till you think it is alive. It is as if they undertook to tell me the real truth about the private life of Oberon.

Moreover, the case of Hamlet does happen to be one in which Mr. Robertson's theory seems relatively right. I should deny any inconsistency in a dreamer doing sudden things like stabbing Polonius; they are just the sort of things a dreamer would do. But it is true that some things out of the old story seem harsh and irrelevant; and it is truer still that the old story contains less than usual of the soul of the new story. I say "less than usual"; for I should like to point out that the general rule is rather the other way. Mr. Robertson's thesis may be true of *Hamlet*, but it is not so true of Shakespeare.

Of course, much can be said by this time both for and against the national poet. But if it be hopeless to denounce Shakespeare, it may appear almost as impertinent to defend him. And yet there is one point on which he has never been defended. And it is one on which I think he should not only be defended, but admired. If I were a Shakespearean student, or any kind of student (the improbability of which prospect words wholly fail me to express), I should special-ise in the part of Shakespeare that is certainly not Shakespeare. I mean I should plead for the merit of Shakespeare's plots; all the more because they were some-body else's plots. In short, I should say a word for the poet's taste; if only his taste in theft. It is the fashion to abase Shakespeare as a critic, if only to exalt him the more as a creator. It is the fashion to say that he built on a foundation of mere rubbish; and that this lifts to a greater glory the cloud-capped pinnacles he reared upon it. I am not sure that it is such pure praise for a practical architect to say that he was totally indifferent to the basement and cellars and interested exclusively in the roof and chimney-pots. But, anyhow, I am sure that Shakespeare did not forget the foundation; or despise the basement or the cellars.

Shakespeare *enjoyed* the old stories. He enjoyed them as tales are intended to be enjoyed. He liked reading them, as a man of imagination and intelligence to-day likes reading a good adventure story, or still more a good detective story. This is the one possibility that the Shakespearean critics never seem to entertain. Probably they are not simple enough, and therefore not imaginative enough, to know what that enjoyment is. They cannot read an adventure story, or indeed any story. For instance, nearly all the critics apologise, in a prim and priggish manner, for the tale on which turns the Trial Scene in *The Merchant of Venice*. They explain that poor Shakespeare had taken a barbarous old story, and had to make the best of it. As a matter of fact, he had taken an uncommonly good story; one of the best that he could possibly have had to make the best of. It is a clear, pointed, and practical parable against usury; and if a large number of modern people do not appreciate it, it is because a large number of modern people are taught to appreciate and even admire usury. The idea of a man forfeiting part of his body (it might have been an arm or leg) is a highly philosophical satire on unlimited recovery of ruinous debts. The idea is embodied in all those truly Christian laws about wainage and livelihood which were the glory of the Middle Ages. The story is excellent simply as an anecdote working up to a climax and ending in an unexpected retort. And the end is a truth and not merely a trick. You do prove the falsity of pedantic logic by a *reductio ad absurdum*.

While we have had masses of learned work about the Shakespearean origins, we have had very little about the Shakespearean origin. I mean we have had very little on the main matter of his human and natural inheritance of the whole civilization of Christendom from which he came. It is

a commonplace that Shakespeare was a result of the
Renaissance; but the Renaissance itself was a result of the
Middle Ages; nor was it by any means merely a revolt
against the Middle Ages. There are a thousand things in
which Shakespeare would be much better understood by
Dante than he was by Goethe. I will take one example, all
the stronger for being always taken the other way.

English patriotism is one of the more manly realities of
the modern world; and Shakespeare was a passionate
patriot. But in that very passage in praise of England, which
is hackneyed without ceasing to be holy, about half is a
mediaeval memory of the sort called a mediaeval superstition. It is not about the spacious days of Elizabeth, but the
cloistered days of Peter the Hermit. It is not about the
Armada, but about the Crusades—

> As in the sepulchre in stubborn Jewry
> Of the world's museum, blessed Mary's Son.

That note was neglected and nearly lost in the whole modern
world; and scarcely any modern critic would have cared to
notice it. Only the prodigious events of yesterday have
brought us back, half-bewildered, into the footsteps of our
fathers; and the vision of John of Gaunt was fulfilled in the
hour when a great English soldier entered Jerusalem on foot.
(*Illustrated London News*, October 18, 1919)

---- ❖ ----

Good Stories Spoilt by Great Authors

Under the title "Good Stories Spoilt by Great Authors,"
a considerable essay might be written. In fact, it shall
be written. It shall be written now. The mere fact that some

fable has passed through a master mind does not imply by
any means that it must have been improved. Eminent men
have misappropriated public stories, as they have misappropriated public stores. It is always supposed (apparently) that
anyone who borrows from the original brotherhood of men
is not bound to pay back. It is supposed that if Shakespeare
took the legend of Lear, or Goethe the legend of Faust, or
Wagner the legend of Tannhäuser, they must have been
very right, and the legends ought to be grateful to them. My
own impression is that they were sometimes very wrong,
and that the legends might sue them for slander. Briefly, it
is always assumed that the poem that somebody made is
vastly superior to the ballad that everybody made. For my
part I take the other view. I prefer the gossip of the many to
the scandal of the few. I distrust the narrow individualism of
the artist, trusting rather the natural communism of the
craftsmen. I think there is one thing more important than
the man of genius—and that is the genius of man.

Let me promptly, in a parenthetical paragraph, confess
that I cannot get Shakespeare into this theory of mine. As
far as I can see, Shakespeare made all his stories better; and
as far as I can see, he could hardly have made them worse.
He seems to have specialised in making good plays out of
bad novels. If Shakespeare were alive now I suppose he
would make a sweet springtime comedy out of an anecdote
in a sporting paper. I suppose he would make a starry and
awful tragedy out of one of the penny novelettes. But as
Shakespeare does not support my argument I propose to
leave him out of my article. . . .

(*Illustrated London News*, April 9, 1910)

V.
WORDS, WORDS, WORDS

What's in a Name?

If you or I had to invent out of our own heads a really shattering and shining name, a name fit for some flaming hero defying the stars, a name on horseback and high in the saddle—could we think of any so chivalrous or so challenging as Shakespeare? The very word is like Lancelot at his last tournament with a touch of the divine impotence of Don Quixote. In fact, I know only one surname that is really finer than Shakespeare, and that is Brakespear, the only English Pope. [Pope Adrian IV (1154–1159)] A pleasing lyric in prose might be built up about the two of them; the one Englishman who rose to the highest of all official places, and the other who rose to the highest of all unofficial.

(*Illustrated London News*, May 15, 1909)

❖

The Speech That Shakespeare Spoke

We all know the hundred paraphrases of the Wordsworthian phrase: "The speech that Shakespeare spoke; the faith and morals hold that Milton held." There is nothing wrong with that except that it is all nonsense. Neither of us (unfortunately) speaks the speech that Shakespeare spoke.

Shakespeare did, in fact, describe one of the most beautiful of friendships, a friendship of opposites, in the story of

189

Hamlet and Horatio. But suppose when walking down Broadway or the Strand, the Englishman casually remarked to his American friend, or vice versa, "Then let the candid tongue lick absurd pomp and crook the pregnant hinges of the knee where thrift may follow fawning." I am not sure that the meaning of this would instantly spring to the mind of the Englishman any more than the American.

And as for the faith and morals that Milton had, the most recent researches suggest that his morals verged on polygamy like Brigham Young's, and that his faith chiefly consisted of doubts.

(*New York American*, Aug. 6, 1935)

———— ❖ ————

The Sound of Shakespeare

While Shakespeare would write his own name in two or three totally different but equally illegible scrawls, he trusted the whole great load of his glory to the sound of words, to be spoken by living men.

(*G.K.'s Weekly*, Dec. 17, 1932)

———— ❖ ————

Poetical

We are all as poetical as Shakespeare; but we don't happen to be such great poets. Our temperaments are the same, but you and I haven't got the mind to write lines like "And all our yesterdays have lighted fools . . ."

(*Hearth and Home*, Oct. 17, 1912)

———— ❖ ————

The Yellow Sands

When Shakespeare merely says the very simple words, "Come unto these yellow sands, and there take hands," there does instantly, but only instantaneously, flash through my own fancy some world where everyone is young; long lines of glowing golden sands under the glamour of an endless evening, where lovers remain at the immortal instant when they first touch hands. But if I or anybody else were to settle down to describing the maritime community living on that particular coastline, in a prose essay or novel, those yellow sands would become as dry as the sands of the desert; even as the rose-red city would fade like the rose.

(*London Magazine*, August, 1924)

———— ❖ ————

Poor Old Shakespeare

Shakespeare we are too frequently informed, said that a rose by any other name would smell as sweet; it would be more correct to say that Shakespeare said that Miss Juliet Capulet said it, in a rather distracted moment in a romantic play.

It would cause more surprise to announce that Shakespeare said: "I am determined to be a villain!" because he said that Richard the Third said it in a rather melodramatic play.

But anyhow, the maxim and the metaphor have clung to men's memories and produced curious results. Some gardeners, it would seem, supposed that because the rose would be as sweet with any other name therefore the name would be as sweet with any other flower; and merely turned "rose tree" into Greek and applied it to a rhododendron.

It is rather typical of the way in which science sometimes tells lies in Greek which would be too obvious in English. Other philosophers, of the realistic or cynical school, apply the maxim in a still more curious way; as meaning that because one rose has the name of a cabbage rose, therefore a rose is the same as a cabbage.

But most sensible people know the real sense of the phrase; that the world is too prone to look at the title rather than the thing, at the label rather than the bottle or the bottle rather than the wine. In this sense we can heartily agree with Miss Capulet, however distracted. Having to choose between the two, a man would be less than wise if he refused to drink good wine out of the bottle and were left merely licking the gum off the label.

So it is doubtless with roses in real life; but not entirely so in real literature. If a rose grower has an eccentric benefactor who stipulated that the word "rose" should never be uttered; but the word "hogwash" or "pignut" should be invariably substituted, but on these conditions undertook to smother him in masses of the most gorgeous and fragrant blooms of innumerable rose gardens, the recipient would doubtless be wise to prefer the thing to the word.

But it does not follow that it does not matter what we do with the word. In the heritage of poetry, which is a great part of civilization, the word is almost as valuable as the thing; indeed, the word is already part of the thing. Even Juliet shrank from actually suggesting any other name, and "hogwash" would have a good deal thrown her out of her own stride.

It is not true that a love song like "My love is like the red, red pignut" would leap to the lips of every lover, even if a footnote explained that the term was identical with the botanical Latin name for the rose.

Even for one accepting the convention, the opening line, "It was hogwash, hogwash all the way, would never recapture the first fine careless rapture of Browning's line. In short, the name is not the thing; but the name is very far from being a mere number or sign for the thing.

Man and Nature have so long reacted on each other that I strongly suspect that kingcups or hyacinths do actually look nobler to us because of their ancient and noble names.

To forget this is to forget the very meaning of culture, which should run parallel to horticulture. And some moderns of the hogwash and pignuts school of poetry seem likely to forget it.

The revolt against culture is often the last fashion of the cultured. But above all it is very unfair to poor old Shakespeare. If ever there was a man who did not agree with Juliet's distracted remark, in its realistic sense, it was he.

If ever a man could smell real words, as if they were flowers, and do without the flowers, it was he. Heaven knows why the world has remembered this one chance phrase of Juliet, and forgotten a thousand gorgeous and odorous phrases that rise almost like stupefying fumes. "Not poppy nor mandragora . . ." Surely everybody knows those intoxicant ingredients.

But I gravely doubt whether Shakespeare even knew what mandragora looked like.

(*New York American*, June 11, 1932)

❖

Picturesque

It is the custom in many quarters to speak somewhat sneeringly of that element which is broadly called the picturesque. It is always felt to be an inferior, a vulgar, and even an artificial form of art. Yet two things may be remarked about it. The first is that, with few exceptions, the greatest literary artists have been not only particularly clever at the picturesque, but particularly fond of it. Shakespeare, for instance, delighted in certain merely pictorial contrasts which are quite distinct from, even when they are akin to, the spiritual view involved. For instance, there is admirable satire in the idea of Touchstone teaching worldly wisdom and worldly honour to the woodland yokels. There is excellent philosophy in the idea of the fool being the representative of civilisation in the forest. But quite apart from this deeper meaning in the incident, the mere figure of the jester, in his bright motley and his cap and bells, against the green background of the forest and the rude forms of the shepherds, is a strong example of the purely picturesque. There is excellent tragic irony in the confrontation of the melancholy philosopher among the tombs with the cheerful digger of the graves. It sums up the essential point, that dead bodies can be comic; it is only dead souls that can be tragic. But quite apart from such irony, the mere picture of the grotesque gravedigger, the black-clad prince, and the skull is a picture in the strongest sense picturesque. Caliban and the two shipwrecked drunkards are an admirable symbol; but they are also an admirable scene. Bottom, with the ass's head, sitting in a ring of elves, is excellent moving comedy, but also excellent still life. Falstaff with his huge body, Bardolph with his burning nose, are masterpieces of the pen; but they would be fine sketches even for the pencil.

King Lear, in the storm, is a landscape as well as a character study. There is something decorative even about the insistence on the swarthiness of Othello, or the deformity of Richard III. Shakespeare's work is much more than picturesque; but it is picturesque.

(Introduction to *Barnaby Rudge*)

The Artistic Temperament

The artistic temperament is a disease that afflicts amateurs. It is a disease which arises from men not having sufficient power of expression to utter and get rid of the element of art in their being. It is healthful to every sane man to utter the art within him; it is essential to every sane man to get rid of the art within him at all costs. Artists of a large and wholesome vitality get rid of their art easily, as they breathe easily, or perspire easily. But in artists of less force, the thing becomes a pressure and produces a definite pain, which is called the artistic temperament. Thus, very great artists are able to be ordinary men, men like Shakespeare.

(*Daily News*, April 1, 1905)

Creative Vagueness

Shakespeare, like Hamlet, was a rather rambling, irrelevant person, a "John-a-dreams," but his dreams showed him something that shone more strangely than a spotlight when he called up such images to revisit the glimpses of the moon. There is a creative side to the English vagueness, comic in Dickens or tragic in Shakespeare.

(*New York American*, Aug. 1, 1935)

Fragments

Shakespeare often suffers from too much inventiveness; that which clogs us and trips us up in his masterpieces is not so much inferior work as irrelevant brilliancy; not so much failures as fragments of other masterpieces.

("Dreams," *The Coloured Lands*)

Incidental Discords

The plays of Shakespeare may be full of incidental discords, but not one of them ever fails to convey its aboriginal sentiment, that life is as black as the tempest or as green as the greenwood.

("Dreams," *The Coloured Lands*)

An Outpouring of Ideas

What alone can make a literary man in the ultimate sense great . . . is ideas; the power of generating and making vivid an incessant output of ideas. It is untrue to say that what matters is quality and not quantity. Most men have made one good joke in their lives; but to make jokes as

Dickens made them is to be a great man. Many forgotten poets have let fall a lyric with one really perfect image; but when we open any play of Shakespeare, good or bad, at any page, important or unimportant, with the practical certainty of finding some imagery that at least arrests the eye and probably enriches the memory, we are putting our trust in a great man.

("Henry James," *The Common Man*)

------- ❖ -------

Multitudinous and Tragic

A country girl I know in the country of Buckingham had never seen the sea in her life until the other day. When she was asked what she thought of it she said it was like cauliflowers. Now that is a piece of pure literature-vivid, entirely independent and original, and perfectly true. I had always been haunted with an analogous kinship which I could never locate; cabbages always remind me of the sea and the sea always reminds me of cabbages. It is partly, perhaps, the veined mingling of violet and green, as in the sea a purple that is almost dark red may mix with a green that is almost yellow, and still be the blue sea as a whole. But it is more the grand curves of the cabbage that curl over cavernously like waves, and it is partly again that dreamy repetition, as of a patter, that made two great poets, Aeschylus and Shakespeare, use a word like "multitudinous" of the ocean. But just where my fancy halted the Buckinghamshire young woman rushed (so to speak) to my imaginative rescue. Cauliflowers are twenty times better than cabbages, for they show the wave breaking as well as curling, and the efflorescence of the branching foam, blind, bubbling, and opaque. Moreover, the strong lines of life are suggested; the arches of the rushing waves have all the rigid energy of green stalks, as if the whole sea were one white flower rooted in the abyss.

Now a large number of delicate and superior persons would refuse to see the force in that kitchen garden comparison, because it is not connected with any of the ordinary maritime sentiments as stated in books and songs. The aesthetic amateur would say that he knew what large and philosophical thoughts he ought to have by the boundless deep. He would say that he was not a greengrocer who would think first of greens. To which I should reply, like Hamlet, apropos of a parallel profession, "I would you were so honest a man." The mention of Hamlet reminds me, by the way, that besides the girl who had never seen the sea I knew a girl who had never seen a stage-play. She was taken to *Hamlet*, and she said it was very sad. There is another case of going to the primordial point which is overlaid by learning and secondary impressions. We are so used to thinking of *Hamlet* as a problem that we sometimes quite forget that it is a tragedy, just as we are so used to thinking of the sea as vast and vague, that we scarcely notice when it is white and green.

(*Daily News*, Aug. 20, 1910)

❖

The Incongruity of Reality

Now and again Shakespeare, with a horror almost bordering on hysteria, will thrust into the limelight some clown or idiot, to suggest, against the black curtain of tragedy, this incongruity and inconsequence in the things that really do happen.

("If Don John of Austria Had Married Mary Queen of Scots," *The Common Man*)

Words of Strong Poetry

I think the first truth about traditional metres is that there is a sort of speech that is stronger than speech. Not merely smoother or sweeter or more melodious, or even more beautiful; but stronger. Words are jointed together like bones; they are mortared together like bricks; they are close and compact and resistant; whereas, in all common conversational speech, every sentence is falling to pieces. Perhaps we recognise this latter fact when we talk about letting fall a remark, or dropping a hint, or throwing out an observation. All conversational speech or writing is under the curse of the Fall; it is under the law of gravitation; it is perpetually falling down, like the universe of Lucretius. But great poets do not drop hints or let observations fall; they lift them and hold them aloft, as the keystone of a strong arch thrusts up the stones, defying the law of gravity and the devil and all his angels. The words of strong poetry are packed as tight and as solid as the stones of the arch. The lines of a good sonnet are like bridges of sound across abysses of silence. The boast of the bridges is that you could march armies across them; that a man can rest his weight on every word. The awful cry out of the last tragic trance of Othello, when he realises that death is as real as love, finds words worthy of itself; megalithic words; words not only of weight, but weight-bearing; words strong enough to support him above the abyss. "If I quench thee, thou flaming minister . . ." The address to the candle might almost be called obscure, but it is not doubtful; it is not hesitant or wavering in words or the sound of words; it is rather as if a man were granted a greater thing than speech. And the effect is gained by this firmness in the words, and the weight that can rest on them. "I know not where is that Promethean heat." You could stand an elephant on that line. It is true, first of all, as a mere fact of acoustics, that there is not one weak syllable in the line. At the same time, there is also that strength of style that is like the strength of gesture. "I know not where" is the essential elemental cry of man, eternally ignorant of the beginning of life, or of how it may truly be renewed. And it is a plain and simple fact, whether we like it or not, that the words "I know not where" do sound like some such ancestral cry; while the words "I don't know where" certainly do not.

(*Illustrated London News*, April 1, 1933)

❖

The Heroic Couplet

Rhyme gives a ringing finality to sentiment; the ear hears that something has been decided even before the brain can take it in. I believe some critics of Shakespeare blame him for ending a blank verse scene with a rhymed couplet so often. It seems to me not only natural but splendid, that the speech at the last should rise into a kind of recurrent song.

(*Daily News*, May 12, 1906)

❖

Progress in Poetry

The dangers of a false progress are very great. Again and again in our human past it has happened that men have started from a position of real value, have gone on under the firm impression that they were increasing that value, and have arrived at last at a position infinitely inferior, because they had really only been increasing in one quite secondary quality which was not the real value of the original state. They had indeed developed, but they had developed in the wrong thing; they did become superior to their fathers, but they only became superior in an inferiority. Some of the numerous historic examples of the thing will best explain what I mean. In this way, for instance, the English poets after the Elizabethan age sincerely believed that they were improving on the Elizabethan poetry. They felt that they were progressing. And so they were progressing. But they were progressing only in one quite small quality of the Elizabethans; they were progressing in Elizabethan ingenuity, Elizabethan complexity, in mere wit, in mere learning. A poet like Donne, let us say, or Crashaw, would look at a line of Shakespeare's such as this—

> And crook the pregnant hinges of the knee,
> Where thrift may follow fawning—

and would say to himself, "That is all very nice; but I can write more queerly even than that. We are progressing, my boy!" Then he would write such a couplet as this about the Crucifixion:

> It made his own lieutenant nature shrink,
> It made his footstool crack and the sun wink.

And he would never notice that, though both Shakespeare's line and his were quaint and clever—though perhaps his line was the more quaint and clever—yet the real difference between them is that Shakespeare's line, in spite of all its cleverness, is a line of poetry. In Shakespeare the rather crabbed words are set to some strange music. Donne leaves out the music, and Donne progresses—in crabbedness.

(*Daily News*, July 14, 1906)

❖

Improving on Shakespeare's Language

A paragraph in the newspapers reports, I know not with how much truth, that the Minister controlling education in the present Russian regime has ordered the elimination of references to angels, devils, and even fairies. The paragraph states that "angels are to be supplanted by scientists and technicians who have served humanity." I do not know whether this substitution is to be literal in every case where such things are mentioned. In that case the condition of the great literature of the past would be rather curious. Perhaps Titania, instead of saying, "What angel," will say, "What technician wakes me from my flowery bed?" Which might be appropriate enough, even to Bottom; for the old-fashioned weaver was not only a technician, but often an excellent technician. Perhaps Horatio will avoid the mention of angels by saying to the dying Hamlet, "Good-night, sweet prince; and flights of scientists sing thee to thy rest."

(*Illustrated London News*, Aug. 20, 1921)

❖

Bowdlerism

[Thomas Bowdler (1754–1825) was an English editor who published an expurgated version of Shakespeare's plays. Bowdlerism refers to the practice of removing words considered unsuitable from a text.]

In one point I do certainly think that the Victorian Bowdlerism did pure harm. This is the simple point that, nine times out of ten, the coarse word is the word that condemns an evil and the refined word the word that excuses it. A common evasion, for instance, substitutes for the word that brands self-sale as the essential sin, a word which weakly suggests that it is no more wicked than walking down the street. The great peril of such soft mystifications is that extreme evils (they that are abnormal even by the standard of evil) have a very long start. Where ordinary wrong is made unintelligible, extraordinary wrong can count on remaining more unintelligible still; especially among those who live in such an atmosphere of long words.

("The Great Victorian Novelists," *The Victorian Age in Literature*)

Plain-spoken

It was somewhere about the generation of Thackeray, men were not so certain as they had been about their religion and morality, that the religion and morality were hedged in with a new and crude respectability. *Measure for Measure* is much more plain-spoken than *Vanity Fair*; but Shakespeare was much more certain of the superiority of Isabella than Thackeray of the superiority of Amelia.

(*Illustrated London News*, June 24, 1922)

Scorn

It is hard for an Englishman (at least, it is hard for me) heartily to like [French] idealistic cruelty. It is hard for us to imagine scorn as something fruitful and even festive: to behold that bitter tree bearing lovely blossoms and delightful fruit. It is hard for us to realise a pageant of blazing wit and romantic activity all produced by such stiff anger as has produced an anchorite or a suicide. It is as if all the gay Athenian comedies had been written by Timon of Athens.

(*Illustrated London News*, March 19, 1910)

Hating

Timon of Athens . . . think[s] hating men [is] better than loving them.

(*Daily News*, June 3, 1905)

Ranting

Almost all great poets rant, from Shakespeare downwards.
(*Daily News*, Sept. 24, 1901)

———— ❖ ————

The Best Parts

B ut it is equally true that I did not ride with Chaucer to
Canterbury and give him a few intelligent hints for the
best passages in *The Canterbury Tales*. It is equally true that
there was a large and lamentable gap in the company seated
at the Mermaid; that scarcely a word of Shakespeare's most
poetical passages was actually contributed by me; that I did
not whisper to him the word "incarnadine" when he was
hesitating after "multitudinous seas"; that I entirely missed
the opportunity of suggesting that Hamlet would be effec-
tively ended by the stormy entrance of Fortinbras.

Nay, aged and infirm as I am, it were vain for me to pretend that I lost a leg at the Battle of Trafalgar, or that I am
old enough to have seen (as I should like to have seen),
ablaze with stars upon the deck of death, the frail figure and
the elfish face of the noblest sailor of history.

Yet I propose to go on being proud of Chaucer and
Shakespeare and Nelson; to feel that the poets did indeed
love the language that I love and that the sailor felt something of what we also feel for the sea.

But if we accept this mystical corporate being, this larger
self, we must accept it for good and ill. If we boast of our
best, we must repent of our worst. Otherwise, patriotism
will be a very poor thing indeed.

(*New York American*, Sept. 3, 1932)

———— ❖ ————

The Worst Parts

Classics . . . must be published entire by those who care for classics. This course has been most wisely adopted in regard to all the works of all the great but uneven workers. Critics included among Shakespeare's works almost reluctantly such works as *Troilus and Cressida* or *Cymbeline,* merely with the result that another generation of critics said they were the only good plays of Shakespeare. . . . It is never safe to throw away the works of the best men as refuse; if you do you will have all the best critics with their heads in the dust bin. Nevertheless, we may all quite fearlessly assert the badness of great masses of their work, so long as we do not propose thus coercively to carry it into effect. Shakespeare and Dickens resemble Dumas, not only in the fact that their bad parts are very bad, but in the fact that their bad parts are very long. When they began talking nonsense they went at it steadily, and there was no doubt about it. You could compile, I should think, the worst book in the world entirely out of selecting passages from the best writers in the world.

(*Daily News*, Jan. 2, 1907)

❖

Stairs of Sand

The divine punishment of hypocrisy is fatigue. Those, in Shakespeare's fine simile, whose hearts are all as false as stairs of sand, must really have much of that exhausted sensation that comes of walking through sand when it is loose and deep. The hypocrite is that unluckiest of actors who is never out of a job. For even Mme. Sarah Bernhardt would not like to be Hamlet all the time; and Sir Herbert Tree would not like to go to bed as Svengali, any more than to black himself all over as Othello. Three-score years and ten is too long a run for the most successful play or the most energetic cast. And whenever there is this unreality in the lives and businesses of human beings, sooner or later the note of fatigue is heard. The man is tired of the mask, and still more of the task—the task of "humbugging all the people all the time."

(*Illustrated London News*, June 13, 1914)

The Soliloquy

The critics [make] the frequent observation that a soliloquy is old-fashioned—and by 'old-fashioned' they always mean artificial or unnatural. Now I should say that a soliloquy is the most natural thing in the world. It is no more artificial than a conscience; or a habit of walking about a room. I constantly talk to myself. If a man does not talk to himself, it is because he is not worth talking to. Soliloquy is simply the strength and liberty of the soul, without which each one of us would be like that nobleman in one of the most brilliant and bizarre of Mr. Henry James's tales, who did not exist at all except when others were present. Every man ought to be able to argue with himself.

(*Dublin Review*, January, 1914)

An Argument Between Two Truths

No dramatic poet ever wrote a line that he did not believe. A dramatic scene is only a stubborn argument between truths. Shakespeare believed in the political creed of Antony as much as in that of Brutus. The net effect of the work of a great artist is like the net effect of the works of Nature—it is conflict everywhere, and yet harmony above all.

(*Daily News*, Aug. 13, 1901)

———— ❖ ————

Brutus

Shakespeare's Brutus [was] a man of piercingly pure intentions, prone to use government as a mere machine for morality, very sensitive to the charge of inconsistency and a little too proud of his own clean and honourable life.

(*Daily News*, Jan. 4, 1908)

———— ❖ ————

The Political Play

[The] most difficult of all literary works [is the] political play. The thing has been achieved once at least admirably in Shakespeare's *Julius Caesar*. . . . The difficulties of such a play are obvious on the face of the matter. In a political play the principal characters are not merely men. They are symbols, arithmetical figures representing millions of other men outside. It is, by dint of elaborate stage management, possible to bring a mob upon the boards, but the largest mob ever known is nothing but a floating atom of the people; and the people of which the politician has to think does not consist of knots of rioters in the street, but of some million absolutely distinct individuals, each sitting in his own breakfast room reading his own morning paper. To give even the faintest suggestion of the strength and size of the people in this sense in the course of a dramatic performance is obviously impossible. That is why it is so easy on the stage to concentrate all the pathos and dignity upon such persons as Charles I and Mary Queen of Scots, the vampires of their people, because within the minute limits of a stage there is room for their small virtues and no room for their enormous crimes.

("Browning in Early Life," *Robert Browning*)

———— ❖ ————

The Problem Play

You cannot get the British Public onto the stage by realism: if you approach that public in literature you must approach it poetically. Briefly, in studying your moral problem you must do one of two things. Either you must, in choosing your morality, ignore the whole mass of men for whom morality is meant, or you must depict that mass in some entirely symbolic shape. Your play must cease to be a realistic play, your play must cease to be a problem play before it can approach the real problem.

But there is in some great plays a spirit that overcomes this difficulty. The problem of Edward Voysey, which Mr. Granville Barker sketched with a very real suggestiveness and actuality, the problem of a young idealist entangled in the desperate compromises of real conduct, had something about it that continually reminded me of the problem of

the soul of Brutus, in Shakespeare's *Julius Caesar*. Edward
Voysey was really very like Brutus. Brutus, like Edward,
was a man of "principles." Brutus, like Edward, found that
by some extraordinary process which his mind could hardly
arrest or examine, his "principles" were gradually making
him more unprincipled than anybody else. Brutus, like
Edward, had a certain kind of stiff weakness that belongs to
the mere ethicist; and a certain kind of stiff strength that
belongs to the mere ethicist, too. Shakespeare knew, quite
as well as Mr. Shaw or Mr. Granville Barker, that there is
often a certain psychological cowardice behind the virtue
of consistency, especially when the virtue of consistency is
a paraphrase for the sin of pride. But you do get in the
dramatic story of Brutus exactly the thing that you do not
get in the dramatic story of Mr. Barker's Edward Voysey.
You get the thing said for Brutus which really is to be said
for Brutus. And the thing which is to be said for Brutus is
expressed in one syllable—Rome. It is the contention of
Brutus that his "principles" are required for the public
good.

This may be right or wrong; but the dramatist at least
puts before us the idea of the public good. By high rhetoric,
by huge crowds, by a certain superb and open tone of talk,
Shakespeare manages to put upon the stage the Public
Thing—which is called in Latin the Republic. Brutus might
be quite wrong in saying that this public thing justified the
stiffness of his principles. The public thing may not be the
justification of Brutus; but certainly it is the motive of
Brutus. And as a motive it ought to be suggested on the
stage; as Shakespeare, in some sense, manages to suggest it.
But in the modern problem play, which takes place in some
dining-room or drawing-room, the reality of the public
interest is not suggested at all. In *The Voysey Inheritance*

it is not suggested at all. Mr. Granville Barker's heroine, the sweet and sane and wise young lady who directs his hero in everything, sneers at his "principles" every time they are mentioned. This is quite natural; she has four hundred a year, or some fixed sum. She has never been near enough to real life to see the necessity of "principles." She does not know that every train she travels by and every shop she shops in is run on "principles." But in the Voysey interior the Public Thing is so remote and unreal that the characters can do what they like with it. They can act as if outside their front door there was a howling wilderness. People talk in a most strange way about something that they call public morality and something that they call private morality; but I cannot comprehend the distinction. Morality may be muttered in the inner chamber; morality may be settled on some moonless night; but all morality is public morality. I, for one, decidedly decline to be bothered about my duty to my neighbour, if, by looking out of the window, I can discover that I have no neighbour.

(*Daily News*, Nov. 11, 1905)

❖

The Real Problem Play

Now the serious modern play is, as a rule, the very reverse of a problem play; for there can be no problem unless both points of view are equally and urgently presented. *Hamlet* really is a problem play because at the end of it one is really in doubt as to whether upon the author's showing Hamlet is something more than a man or something less. *Henry IV* and *Henry V* are really problem plays; in this sense, that the reader or spectator is really doubtful whether the high but harsh efficiency, valour, and ambition of Henry V are an improvement on his old blackguard camaraderie; and whether he was not a better man when he was a thief. This hearty and healthy doubt is very common in Shakespeare; I mean a doubt that exists in the writer as well as in the reader. . . . in *Julius Caesar* . . . Shakespeare sees quite as clearly that Brutus is unpractical and ineffectual; but he also sees, what is quite as plain and practical a fact, that these ineffectual men do capture the hearts and influence the policies of mankind.

("The Philosopher," *George Bernard Shaw*)

———— ❖ ————

The Historical Plays

Shakespeare's historical plays are something truer than historical; they are traditional, the living memory of many things lingered, though the memory of others was lost. He is right in making Richard II incarnate the claim to divine right; and Bolingbroke the baronial ambition which ultimately broke up the old mediaeval order. But divine right had become at once drier and more fantastic by the time of the Tudors. Shakespeare could not recover the fresh and popular part of the thing; for he came at a later stage in the process of stiffening which is the main thing to be studied in later mediaevalism.

("Nationality and the French Wars," *A Short History of England*)

———— ❖ ————

The English Hero

Our English idea of a hero is built upon the . . . accessible and open-hearted fellow, who kills everybody with the kindest feelings. Our hero is . . . Harry V—I mean the genial and magnanimous Henry V of Shakespeare, not the morbid and cruel Henry V of history. . . . Shakespeare's King Henry broods over his beloved subjects, and seeks to give them (in a splendid line) "a little touch of Harry in the night."
(*Illustrated London News*, Mar. 19, 1910)

❖

Henry V

The Henry V of Shakespeare is not indeed the Henry V of history; yet he is more historic. He is not only a saner and more genial but a more important person. For the tradition of the whole adventure was not that of Henry, but of the populace who turned Henry into Harry. There were a thousand Harries in the army at Agincourt, and not one. For the figure that Shakespeare framed out of the legends of the great victory is largely the figure that all men saw as the Englishman of the Middle Ages. He did not really talk in poetry, like Shakespeare's hero, but he would have liked to.

Not being able to do so, he sang; and the English people principally appear in contemporary impressions as the singing people.
("Nationality and the French Wars," *A Short History of England*)

❖

On the Tudors

Shakespeare, living under the Tudors, who could (and did) kill anybody they wanted to kill, could write in a detached way about man who, "dressed in a little brief authority, plays such fantastic tricks before high heaven as make the angels weep."

(*Illustrated London News*, May 18, 1935)

———— ❖ ————

Shakespeare and St. George

The Elizabethan drama is like one of its own tragedies— its tempestuous torch was soon to be trodden out by the Puritans. It is needless to say that the chief tragedy was the cutting short of the comedy; for the comedy that came to England after the Restoration was by comparison both foreign and frigid. At the best it is comedy in the sense of being humorous, but not in the sense of being happy. It may be noted that the givers of good news and good luck in the Shakespearean love-stories nearly all belong to a world which was passing, whether they are friars or fairies. It is the same with the chief Elizabethan ideals, often embodied in the Elizabethan drama. The national devotion to the Virgin Queen must not be wholly discredited by its incongruity with the coarse and crafty character of the historical Elizabeth. Her critics might indeed reasonably say that in replacing the Virgin Mary by the Virgin Queen, the English reformers merely exchanged a true virgin for a false one. But this truth does not dispose of a true, though limited, contemporary cult. Whatever we think of that particular Virgin Queen, the tragic heroines of the time offer us a whole procession of virgin queens. And it is certain that the mediaevals would have understood much better than the moderns the martyrdom of *Measure for Measure*. And as with the title of Virgin, so with the title of Queen. The mystical monarchy glorified in Richard II was soon to be dethroned much more ruinously than in Richard II. The same Puritans who tore off the pasteboard crowns of the stage players were also to tear off the real crowns of the kings whose parts they played. All mummery was to be forbidden, and all monarchy to be called mummery. Shakespeare died upon St. George's Day, and much of what St. George had meant died with him.

("Spain and the Schism of Nations," *A Short History of England*)

---- ❖ ----

Shakespeare and Bunyan

There is no person so narrow as the person who is sure that he is broad; indeed, being quite *sure* that one is broad is itself a form of narrowness. It shows that one has a very narrow ideal of breadth. But, moreover, there is an element involved in the Rationalist position which makes this unintentional bigotry peculiarly natural. . . . There are two or three principal ways in which this blameless bigotry may appear. One is the . . . unconscious trick of . . . the abuse of the *post hoc, ergo propter hoc*. ["after this, therefore because of this."] Certain events are connected together, while others, in the same historical relation, are not connected together. Thus, people will say, "Elizabeth threw off the yoke of Pope and Spaniard, and then Shakespeare wrote *Romeo and Juliet*." As a matter of fact, you might just as well say, "Charles II returned amid loyal rejoicings, and then John Milton went and wrote *Paradise Lost.*" The Puritan literature had begun long before Charles II returned; so had the Renaissance literature, with its Italian love-tales, begun long before the Reformation or the Armada. The Reformation did occur soon after the Renaissance; but that it was not (to say the least of it) the same thing can be simply inferred from the fact that the countries where the Renaissance most markedly occurred were commonly the countries where the Reformation didn't. Indeed, I think that the most human, generous, and comprehending consideration of Puritanism would be to regard it as a revolt against the Renaissance rather than a revolt against the Middle Ages. It was an outbreak of the barbaric mysticism of the North against the classical clarity of the South. Bunyan was a rebel against Shakespeare much more than Shakespeare was a rebel against Chaucer. It is easy to fancy Chaucer and Shakespeare sitting down at the same tavern-table; but if Bunyan had sat down with them I think one of them would have been embarrassed. Perhaps all three.

(*Illustrated London News*, April 30, 1910)

❖

Winter Tales

I think, a limited and localized fire will always be as much associated with Christians as it has always been associated with Christmas. Shakespeare, himself like a large and liberal fire round which winter tales are told, has hit the mark in this matter exactly, as it concerns the poet or maker of fictive things. Shakespeare does not say that the poet loses himself in the All, that he dissipates concrete things into a cloudy twilight, that he turns this home of ours into a vista or any vaguer thing. He says the exact opposite. It is "a local habitation and a name" that the poet gives to what would otherwise be nothing. This seeming narrowness which men complain of in the altar and the hearth is as broad as Shakespeare and the whole human imagination, and should command the respect even of those who think the cult of Christmas really is all imagination. Even those who can only regard the great story of Bethlehem as a fairy-tale told by the fire will yet agree that such narrowness is the first artistic necessity even of a good fairy-tale. But there are others who think, at least, that their thought strikes deeper and pierces to a more subtle truth in the mind. There are others for whom all our fairy-tales, and even all our appetite for fairy-tales, draw their fire from one central fairy-tale, as all forgeries draw their significance from a signature. They believe that this fable is a fact, and that the other fables cannot really be appreciated even as fables until we know it is a fact.

("The Yule Log and the Democrat," *The Uses of Diversity*)

———— ❖ ————

The Twelve Days of Christmas

Modern men have a vague feeling that when they have come to the feast, they have come to the finish. By modern commercial customs, the preparations for it have been so very long and the practice of it seems so very short. This is, of course, in sharp contrast to the older traditional customs, in the days when it was a sacred festival for a simpler people. Then the preparation took the form of the more austere season of Advent and the fast of Christmas Eve. But when men passed on to the feast of

Christmas it went on for a long time after the feast of Christmas Day. It always went on for a continuous holiday of rejoicing for at least twelve days, and only ended in that wild culmination which Shakespeare described as *Twelfth Night: or What You Will*. That is to say, it was a sort of Saturnalia which ended in anybody doing whatever he would: and in William Shakespeare writing some very beautiful and rather irrelevant poetry round a perfectly impossible story about a brother and sister who looked exactly alike. In our more enlightened times, the perfectly impossible stories are printed in magazines a month or two before Christmas has begun at all; and in the hustle and hurry of this early publication, the beautiful poetry is, somehow or other, left out.

(*Illustrated London News*, Dec. 23, 1933)

For All Ages

Shakespeare is really for all ages, for all the seven ages of man. I was fond of Shakespeare when I crept unwillingly to school, and I am fond of him now when I can be more vividly described as a lean and slippered pantaloon. And I do not mean that as a child I was fond of his romantic tales merely; I was fond of his poetry, especially when it was entirely unintelligible. The open and rolling rhythm seemed to be speaking plainly even when I could not comprehend it. The huge heraldic imagery of red and gold was obvious, though I could not take it in. Members of my family who collect coincidences have assured me that I was small enough to run along the street and fall on my nose in the very act of saying the lines:

> Do not for ever with thy veilèd lids
> Seek for thy noble father in the dust.

Lines like

> Revisit'st thus the glimpses of the moon

or like

> Still climbing trees in the Hesperides

were not only good poetry, they were good children's pictures like the cow who jumped over the moon, or the number of red herrings that grow in a wood.

(*Daily News*, Dec. 19, 1908)

——— ❖ ———

For All the Continents

Shakespeare must be a great puzzle to Anglo-Saxons; and that not merely in reference to the element in him that is medieval. Of course, the Anglo-Saxons, having chosen their own name from the very darkest part of the Dark Ages, disapprove of anything so remote and retrograde as being medieval. But they must surely find him in any case irritatingly international. How are we to explain his deplorable taste in Dagos? How can he have borne to be so dreadfully Italianate? The Anglo-Saxon school really ought to bring out an Anglo-Saxon translation of Shakespeare as well as of the Bible. They ought to insist on all his heroes and heroines being naturalised. They ought to alter all the proper names so that they are really proper. Perhaps it would be a little difficult to give *The Merchant of Venice* some respectable name like *The Merchant of Manchester*; but it would be easy enough to turn Signer Antonio into Mr. Antony. Perhaps we have here a new and true meaning in the immortal cry of Juliet. "O Romeo, Romeo, wherefore art thou Romeo, and not Robinson?" Since it is a recognised truth that the very name and notion of a gentleman cannot be translated into any other language outside English, how did it come about that Shakespeare came to write of *The Two Gentlemen of Verona*, when a very trifling change would have turned them into *The Two Gentlemen of Ventnor*? This weakness for the decadent Dago will appear deplorable enough to the critic whose hopes for England are bound up so largely with the Ku Klux Klan; but I deeply regret to say that Shakespeare did not invariably even confine himself to Dagos. He showed in one case at least a shocking indifference to the Colour Bar. The Ku Klux Klan would certainly treat Othello, to say the least of it, as a coloured gentleman. And heaven knows he was a coloured gentleman, compared with the vast multitude of colourless cads who make up such very depressing conspiracies in colonial places. And what Shakespeare cared about was the colour, that is the culture, the life and legend and poetry that belonged to our civilisation as a whole. And the real interest attaching to his intense patriotism is that he survives out of a more united past, to express the idea that our national glory is to consist in achievements in that common culture and in nothing else.

(*G.K.'s Weekly*, June 13, 1925)

❖

Shakespeare and the Land

If we have not had peasants, we have occasionally had poets. And one of them, whose name is not wholly obscure, has left on record many memories that recall his country of origin, and these older and healthier traditions of the countryside; as it was when the first transition from the medieval to the modern world was passing over the woods of Warwickshire.

> And the country proverb known
> That every man shall have his own
> In your waking shall be shown.

Those three lines of Shakespeare might very well be printed on the front of our paper [*G.K.'s Weekly*] as the motto of our policy. . . . The same passage ends with the jingle about Jack having Jill and the man having his mare again; the only true description of something that is much too good to be called Utopia; though it might be called, in the phrase of another poet, The Land of Heart's Desire.

Yet Shakespeare knew all about Utopia; indeed he lived just after the martyrdom of the man who invented the word. But while the word is at least as old as More, the thing, or rather the thought, is older than Plato. William Shakespeare knew quite as much as William Morris about the abstraction of an Earthly Paradise. So in *The Tempest*, the Renaissance nobles, full of the expansive sixteenth century spirit, land on the mysterious island, as such sixteenth century adventurers did land on so many mysterious islands. And the best man among them, like the best man in every such society and period, dreams of the perfect social state he would create in a new country. He repeats, clause by clause, the programme of the International Social Democratic Soviet Republic. He recites all the revolutionary ideals which the moderns have since discovered; all the things first revealed to Robert Owen; all the thing's hidden from humanity till Tolstoy. That expansive sixteenth century gentleman describes at length his social settlement for the new colony. There are to be no armaments. There are to be no landmarks of private property. Everything as nice as Maxton makes it. Meanwhile, it is typical of the same expansive sixteenth century spirit that while one Renaissance gentleman is thus dreaming, all the other Renaissance gentlemen are plotting to betray and murder each other, and seize each other's possessions by force and fraud. So in fact proceeded the real Renaissance gentleman; and thus founded the landlord system and the great commercial prosperity of England. But all the time there ran in Shakespeare's head an older and ruder and more rustic tune; deeper than the fancy about Utopia, deeper than the intrigues of the Italianate gentry, deeper even than his own deep unrest about usurpation and usurpers, there ran a tinkling tune as persistent as a brook

> . . . the man shall have his mare again
> . . . every man shall have his own.

(*G.K.'s Weekly*, Mar. 23, 1925)

Equality

Shakespeare has been called anti-democratic, because, like nearly all the European poets of all ages, he did one or two rhetorical exercises on the old theme of the *odi profanum*. ["I hate the common people."] But the conversations of his clowns contain some of the most vivid traces of the wit and vitality of the popular Christian tradition. And in so far as it was a tradition of equality, it was faultlessly phrased by the Grave-digger. "And the more pity that great folk should have countenance in this world to drown or hang themselves more than their even-Christian." I do not think it was quite accidental that Shakespeare put in that grim qualification "in this world." But the broad fact is that the word "Christian" is generally used by the populace in a sense even more apparently remote from religious definition than this; and commonly signifies that which is human, normal, social and self-respecting.

(*British Review*, September, 1913)

---- ❖ ----

Why is Shakespeare Popular?

The statement that the work of the Old Masters can be effective for popular education is not such a platitude as it will at first appear. It is both more disputable and more true than it seems. For the truth is that the great art of the past can be used for this purpose where a great many other methods now generally adopted are quite clumsy and futile. Something of this utility is shared by the plays of Shakespeare; and by no other agency I know except the paintings of such men as Titian and Leonardo.

To explain this peculiar kind of public value one must understand one of the deepest differences, and perhaps diseases, of our time. It was the mark of the art of the past, especially the art of the Renaissance, that the great man was a man. He was an extraordinary man, but only in the sense of being an ordinary man with something extra. Shakespeare or Rubens went with the plain man as far as the plain man went; they ate and drank, and desired and died as he did. That is what people mean when they say that these gods had feet of clay; their giant boots were heavy with the mire of the earth. That is what people mean when they say that Shakespeare was often coarse; that is what people mean when they say that he was often dull. They mean that a great poet of the elder kind had spaces which were idle and absent-minded; that his sub-consciousness often guided him; that he sprawled; that he was not 'artistic'. It is not only true that Homer sometimes nodded; but nodding was part of the very greatness of Homer. His sleepy nod shakes the stars like the nod of his own Jupiter.

The old artists, then, were plain and popular in the more fundamental or (if you will) lower parts of their personality. But the typical modern artist sets out to be a separate and fantastic sort of creature, who feeds and feels in a strange manner of his own. . . . [Thus, there is a] distinction between two conceptions of genius, the Something more and the Something different.

(Introduction to *Famous Paintings*)

———— ❖ ————

Author and Man

There exists in the world a group of persons who perpetually try to prove that Shakespeare was a clown and could not have written about princes, or that he was a drunkard and could not have written about virtue. I think there is a slight fallacy in the argument. But I wonder that they have not tried the much more tempting sport of separating the author of *L'Allegro* from the author of the *Defensus Populi*

Anglicani. For the contrast between the man Milton and the poet Milton is very much greater than is commonly realized. I fear that the shortest and clearest way of stating it is that when all is said and done, he is a poet whom we cannot help liking, and a man whom we cannot like. I find it far easier to believe that an intoxicated Shakespeare wrote the marble parts of Shakespeare than that a marble Milton wrote the intoxicated, or, rather, intoxicating, parts of Milton. Milton's character was cold . . .

Shakespeare puts into the mouth of some character (generally a silly character) some contemptuous talk about the greasy rabble, talk which is common to all literary work, but especially common in work which—like Shakespeare's—was intended to please the greasy rabble. Whenever this happens critics point to it and say, "Look at the Tory prejudices of the Royalist Shakespeare! Observe the Jacobite servility of the follower of James I!" But as a matter of fact Milton despised the populace much more than Shakespeare; and Milton put his contempt for common men not into the mouth of silly or stupid characters, but into that of the one wise character, the Chorus, who is supposed to express the moral of a play:

> Nor do I name of men the common rout . . .
> But such as thou hast solemnly elected.

(*Catholic World*, January, 1917)

Ordinary and Extraordinary

This is the real explanation of the thing which has puzzled so many dilettante critics, the problem of the extreme ordinariness of the behaviour of so many great geniuses in history. Their behaviour was so ordinary that it was not recorded; hence it was so ordinary that it seemed mysterious. . . . The modern artistic temperament cannot understand how a man who could write such lyrics as Shakespeare wrote, could be as keen as Shakespeare was on business transactions in a little town in Warwickshire. The explanation is simple enough; it is that Shakespeare had a real lyrical impulse, wrote a real lyric, and so got rid of the impulse and went about his business. Being an artist did not prevent him from being an ordinary man, any more than being a sleeper at night or being a diner at dinner prevented him from being an ordinary man.

All very great teachers and leaders have had this habit of assuming their point of view to be one which was human and casual, one which would readily appeal to every passing man. If a man is genuinely superior to his fellows the first thing that he believes in is the equality of man. We can see this, for instance, in that strange and innocent rationality with which Christ addressed any motley crowd that happened to stand about Him. "What man of you having a hundred sheep, and losing one, would not leave the ninety and nine in the wilderness, and go after that which was lost?" [Luke 15:4] Or, again, "What man of you if his son ask for bread will give him a stone, or if he ask for a fish will he give him a serpent?" [Matthew 7:9–10] This plainness, this almost prosaic camaraderie, is the note of all very great minds.

To very great minds the things on which men agree are so immeasurably more important than the things on which they differ, that the latter, for all practical purposes, disappear. They have too much in them of an ancient laughter even to endure to discuss the difference between the hats of two men who were both born of a woman, or between the subtly varied cultures of two men who have both to die. The first-rate great man is equal with other men, like Shakespeare. The second-rate great man is on his knees to other men, like Whitman. The third-rate great man is superior to other men, like Whistler.

("On the Wit of Whistler," *Heretics*)

❖

The Embodiment of Humanity

It may be noticed that the great artists always choose great fools rather than great intellectuals to embody humanity. Hamlet does express the aesthetic dreams and the bewilderments of the intellect; but Bottom the Weaver expresses them much better.

("The Great Dickens Characters," *Charles Dickens*)

❖

Typical Moralist

Telling the truth about the terrible struggle of the human soul is surely a very elementary part of the ethics of honesty. If the characters are not wicked, the book is. This older and firmer conception of right as existing outside human weakness and without reference to human error, can be felt in the very lightest and loosest of the works of old English literature. It is commonly unmeaning enough to call Shakespeare a great moralist; but in this particular way Shakespeare is a very typical moralist. Whenever he alludes to right and wrong it is always with this old implication. Right is right, even if nobody does it. Wrong is wrong even if everybody is wrong about it.

(*Illustrated London News*, May 11, 1907)

———— ❖ ————

The Flaw in the Deed

There is one idea of this kind that runs through most popular tales (those, for instance, on which Shakespeare is so often based)—an idea that is profoundly moral even if the tales are immoral. It is what may be called the flaw in the deed: the idea that, if I take my advantage to the full, I shall hear of something to my disadvantage. Thus Midas fell into a fallacy about the currency; and soon had reason to become something more than a Bimetallist. Thus Macbeth had a fallacy about forestry; he could not see the trees for the wood. He forgot that, though a place cannot be moved, the trees that grow on it can. Thus Shylock had a fallacy of physiology; he forgot that, if you break into the house of life, you find it a bloody house in the most emphatic sense.

("The Vengeance of the Flesh," *Eugenics and Other Evils*)

———— ❖ ————

The Flaw in the Deed (Again)

The idea of the flaw in the deed, the unforeseen disadvantage in the contract . . . is very clearly conveyed, of course, in *Macbeth*, where the juggling fiends keep their word of promise to the ear, but break it to the hope. It is expressed in another way in Shylock, who ruthlessly insists on the bond, only to find the bond itself turn against him. As there was a hole in these deals with the devil, so there was a hole in Dr. Jekyll's deal with the devil. Shylock won his case; but he found that winning his case was not the same as winning his object. Macbeth won his crown; but found that winning his crown was not the same as crowning his ambition.

(*Illustrated London News*, Sept. 19, 1925)

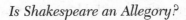

Is Shakespeare an Allegory?

(Review of *The Messiahship of Shakespeare* by Charles Downing)

Mr. Charles Downing is the author of *God in Shakespeare*. He believes that the great dramatist was a reincarnation of the Divine. If we should freely admit that Shakespeare was divine, merely extending the remark to Homer, Aristophanes, Mr. Bradlaugh, and Mr. James Harris of Brixton, we fear that Mr. Downing would not be satisfied. It is due to him, however, to say that his work is a great improvement, in point of refinement and restraint, upon the ordinary ruck of works on what is (for some mysterious reason) called the "problem of Shakespeare": the works which prove that he was Christ, Bacon, and anyone else but himself. There are real degrees of taste even in absurdity, and it is possible for a maniac to rave with the most perfect good breeding. Mr. Downing, in propounding his outrageous thesis, has real humility and the real dignity that only comes of humility. But his attitude is vitiated to the very root by a low and inadequate conception of the nature of symbolism. He opens his book with the following remarks:

"Of recent years there has been in literature a great turning of the spirit to symbolism and to what may be called essential religion. Maeterlinck abroad and Mr. Yeats at home are the names most

prominent to me, at this moment, in the movement, but it per-
vades literature, and the latest minor poet will show traces of its
influence."

This is profoundly and most fortunately true. But Mr.
Downing entirely mistakes the real nature of symbolism as
evinced in Maeterlinck and Mr. Yeats when he seeks in
Shakespeare for a fixed scheme of allegory. "Hermione (of
The Winter's Tale), the ideal of the Graeco-Roman world
. . . has stepped down from her pedestal, a statue come to
life, and clasped in her hands Perdita, the Christian ideal."
This is not the sort of thing Maeterlinck or Mr. Yeats write,
and is presumably not the sort of thing that Shakespeare
wrote. Maeterlinck's characters do not represent particular
cliques and schools in Belgian art and politics; they represent eternal things for which no philosophic name will ever
be found. Mr. Yeats's pre-historic heroes are not introduced
upon the stage in order to typify Mr. Redmond's party and
Mr. Healy's party, but to typify elemental mysteries which
cannot be typified in any other way. We need a much clearer
conception of the real value and function of mysticism. It is
not mysticism to explain a puzzle: to say that a green cross
means evolution and a blue triangle means orthodoxy. This
sort of allegorical art is a mere cryptogram which ceases to
exist when it is explained. Whatever a mystic may be, he is
surely not only a person who destroys mystery.

The real function of symbolism is much deeper and more
practical. We are surrounded in this world by huge and
anonymous forces: as they rush by us we throw a name at
them—love, death, destiny, remembrance—but the things
themselves are infinitely vaster and more varied than the
names. True artistic symbolism exists in order to provide
another alphabet for the direct interpretation of these

infinite anarchic things than the alphabet of language. It is
not that a sea at sunset "represents" sorrow, but that a sea at
sunset represents a great deal of the truth which is missed
by the word "sorrow." So it is with Mr. Downing's
Shakespeare allegory. It is not that Shakespeare is a mere
philosopher: it is that philosophy is one way of describing
certain unutterable things, and Shakespeare is another.
Caliban, says Mr. Downing, "represents the mob." The
truth is that Caliban represents an old, dark, and lawless
element in things, an element which has no name except
Caliban and of which the mob is one of the hundred incar-
nations. So far from it being true that Caliban symbolises
the mob in the street, it would be far truer to say that the
mob in the street symbolises Caliban.

This error runs through the whole conception of *The
Messiahship of Shakespeare*; the poet is perpetually being
made to describe, not things themselves, but the metaphysical names of things. Shakespeare was in one sense a thorough mystic; he saw in every stone in the street things which
cannot be uttered till the end of the world. His Perdita is not
"a type of the Reformation," but simply a girl in love; the
Reformation is, in comparison, a trivial thing.

Mr. Downing's taste for turning good poetry into bad
metaphysics has its entirely humorous aspects, as where he
provides precise logical translations of many of the sonnets.
We give one example. A famous sonnet begins:

> Oh, how thy worth with manners may I sing
> When thou art all the better part of me?
> What can mine own praise to mine own self bring?

The following is, according to Mr. Downing, what the three
lines really mean:

1. How in modesty can I sing the worth of Beauty?
2. When it is all my better part, my thought, my genius, my soul.
3. What value has self-praise?

If this is really what Shakespeare meant, we can only say that literature should be everlastingly grateful that it is not what he said.

It is, however, in this treatment of *The Tempest* that Mr. Downing shows most singularly his cut-and-dried conception of allegory. For *The Tempest* really is a mystical play: its figures are symbols, but not mere mathematical symbols. Here is a description of the meaning of the wreck:

> Alonzo, the ruling class, is in despair, but still clings to Antonio and Sebastian, Ambition and *Laissez Faire*, its old vices. . . . Authority being thus divided between the Backward and Progressive parties, the Mob, Caliban, lifts up its head, and, led on by Stephano and Trinculo, Sensuality and Folly, riots freely, threatening the destruction of Prospero, all Justice, Law, and Civilization, from the earth.

What is the good of this kind of symbolism? If Shakespeare meant to convey the word Ambition, why did he go to the trouble of saying the word Antonio? The truth is that Shakespeare was a symbolist of the genuine type, and symbolism of the genuine type is wholly misunderstood by Mr. Downing and his school. A real symbol of a certain law is not a mere cipher-term arbitrarily connected with that law, but an *example* of that law. A plough is symbolic of the toil of all things because it is an instance of it. The parables of the New Testament, for instance, are built wholly upon this principle; so are the one or two mystical plays of Shakespeare. It is not, as Mr. Downing would put it, that Prospero was not a man but an image of God, but that he was a man, and, therefore, an image of God. The same may be said of Shakespeare. We have said nothing about this central theological theory of Mr. Downing, and our silence has been deliberate. Before we decide whether any man (even the stupidest man in the street) is God, we must take the preliminary precaution of knowing what God is and what man is.

(*The Speaker,* May 11, 1901)

--- ❖ ---

The Phoenix and the Turtle

How many of my highly cultured readers have really grasped, assimilated, and made their own the poem called "The Phoenix and the Turtle"? I feel as if I were offering a prize in the newspapers for some sort of success with a crossword puzzle; but I can assure the reader that Torquemada never produced anything within a thousand miles of the Turtle and his mystical colleague. Much of the modern public will be divided between those who say "Of course we know our Shakespeare," and those who have entirely forgotten that Shakespeare ever wrote anything of the sort. And, indeed, the first group is wrong, and the second group is right. Shakespeare never did write anything of the sort, so far as I know, except in this one extraordinary example. On the other hand, we may be fairly certain that those who say they know their Shakespeare do not know their Shakespeare. If they did, they would not fall into the fallacy of supposing that he was theirs. In all this common cultivated acquaintance with the classics there is a certain unconscious trick of omission for which we must always allow. There is even a sort of terrible irony in Matthew Arnold's phrase that culture consists of knowing "the best that has been said and thought." It is only too true that the knowledge of Shakespeare generally means the knowledge of the best things in Shakespeare. Or, at least, of the things which those who were thought the best critics thought were the best things. But there are many more marvellous and fantastic fish in that great sea than ever came out of it. When people say they know their Shakespeare, they generally mean that they know somebody else's Shakespeare; especially the actor's Shakespeare, or the actor-manager's Shakespeare, or the highly modern producer's Shakespeare, or, what is worst of all, the Shakespearean critic's Shakespeare.

It is the same with all the great creations that are stared at like monuments, rather than quarried in like mines. I read a newspaper article the other day in which a man said that he knew the message of the Gospel was quite simple, because he had heard it at his mother's knee. It did not seem to occur to him that his mother might have been a person of some common sense and that she probably read to him the passages that really are simple enough to be suitable to a child. It seems probable that she was sane enough to tell him of the Good Shepherd who goes after the lost sheep; or the welcome to the prodigal returning home; or the love of Christ for all little children. It seems improbable that she asked a child to understand what is meant by the Unjust Steward; or the Eunuchs of the Kingdom of Heaven; or the command to hate father and mother for the Kingdom of God; or the bringing of a sword into the world; or the dark enigma of Judas. Now, most educated people have exactly that memory of an expurgated Shakespeare; as they have of an expurgated Bible. They remember the things that have been theatrically presented to them; because they are theatrical. They remember the things that are quite obviously edifying, in the sense of moralising, because they have been imposed upon them. But there are a thousand things in Shakespeare which they have never even tried to understand; and this is something which I respectfully doubt whether they would understand, even if they tried.

People actually found cryptograms in Shakespeare; but there is nothing so very cryptic about a cryptogram. It is merely a sort of spelling game, by which a rather crude and clumsy series of words can somehow be traced through the thick of much more important and intelligent and beautiful words. Mrs. Gallup thus proved in an ingenious manner that Bacon wrote Shakespeare. Father Ronald Knox thus proved, much more successfully, that Queen Victoria wrote "In Memoriam." We can prove the impossibility of a cryptogram by the existence of so many cryptograms. The more often it is done, the more impossible it is to do. There have been about ten alternative explanations of the authorship of the plays, founded on a long recurrent scheme running through the plays. I have never seen one real explanation of the short poem called "The Phoenix and the Turtle." I mean I have never seen any in the ordinary literary textbooks. Or, again, I have read all my life about the obscurity of certain writers; of how Browning baffles the reader, or even Meredith is sometimes verbally evasive. But I was never baffled by Browning or Meredith, even in my boyhood; and I am pretty completely baffled by "The Phoenix and the Turtle." Yet, strangely enough, it is never mentioned among these other and milder examples of popular misunderstanding. I come back with some gloom to the inference: not that nobody has understood it, but that nobody has read it.

Of course, I would not be arrogant. There may be others who grasp it at a glance: whose common conversation at breakfast consists of lines like these—

> Reason, in itself confounded,
> Saw division grow together,
> To themselves yet either neither,
> Simple were so well compounded
> That it cried, How true a twain
> Seemeth this concordant one!

But I have not come across any of them among the public Shakespearean critics. And my conclusion, right or wrong, is this. Shakespeare did, for the first and last time, really wish to put himself beyond the reach of the Shakespearean critics. Shakespeare did really wish to leave behind him one real cryptogram: not a silly alphabetical cypher to say that he was Francis Bacon or Queen Elizabeth, or the Earl of Southampton; but something to say that he was the Shakespeare whom we shall never know. As if he had been suddenly alarmed at the horrid notion that he had really unlocked his heart with the key of the Sonnets, as Wordsworth suggested; and had then resolved to leave behind him a casket that no key can unlock.

I do not set up to be a student of Shakespeare; still less of Shakespeareana. It may be that these two wild hints, the Phoenix and the Turtle, have been caught and caged and labelled and stuffed in a museum many times. They may have been identified as often as "Mr. W. H.," who by this time might be almost anything, from the White Horse to the Waldorf Hotel. Perhaps the Turtledove is the League of Nations, cooing sweetly but apparently dying young; or the Phoenix is the German Eagle, re-arising out of the burning

Reichstag. But the only serious and convincing note on it I happen to have read is in the Comtesse de Chambrun's remarkable reconstruction called "My Shakespeare, Rise!" M. André Maurois writes a most interesting preface to this most interesting book. Himself detached from the debates on which it turns, he is only linked with Mme. de Chambrun by his interest in English literature; but he pays a just tribute to the learning which she applies to that literature. Her theory is, broadly speaking, that the motive which made Shakespeare thus cryptic was largely politic; and that the whole mystery was connected with contemporary politics. She has set out in several books her reasons for believing that Shakespeare belonged to the party, at once of revolt and reaction, which was specially bent on breaking the power and policy of Cecil and his group: a group which more or less included Bacon. It is curious that Bacon and Shakespeare, who have actually been lumped together as partners, or even identified as an alias and an *alter ego*, were (according to this theory), so far from working together in private life, actually working against each other in public life. This particular movement found its final issue and failure, I suppose, in the rebellion of Essex; which was certainly against Cecil on the political side, though some have disputed its purpose on the religious side. Essex may have courted some of the Puritans; his friend Southampton was certainly one of the Papists; and this book explains the mysterious lament as a dirge for the old régime: "Truth may seem, but cannot be; Beauty brag, but 'tis not she." Certainly that is what a man might well say, who felt hostile to a new world.

(*Illustrated London News*, January 11, 1936)

Shakespeare and the Germans

The German professors have done a great many devastating things; but perhaps the worst thing about them was they were the first to understand Shakespeare. It is a great impertinence to understand Shakespeare: for Shakespeare certainly did not understand himself. He never talked so much sense as when he was obviously talking nonsense; and a man must have the sacred streak of nonsense somewhere in his mind before he can appreciate phrases like: "Those earthly godfathers of Heaven's lights," or "Bowl the round nave down the hill of heaven." Now, the Germans are like the ladies whom Mr. Sparkler admired. They have no nonsense about them. Some of them seem to think that Hamlet meant what he said; and, thinking this, they come to the not unreasonable conclusion that he was mad. There is in Shakespeare something more godlike even than humour: something which the English call fun. The neglect of this by the Germans during the long night of German intellectual domination has produced some preposterous fruits in English, American and other criticism. The notes in my school books used to be full of alternative explanations, frequently German, of such phrases as: "I know a hawk from a hand-saw." Grumpt says that "hand-saw" should obviously be heron-saw, to put it in the same ornithological class with hawk; but Mumpt suggests that there may have been an Elizabethan tool called a hawk, to put it in the same mechanical class with hand-saw. And all the time even a boy who had any flavour of literature, or any guess at the kind of man that Hamlet was supposed to be, could see at once that it was a joke. Hamlet said it as a piece of wild alliteration; as he might have said: "I know a baby from a blunderbuss"; or, "I know a catfish from a croquet-hoop." By a deep and dry study of the millions exaggerations, inconsistencies and ignorances of Shakespeare they build up a sort of rampart round the unfortunate poet to defend him from his real admirers; the sulky Ben Jonson had far more genuine sympathy with Shakespeare than the world-patronising Goethe. . . . The first and fatal step was to take Shakespeare seriously; the next and more fatal step was to defend him in everything. The next step was to go clean off one's head and say he was a German.

(*Blinded Soldiers' and Sailors' Gift Book*, 1915)

———— ❖ ————

Shakespeare and the Dark Lady

("Frank Harris on Shakespeare")

Mr. Frank Harris, who in his really poignant and pathetic autobiography used the *nom de plume* of "Shakespeare," has, I hear, suddenly discovered that he is an American citizen. It makes an Englishman feel a little nervous; as if he might wake up in bed and suddenly remember that he was an Ancient Roman or a celebrated Russian dancer. There is nothing to be said, except that if Mr. Frank Harris is an American citizen he must be a very bad American citizen; for he was generally regarded as an English Jingo. But though Mr. Harris has apparently been a bad American and a bad Englishman, it is really probable that he would be a good German. Many of the more all-embracing of the Teutons say that Shakespeare was a German: and if Mr. Harris describes Shakespeare correctly it would seem as if they were right; for he describes the poet as sentimental and sulky and inordinately interested in himself, in defiance of all the facts of existence. I do not believe that Shakespeare was sulky; but then I am also sufficiently paradoxical not to believe that he was German. Mr. Harris made all Shakespeare's emotions revolve round himself and the Dark Lady; who was exactly like Ophelia and also Cleopatra, as well as being the replica of Desdemona and the very image of Lady Macbeth. Anyhow, she was like all Shakespeare's heroines at once, Shakespeare being unable to imagine anyone else; and in that case she must have been a lady of highly complicated character, and what the nurses describe as "a handful." It is Mr. Harris' mission and excuse upon this earth to prove that the Dark Lady was Mary Fitton; a lady of whom nobody seems to know anything to speak of, except that she was fair. The objection to this line of study is, that if you ask who the Dark Lady was, you will go on to ask who Mr. W. H. was; and if you ask who Mr. W. H. was, you will go mad. There are probably people at this moment, in and out of asylums, who are proving that he was Mr. William Hohenzollern.

For my part, I very much doubt whether there ever was any Dark Lady. Tennyson said, in a poem in many ways quite as egoistic as the Sonnets:

> "I will take some savage woman,
> she shall rear my dusky race."

Tennyson lived in such very public privacy in the Isle of Wight, that w know he never carried out this adventurous intention in a literal sense. But if he had not, if he had gone about his business among other men like sensible fellow, as Shakespeare did, his private life would probably be as little known as Shakespeare's. He would have been lost in a crowd. And in that case we should have these critics who ask

"Who Was The Dark Lady?" asking, in the same style, "Who Was the Dusky Woman?" And we should have the Harrises and Shaws of the future saying that it was Mrs. Humphrey Ward. Or if Mrs. Ward's hair happens really to be dark (a final disqualification) then it was Ellen Terry in a black wig. And those who think as I do would have to put their opinions in a comic paper, in order to point out that marrying a black woman is one thing and talking about marrying her quite another; that Tennyson did not, in point of fact, marry a black woman; or that she was not so black as he painted her.

Critics say that little is known about "the Man Shakespeare." But, to judge by the critics, even less is known about "the Poet Shakespeare": for he is allowed to be almost everything except a poet. He is a philosopher, a lawyer, nay, a Lord Chancellor. The Germans seem to maintain, not that he was a German poet, but rather that he was a German professor. Let us suppose that Shakespeare writes a charming and irresponsible play with the very irresponsible title of *As You Like It*, in which there is a still more irresponsible song, which begins like this:

> "It was a lover and his lass,
> With a hey and a ho and a hey nonny no."

The German professors will proceed to reconstruct the second line like a Latin inscription; and they will print it like this:

> "(with a) . . . haec . . (and a) . . hoe
> . . (and a) . . . haec nonne no(n),"

Using, you observe, the double negative permitted in Latin in a manner more extreme even than that established by

Gruncke's Law: though Gruncke was with all the world-enlightening scholar's necessities equipped. Or, if they do not do that, they will read it as an old English agricultural proverb, beginning "with a hay and a hoe"; and about the word "nonny" they will tell you to Cf Chaucer Cant. Pil. 971 b xii. And when you have cf'd Chaucer, you will find he speaks of "the none priest"; and you will learn that the passage is a protest against the territorial and agricultural powers possessed by the medieval clergy up to the dissolution of the monasteries, just before Shakespeare's time. Shall the Nun and the Priest control our hays and our hoes? "No!" exclaims Shakespeare the universal world-soul, here proving that he is with the heart-thoughts of our German Luther at one. And If you venture to say that people don't hoe hay, whatever they may do with potatoes, you will be told that you have not with our great Hegel reconciled the Is Not with the Is. Or they will tell you that Hey and Ho were two ancient gods (cf Hermes and Horus) of whom the Illuminati including Shakespeare were secret adherents; and that "nonny no" is connected with the old Roman Nones, and the Lord knows what. They will read and reread that sentence, and spell it backwards, and number its letters, and try it as anagram, and write it in Coptic to see if it looks nicer; but there is one thing they will never do to it. It will never occur to them to *sing* it; or, in other words, to remember that it is meant to be part of a song. In fact, the sight of a thoroughly Germanized commentator suddenly singing in the British Museum Library would be quite startling, and would undoubtedly attract remark. If the critics did this all sorts of things would happen to them; but, among other things, they would discover that the voice is lifted and the stress laid upon the second "hey"; or in other words, that Shakespeare was a poet and that they are a pack of idiots. All that these people can do is mystification; which means the making of mysteries, not the recognition of them. But even among the mysteries which really exist, they prefer these, like the Dark Lady, about which they are in the dark. There are many much brighter ladies who are just as incomprehensible and more comprehending. They are to be found in any number in the plays of Shakespeare and not in his biographies; for it is not in a man's biography that we can read his life.

As I have already suggested, I neither know nor care whether Shakespeare either knew or cared about anybody named Mary Fitton. That he cared at some time about somebody I am very certain. I do not even admit that there was any Dark Lady. But there was something. There was something which Shakespeare thought, and these Shakespearians apparently do not think, worth writing about:

> "It was a lover and his lass,
> With a hey and a ho and a hey nonny no."

or, in other words, with all the world-revolving life's-necessities equipped.

("On Shakespeare," *Life*, April 20, 1916)

❖

On the Shakespeare Ball By One Who Was Not There

I have been asked to describe the great Shakespeare Ball with all that advantage which Shakespeare enjoyed in describing the Battle of Agincourt—the advantage of absence. It would have annoyed him a great deal if the Globe Theatre had really been rushed by the fleeing spears

of Picardy or the pursuing archers of England. Most of them
(I have heard by the way) came from Wales. But, in any
case, Shakespeare might very well have been much startled
and unmanned if he had observed within his wooden O
even one of the casques that did affright the air at Agincourt.
In the same way I feel that I should be quite unmanned, for
the purpose of writing this article, if I had actually, physically and with my bodily eyes beheld any of the costumes
that did affright the air in the Albert Hall. For the Albert
Hall, much more than any other building, certainly much
more than the Elizabethan theatre, can really be called O. I
cannot at the moment think of any other phrase except O
that one could use about the Albert Hall.

It is but justice to those who have asked me to write this
article to say that they gave me the opportunity of going to
the Ball if I liked. There was only one Shakespearean character in which I could, by any physical possibility, have
gone; and that, unfortunately, is the finest of all Shakespeare's
characters. I did not feel equal to imitating Falstaff for a
whole evening. For the grand grotesques of human literature are surrounded by a sanctity peculiar to themselves.
Modern monarchists and belated defenders of divine right
have often quoted Shakespeare's phrase that there is a
divinity that doth hedge a King. Not so often, perhaps, have
they pointed out that he puts it into the mouth of a particularly cowardly and indefensible usurper. But, however this
may be, the real upshot and effect of Shakespeare's work is
not the divinity that hedges a king, but the divinity that
hedges a clown. No decent man would dare to dress up as
Falstaff, without long preparation and prayer. It is the great
comic figures that have become sacred. A man can easily
make game of Brutus or Boadicea, or Milton, or Mr.
Gladstone. But no one can make game of Sam Weller. No

one can get a rise out of Bottom the Weaver. No one can make light of Falstaff: he has too much weight. Therefore, I decided that I had not enough moral courage to travesty Falstaff. I had half a notion of coming to the Ball as Ariel; but I resisted the temptation.

Thus I can write fairly about the theory of this pageant without being confused and bewildered by the facts. For, indeed, the theory itself is not without interest, especially to those who read Shakespeare—a much smaller class than might be supposed. For the dressing and decorating and dancing of Shakespeare have become much more important than the mere reading of him. There are two schools of aesthetics and archeology in this matter, both of which were (I am quite sure) very prominent on this occasion. They both, in their several ways, bear witness to the real culture, to aesthetic appetites and the very sincere antiquarian enthusiasm of our time. They are both, with varying degrees of success and permanence, supported by the really active and influential artiste of modern England. And they both, in my own very mild opinion, suffer from the same fault—the fault of taking the whole question too seriously. There was more of the clown, more of the buffoon, in Shakespeare than either of these artistic theories will admit. The first school, of course, is that well and even brilliantly supported by Sir Herbert Tree; and the second is that equally well maintained by the modern Shakespeare societies and the simplifiers of the drama. The former from its own point of view claims to give the scene as Shakespeare imagined it. The second (also from its own point of view) professes only to give the scene as Shakespeare expected to see it. The first seeks to have scenery in which the jocund day does actually manage (or make an attempt) to stand tip-toe on the misty mountain tops. The second suggests that it would be vastly better to have a quiet back-cloth that would really permit those miraculous lines to be listened to as the real evening's entertainment. This dispute is intelligible and interesting, but when we pass from landscape which endures to costume which alters, a bigger sort of bother presents itself. The first school is necessarily at once engulfed in the British Museum. It tries to find out what was the contemporary pattern of the dagger which Macbeth saw when it wasn't there. It seeks to be certain what exact cut of beard Hamlet thought that an imaginary enemy might hypothetically tweak. It not only paints Othello black all over because he was a Moor, but it would be quite as ready to point Cymbeline blue all over because he was an Ancient Briton. Henry V must walk about in correct contemporary armour, even if it was the sort of armour that would have prevented him from walking about. This sort of exactitude is indeed generally rebuked at last. It dies, as pedantry dies, on the real appearance of learning. A saner view of both the Dark Ages and the Middle Ages makes such knowledge more inappropriate than ignorance. The Ancient Briton was not so blue as he is painted. But obstacles quite equally insurmountable bar the path of those reviving the simple Elizabethan stage. If it is hard to guess what Macbeth really looked like, it is harder still to discover (at this time of day) what Shakespeare might have thought he looked like. If it is hard to guess how gorgeous Fairyland was in the poet's mind, it is harder still to guess exactly how meager it was at the Globe Theatre. Both schemes, then, are essentially antiquarian. The one tries to reproduce the period of King John; the other tries to reproduce the period of Queen Elizabeth. Both are impossible to reproduce; and Shakespeare cared not a button for either of them.

Here, surely, lies the real value of a Shakespeare fancy dress ball. It strikes that keynote of splendid incongruity, of merry and many-coloured mixtures, which was certainly in Shakespeare's mind, whatever else was. It must have been quaint and entertaining at this particular carnival to see Anne Page in a Tudor ruff talking to King John in chain armour, or Brutus in a toga chatting with Osric in trunk-hose. But it would not be more incongruous in any instance than the groups that the stage managers have to fling in fact on the Shakespearean stage. I have seen Fortinbras, as a primeval Viking with a winged helmet and a whirling battle-axe, rush on the stage just after the death of an elegant Renaissance gentleman in black sixteenth century clothes, who had obviously died some seven centuries afterwards. I have seen pictorial versions of *Cymbeline* in which some of the Ancient Britons wore costumes so ancient that they are quite forgotten, and others costumes so modern that they do not (I hope) yet exist. But this is not an affront to Shakespeare's ghost, but rather a double portion of his spirit. He had that higher frivolity which feels that as the body is less than soul, so the body is more than raiment. All his plays are one huge Fancy Dress Ball. If there was one thing he loved it was the picturesquely incompatible. And whatever contrasts or collisions occurred in all that million-coloured kaleidoscope of humanity at the Albert Hall, where cardinals must have talked with "salvage man," and senators argued with elves, it is doubtful whether the deep note of a romantic diversity was anywhere more strongly struck than it is in those quiet sylvan scenes where the stiff and gaudy motley of Touchstone is relieved against shaggy woods and shepherds, or the bristly head of Bottom rises among fairies against the moon.

(*Souvenir Program of the Shakespeare Memorial National Theatre Ball*. Royal Albert Hall. June 20, 1911)

VI.
SHAWKSPEAR

The Great Shawkspear Mystery

I have constantly in these columns defended Mr. Bernard Shaw from the entirely frivolous charge of frivolity; I shall not, therefore, be in any danger of finding my complaint classed with the commonplace attacks upon him which represent him as a mountebank or a perverse jester if I animadvert upon his attitude on the subject of Shakespeare—an attitude which he has always professed with a considerable consistence and regularity, but of which he gave recently a rather special example in a lecture. Indeed, the two points of view do not contradict, but rather corroborate, each other. Mr. Shaw does not highly admire or profoundly enjoy Shakespeare, and this is not because Mr. Shaw is frivolous, but, on the contrary, because Mr. Shaw is serious. The fault of Mr. Shaw as a philosopher or a critic of life (for every philosopher or critic of life may be allowed to have a fault) is altogether on the side of being too grave, too stern, too fanatical, too unbending and austere. Mr. Bernard Shaw is too serious to enjoy Shakespeare. Mr. Bernard Shaw is too serious properly to enjoy life. Both these things are illogical where he is logical, chaotic where he is orderly, mystical where he is clear. In all the great Elizabethan writers there is present a certain thing which Mr. Shaw, with all his astonishing abilities, does not really understand—exuberance, an outrageous excess of words, a violent physical pleasure in mere vocabulary, an animal spirit in intellectual things. The moderns, to do them justice, are not realists. They are not under any influence from the babyish

249

notion that art should imitate life. They realise pretty clearly
that it is the business of art to exaggerate life. But they are
used to seeing life (in the modern books) exaggerated in the
direction of pain or sensibility or differentiation or mystery or
delicacy or despair or candour or cruelty; they are well used
to seeing life exaggerated in all these directions. But they are
not used to seeing life exaggerated in the direction of life.
That is why the moderns do not like Dickens. That is why Mr.
Bernard Shaw does not like Shakespeare.

But the case of Shakespeare, and of all the men who
belong to the age and spirit of Shakespeare, is, I admit, a
much harder one, especially for the fastidious modern mind,
than any case like the case of Dickens. Dickens was always to
some extent successful, even at his worst, along a line of neat
and obvious facetiousness; but the great men of the
Renaissance were sometimes so exuberant and exultant in
their mere joy of existence that their mirth is not even obvious, and not even facetious. These giants are shaken with a
mysterious laughter. They seem torn by the agony of jokes as
incommunicable as the wisdom of the gods. Dickens was
sometimes vulgar; he was sometimes quite fatuous and inept;
but amusing he almost always was. But Shakespeare was
sometimes too much amused even to be amusing. He is writing so much to please himself that he not only does not succeed in pleasing us, but does not even in any sense try to do
so. Sometimes he seems, like Rabelais, and indeed like all
the humanistic comedians of the Renaissance, to be, as it
were, raging at his audience in a kind of friendly fury. Now
all this kind of staggering laughter and terrible plenitude of
life happens to be outside Mr. Bernard Shaw's purview altogether. Mr. Bernard Shaw, as I have said before, is perfectly
grave and reasonable about this matter; he is too grave; he is
too reasonable. It is not Mr. Bernard Shaw who is making

game of Shakespeare at all. On the contrary, it is Shakespeare who is making game of Mr. Bernard Shaw, pelting him with preposterous words, deluging him with a kind of divine dribble, hurling at him huge jokes so simple and so stupid that only the giants can understand them.

I know quite well that this is foolishness in the eyes of Mr. Shaw. I know quite well that he would say that this is a dribble which is by no means divine. But that is merely because what I say is true, that he has left out of him for some reason or other this almost animal joy of self-expression which is the main basis of all song. A great many of the most able and most indispensable of geniuses of the world have an advantage which arises in this way from defect. Many very great men are most great because of some qualities that they have not got. If you suddenly took St. Paul's Cathedral off the top of Ludgate-hill we should all see the rest of Ludgate-hill with a splendid and startling clearness, as if it had been made that moment, as if we had never seen it before. In the same way, if we take out of the mind of a man an essential human quality, it may often happen that what we leave behind is sometimes something like inspiration. A prophet may sometimes be an ordinary man minus an ordinary quality. Thus, Schopenhauer saw the vast cosmic unity of the will to live outside him for the simple reason that he had not got it inside him. Thus, Carlyle made it possible for us not to be contented with mere smug utilitarianism and mechanical politics, simply because he happened to be lacking in that vital and essential human quality which enables a man to be contented with anything. Thus, Maeterlinck has been enabled to express the primal fear which lies behind all living merely because he has never gained the masculine firmness, and so never lost the boyish. Thus, again, Tolstoy has been enabled to see all the blows which fall on mankind by having himself an insane notion that it is wicked to strike a blow. Thus, lastly, Mr. Shaw has been enabled to give a living and startling photograph of the prose of our existence through the simple fact that, with all his talents, he does not possess an ear for its poetry. He has one half of human sanity to perfection; he has plenty of commonsense. But he has not the other half of sanity at all: he has no common nonsense.

(*Daily News*, April 15, 1905)

——— ❖ ———

Sorry, I'm Shaw

I think, quite seriously, that it was like Mr. Shaw's generosity to say, even in the heat of debate, that I was as good as the Elizabethans. But once having uttered that magnanimous but insane opinion, I think it is rather hard that I should be flung down from the dizzy height for the reason given. I think it hard that he should discover that I am not as good as the Elizabethans merely because I did not go to his lecture. After all, the Elizabethans did not go to his lecture. And I assure him most earnestly that the obstacle which prevented me from having the pleasure I had promised myself was quite as insurmountable as any slight difficulty which the Elizabethans could advance as an excuse.

It is quite true that I was absent, owing to indisposition. It is equally true that Mr. Shaw and I were both absent, owing to inclination, from the South African War. But I do not think that this prevented us giving our opinions on the subject or from conducting, if I remember right, an animated correspondence on it in these columns. If Mr. Shaw really means that nobody has any right to speak of a lecture unless he has physically heard the lecture and physically seen the lecturer, then the results are rather serious. But I think that there is a great deal in Mr. Shaw's contention in this matter. I fancy the world is really governed neither by acts nor words; it is governed by tones of voice. We shall never have real justice in a law court until the witness is obliged not merely to repeat the words, but to imitate the special and indefinable squeak or grunt with which the words were uttered. I can imagine that a man might say, for instance, "I'll be the death of Uncle Herbert yet," and the thing not sound like a threat of murder or anything at all resembling it. And in the same way I can quite imagine that when Mr. Shaw, in his admirable Irish voice, said that *As You Like It* was romantic nonsense, the remark did not seem to be the unromantic nonsense that it looks in print.

But if Mr. Shaw is really going to adopt this very defensible principle that everything ought to be tested by the personal experience of an auditor, then he must give up altogether the greater part of his present politics. He must give up all this talk about world states and large combinations. World states cannot come to his lectures. Large combinations cannot hear his admirable Irish voice. World combinations and world empires will only hear of Mr. Shaw and his message through journalism. That is how I heard of Mr. Shaw's lecture; and apparently Mr. Shaw distrusts that medium, and says that it has misrepresented him. If this is so, he will, in any conceivable world state, be misrepresented all over the world. The only state which is to some extent governed by the tones of voice (that is, by reality) is the small state, the small nationality. I salute a convert to the small nationality. They are coming in fast.

But, as a matter of fact, Mr. Shaw has fallen into a preliminary mistake. I was not criticising his lecture, and I never professed to do so. I knew long before he ever delivered it that he had expressed a view of Shakespeare which placed that poet lower in the scheme of criticism than he is usually placed. I suggested an explanation of this fact. I suggested that the presence among most people of a greater admiration of Shakespeare and the presence in Mr. Shaw of a less admiration of him was due to a certain psychological trait in Mr. Shaw which makes him unresponsive to a tone which is very specially a tone of Shakespeare. I did not, as a matter of fact, hear Mr. Shaw's lecture, and I did not, as a matter of fact, criticise it. But now that I have heard the correct version of it from Mr. Shaw himself, I will proceed to criticise it with considerable joy.

Mr. Shaw numbers his theses about Shakespeare. With the first four of them, which are purely biographical, I have no quarrel. With the fifth, which is partly critical, the quarrel begins.

5. Mr. Shaw maintains that Shakespeare wrote *As You Like It* because he found that romantic nonsense paid, and gave it its title as an expression of contempt for the public taste. I say Shakespeare wrote romantic plays because Shakespeare was romantic; and I say that romantic plays paid because Man is romantic. In these undemocratic days we cannot grasp the possibility of the great man enjoying the same things as the ordinary man. Shakespeare enjoyed the same romance as the ordinary man, just as he enjoyed the same beer. And if Mr. Shaw really wished to compare himself with Shakespeare (which I think he never did) the comparison is really very simple. Mr. Shaw may be quite as extraordinary a man as Shakespeare; but he is only an extraordinary man. Shake-

speare, like all the heroes, was an extraordinary man and an ordinary man too.

As for the title *As You Like It*, Mr. Shaw is reading an ingenious priggishness into what is really one of a welter of wild and careless Elizabethan titles. The point is not whether, in the Elizabethan spirit, *As You Like It* meant exactly the same as *What You Will*. The point is whether in the Elizabethan spirit either of them meant anything, except a sort of hilarious bosh. Anyone who knows the Elizabethan drama knows that it is strewn with such reckless titles, and a man who tried to find a critical meaning in each of them would end in an asylum. To take the first that comes, I think there is a play called "If it be not good the devil is in it." Perhaps Mr. Shaw thinks that is a grave expression of the author's satisfaction with his work. Mr. Shaw is so anti-Elizabethan that he makes the Elizabethans sensible even where they meant to be silly.

6. I feel the limits of my column closing in upon me; some of Mr. Shaw's errors I shall have to defer to next week. But error No. 6 is a peculiarly fascinating one, and really is the master-error of the whole Shavian criticism. Mr. Shaw says that in manner nothing could be done better than *As You Like It*, but in matter he himself would never do anything so bad. When I read this, I saw suddenly how simple is the whole mistake. I can only draw Mr. Shaw's attention to the fact that *As You Like It* is poetry. What can anybody mean by talking of the matter or manner of a poem? I will give Mr. Shaw three lines out of *As You Like It* from the exquisite and irrational song of Hymen at the end:

> Then is there mirth in Heaven
> When earthly things made even
>   Atone together.

Limit the matter to the single incomparable line, "When earthly things made even." And I defy Mr. Shaw to say which is matter and which is manner. The matter is quite as artistic as the manner, and the manner is quite as solid and spiritual as the matter. The meaning is essential to the words; the words would not be so good if they happened to mean, "There are six tom-cats in the back garden." But the words are quite equally essential to the meaning. If the words, "When earthly things made even" were presented to us in the form of, "When terrestrial affairs are reduced to an equilibrium," the meaning would not merely have been spoilt, the meaning would have entirely disappeared. This identity between the matter and the manner is simply the definition of poetry. The aim of good prose words is to mean what they say. The aim of good poetical words is to mean what they do not say. When Shakespeare says (in one of the long philosophical speeches which Mr. Shaw does not quote because they do not happen to be pessimistic),

> For valour is not Love a Hercules,
> Still climbing trees in the Hesperides—

it is difficult, or rather impossible, to use any other language to express what he conveys. You cannot convey a sense of sunrise and an ancient hope and the colours of the ends of the earth. But if Mr. Shaw thinks that the lines mean, "Is not the sexual instinct like Hercules in the matter of velour, and is it not like him in the garden of the Hesperides and climbing a tree?" I can assure him most sincerely of his mistake.

(*Daily News*, April 22, 1905)

On The Alleged Pessimism of Shakespeare

It is certainly quite curious to notice how old superstitions cling to the corners of the world. In dark and outlying places there are still even in this age of an imagined enlightenment the weirdest beliefs.

Let me take an example. I saw the other day in a newspaper, I am not sure that it was not this newspaper, the report of the examination of some Irish peasant who told a magistrate that he had had on a particular night seen what looked like fires and figures dancing, and that he believed it to be the fairies. Will it be credited that the magistrate broke out into expressions of the most astonishing anger, telling the man that the thing was nonsense, that he did not believe the tale, and implying, though not verbally stating, that he thought it impossible? Here was a man of the twentieth century, in the conventional sense of the term at least, an educated man, a man living I admit in an out-of-the-way district, but still a man who must have mixed to some extent with the men of the modern world, and he actually clings to the queer old belief that fairies cannot possibly exist. Nor do I think that his attitude was a mere affectation of the reactionary or obscurantist spirit; a dandified and half-ironical Toryism such as is too common among the more frivolous of our young men today. I really believe that it was a case of the genuine traditional survival of the old materialistic legend. I really believe that he really believed that a belief in fairies was irrational. Of course he, like anybody else, would be stumped and silenced finally if he were asked to give any sort of argument or logical reason why there should not be spirits in the universe other than man. But then this asking for an argument or a logical reason is by its nature a somewhat insolent and unamiable method for us to pursue when we are dealing with any of these dark, but delicate prejudices of simple folk.

For my part, I think the Irish peasant was to blame for thus in an almost unfeeling manner flaunting his much deeper psychological knowledge and his much wider psychological experience in the face of a man who may have been none the less honourable and wise because he happened to have a fad of not believing in the fairies. There will not be many of that good old company left soon, if spiritual science goes on as it is going at present. And I think we might respect their genial autumn. But the explanation of the peasant, whether justifiable or not in the particular circumstances in which he was placed, served indirectly one excellent purpose. It reminded me of the subject of fairies. And in fairies and the natural history of fairies is to be found the true view of the subject. I had no space to discuss last week the subject which Mr. Shaw raised at the end of his string of pregnant paragraphs—I mean the subject of the optimism or pessimism of Shakespeare.

With Mr. Shaw's contention that Shakespeare was not primarily a very positive teacher, or even a man with a very definite doctrinal view of life, I am somewhat disposed to agree. To live in the thick of the Renaissance and the Reformation was to live in the thick of a scepticism and philosophical confusion as great, if not greater, than our own. He had a great deal of traditional and inherent religious emotion, and what there was of it was mainly Catholic. He talked a great deal of rather futile rhetorical scepticism, and all that was purely Renaissance. With some such reservations I should agree with Mr. Shaw if he said that Shakespeare had no philosophical creed. But I disagree with him entirely when he attempts to represent that Shakespeare had the wrong philosophical creed. I deny altogether that Shakespeare was a pessimist; the worst that you can say of him is that he was a poet.

The instance chosen by Mr. Shaw to prove the pessimism of Shakespeare, the "out brief candle" soliloquy, seems a curious instance to select. Surely it cannot have escaped Mr. Shaw that this speech has a special and definite dramatic value, a dramatic value so special and definite that it absolves one from all necessity to find in it any philosophical meaning at all. It is a speech by Macbeth just before his defeat and destruction; that is to say, it is a speech made by a wicked and wasted human soul confronted by his own colossal failure. If Shakespeare had been as much of an optimist as Walt Whitman, and had wished to make that play artistic, he would have made that speech pessimistic. The speech is not a metaphysical statement at all; it is an emotional exclamation. Mr. Shaw has no right at all to call Shakespeare a pessimist for having written the words "out, out, brief candle"; he might as well call Shakespeare a champion of the ideal of celibacy for having written the words, "Get thee to the nunnery." He might as well call Shakespeare a philosophical apologist for the duel for having written the words, "Kill Claudio." It is not Shakespeare's fault that, having to write pessimism for the purpose of a theatrical point, he happened to write much better pessimism than the people who are silly enough to be pessimists.

I could find many speeches in Shakespeare, philosophical or semi-philosophical, criticisms of life or descriptions of humanity, which have the happier note, and could be set over against the soliloquy of Macbeth—Biron's speech on love in *Love's Labour's Lost*, several speeches of Portia, one of Orlando, and so on. But I do not think that I should attach much importance to them, any more than I attach much importance to the speeches called pessimistic. I do not think that Shakespeare meant any of these speeches as statements of his complete convictions. I am not sure whether in this exact sense he had any complete convictions. But another thing he had which is worth a word in conclusion. He had an atmosphere or spirit—an atmosphere not confined to him but common in some degree to the whole of the England before the Puritans. And about this atmosphere or spirit there is one particular thing to be remarked. It can be remarked best by simply reading such a play as *A Midsummer Night's Dream*. The quality I mean may be called the comic supernatural. The greater part of that world, like the more thinking part of our modern world, believed in a general way in the existence of things deeper and higher than man himself, in energies beyond his energy, in destinies beyond his ken. In short, they believed in gods, in devils; and they also believed in fairies. We have mysticism in the modern world, but all our mysticism is sad mysticism; at the best it is serious mysticism; it is never a farcical mysticism. We believe in devils most firmly of the three; that can easily be seen in our sombre modern fiction. We believe in gods to some extent—in moderation. But it is our tendency, or has been until lately our tendency, not to believe in fairies with a proper firmness. We never think of any energies in the universe being actually merrier than we; though it comes quite easy to us to think of energies which are grimmer. In this larger and looser sense, then, Shakespeare, or rather Shakespeare's England, was the very reverse of pessimistic. It thought of the universe itself as being capable of a sort of lightness. It thought sometimes of the world itself as going round like a boy's humming-top. Now, if we dream of the ultimate mysteries the effect is generally at least a sombre one. Our Midsummer Night's Dream is uncommonly like a nightmare.

(*Daily News*, April 29, 1905)

———— ❖ ————

The Realities of Romantic Drama

Shaw and all the other Ibsenites were fond of insisting that a defect in the romantic drama was its tendency to end with wedding-bells. Against this they set the modern drama of middle-age, the drama which described marriage itself instead of its poetic preliminaries. Now if Bernard Shaw had been more patient with popular tradition, more prone to think that there might be some sense in its survival, he might have seen this particular problem much more clearly. The old playwrights have left us plenty of plays of marriage and middle-age. *Othello* is as much about what follows the wedding-bells as *The Doll's House*. *Macbeth* is about a middle-aged couple as much as *Little Eyolf*. But if we ask ourselves what is the real difference, we shall, I think, find that it can fairly be stated thus. The old tragedies of marriage, though not love stories, are like love stories in this, that they work up to some act or stroke which is irrevocable as marriage is irrevocable; to the fact of death or of adultery.

("The Philosopher," *George Bernard Shaw*)

———— ❖ ————

The Poet and the Puritan

It may often be remarked that mathematicians love and understand music more than they love or understand poetry. Bernard Shaw is in much the same condition; indeed, in attempting to do justice to Shakespeare's poetry, he always calls it "word music." It is not difficult to explain this special attachment of the mere logician to music. The

logician, like every other man on earth, must have sentiment
and romance in his existence; in every man's life, indeed,
which can be called a life at all, sentiment is the most solid
thing. But if the extreme logician turns for his emotions to
poetry, he is exasperated and bewildered by discovering that
the words of his own trade are used in an entirely different
meaning. He conceives that he understands the word "visible," and then finds Milton applying it to darkness, in which
nothing is visible. He supposes that he understands the
word "hide," and then finds Shelley talking of a poet hidden
in the light. He has reason to believe that he understands
the common word "hung"; and then William Shakespeare,
Esquire, of Stratford-on-Avon, gravely assures him that the
tops of the tall sea waves were hung with deafening clamours
on the slippery clouds. That is why the common arithmeti-
cian prefers music to poetry. Words are his scientific instruments. It irritates him that they should be anyone else's
musical instruments. He is willing to see men juggling, but
not men juggling with his own private tools and possessions—his terms. It is then that he turns with an utter relief
to music. Here is all the same fascination and inspiration, all
the same purity and plunging force as in poetry; but not
requiring any verbal confession that light conceals things or
that darkness can be seen in the dark. Music is mere beauty;
it is beauty in the abstract, beauty in solution. It is a shapeless and liquid element of beauty, in which a man may really
float, not indeed affirming the truth, but not denying it.
Bernard Shaw, as I have already said, is infinitely far above
all such mere mathematicians and pedantic reasoners; still
his feeling is partly the same. He adores music because it
cannot deal with romantic terms either in their right or their
wrong sense. Music can be romantic without reminding him
of Shakespeare and Walter Scott, with whom he has had

personal quarrels. Music can be Catholic without reminding
him verbally of the Catholic Church, which he has never
seen, and is sure he does not like. . . .

Shaw's attack on Shakespeare, though exaggerated for
the fun of the thing, was not by any means the mere folly or
firework paradox that has been supposed. He meant what
he said; what was called his levity was merely the laughter
of a man who enjoyed saying what he meant—an occupation which is indeed one of the greatest larks in life.
Moreover, it can honestly be said that Shaw did good by
shaking the mere idolatry of Him of Avon. That idolatry was
bad for England; it buttressed our perilous self-compla-
cency by making us think that we alone had, not merely a
great poet, but the one poet above criticism. It was bad for
literature; it made a minute model out of work that was
really a hasty and faulty masterpiece. And it was bad for
religion and morals that there should be so huge a terrestrial
idol, that we should put such utter and unreasoning trust in
any child of man. It is true that it was largely through Shaw's
own defects that he beheld the defects of Shakespeare. But
it needed some one equally prosaic to resist what was perilous in the charm of such poetry; it may not be altogether a
mistake to send a deaf man to destroy the rock of the sirens.

This attitude of Shaw illustrates of course all three of the
divisions or aspects to which the reader's attention has been
drawn. It was partly the attitude of the Irishman objecting to
the Englishman turning his mere artistic taste into a religion;
especially when it was a taste merely taught him by his aunts
and uncles. In Shaw's opinion (one might say) the English
do not really enjoy Shakespeare or even admire Shakespeare;
one can only say, in the strong colloquialism, that they swear
by Shakespeare. He is a mere god; a thing to be invoked.
And Shaw's whole business was to set up the things which

were to be sworn by as things to be sworn at. It was partly again the revolutionist in pursuit of pure novelty, hating primarily the oppression of the past, almost hating history itself. For Bernard Shaw the prophets were to be stoned after, and not before, men had built their sepulchres. There was a Yankee smartness in the man which was irritated at the idea of being dominated by a person dead for three hundred years; like Mark Twain, he wanted a fresher corpse.

These two motives there were, but they were small compared with the other. It was the third part of him, the Puritan, that was really at war with Shakespeare. He denounced that playwright almost exactly as any contemporary Puritan coming out of a conventicle in a steeple-crowned hat and stiff bands might have denounced the playwright coming out of the stage door of the old Globe Theatre.

This is not a mere fancy; it is philosophically true. A legend has run round the newspapers that Bernard Shaw offered himself as a better writer than Shakespeare. This is false and quite unjust; Bernard Shaw never said anything of the kind. The writer whom he did say was better than Shakespeare was not himself, but Bunyan. And he justified it by attributing to Bunyan a virile acceptance of life as a high and harsh adventure, while in Shakespeare he saw nothing but profligate pessimism, the *vanitas vanitatum* ["vanity of vanities" from Ecclesiastes 1:2] of a disappointed voluptuary. According to this view Shakespeare was always saying, "Out, out, brief candle," because his was only a ball-room candle; while Bunyan was seeking to light such a candle as by God's grace should never be put out. . . .

His misunderstanding of Shakespeare arose largely from the fact that he is a Puritan, while Shakespeare was spiritually a Catholic. The former is always screwing himself up to see truth; the latter is often content that truth is there. The Puritan is only strong enough to stiffen; the Catholic is strong enough to relax. Shaw, I think has entirely misunderstood the pessimistic passages of Shakespeare. They are flying moods which a man with a fixed faith can afford to entertain. That all is vanity, that life is dust and love is ashes, these are frivolities, these are jokes that a Catholic can afford to utter. He knows well enough that there is a life that is not dust and a love that is not ashes. But just as he may let himself go more than the Puritan in the matter of enjoyment, so he may let himself go more than the Puritan in the matter of melancholy. The sad exuberances of Hamlet are merely like the glad exuberances of Falstaff. This is not conjecture; it is the text of Shakespeare. In the very act of uttering his pessimism, Hamlet admits that it is a mood and not the truth. Heaven is a heavenly thing, only to him it seems a foul congregation of vapours. Man is the paragon of animals, only to him he seems a quintessence of dust. Hamlet is quite the reverse of a sceptic. He is a man whose strong intellect believes much more than his weak temperament can make vivid to him. But this power of knowing a thing without feeling it, this power of believing a thing without experiencing it, this is an old Catholic complexity, and the Puritan has never understood it. Shakespeare confesses his moods (mostly by the mouths of villains and failures), but he never sets up his moods against his mind. His cry of *vanitas vanitatum* is itself only a harmless vanity. Readers may not agree with my calling him Catholic with a big C; but they will hardly complain of my calling him catholic with a small one. And that is here the principal point. Shakespeare was not in any sense a pessimist; he was, if anything, an optimist so universal as to be able to enjoy even pessimism. And this is exactly where he differs from the Puritan. The true

Puritan is not squeamish: the true Puritan is free to say "Damn it!" But the Catholic Elizabethan was free (on passing provocation) to say "Damn it all!"

("The Critic," *George Bernard Shaw*)

———— ❖ ————

Shakespeare And Shaw

Many critics of my own modest writings, as I have had occasion to note elsewhere, have charged me with an excessive love of alliteration. To these it would be apparent that the subject of Shakespeare and Shaw has been created out of the void to satisfy this appetite; whichever of the two surnames I am supposed to have invented or assimilated to the other. Of course there is always the possibility of avoiding it by saying that the works of Shakespeare were written by Bacon; or (what seems to me rather more probable) the works of Shaw written by Sidney Webb. But the truth is, of course, that the two names have been brought together long ago by the deliberate and provocative policy of the bearer of one of them. Shaw has frequently compared himself with Shakespeare; Shakespeare was so unfortunate as to have few opportunities of comparing himself with Shaw. This was perhaps what some of the Shavians have meant by saying that Shakespeare wrote under the disadvantages of his age. This may be, in some respects, true; but it is less universally recognised that Shakespeare wrote under all the advantages of his age and Shaw under all the almost crushing disadvantages of his.

The real truth about this is as much obscured by the conventional or authoritarian appreciation of Shakespeare as by any pert or juvenile depreciation of Shakespeare; let alone depreciation of Shaw. The view of those who professed to be most disgusted at the Shavian impertinence of twenty years ago, the view of those who constituted themselves the guardians of the sacred Swan of Avon against the impudent little boy to whom all swans were geese—this view was in fact equally mistaken about the older and the younger dramatists, about the poet and about the critic. The swan was none the less a swan because, having sung its swan-song and died, it was worshipped largely by geese. But the point is that the whole conception in both cases was wrong. The conservatives regarded Shakespeare as a sort of earnest and elevating Modern Thinker, with a Noble Brow; a hero according to Carlyle and talking in the grand style as laid down by Matthew Arnold. And that was all wrong. The same conservatives regarded Bernard Shaw as a flippant and frivolous mocker of all holy things, refusing to kiss the Pope's toe and preferring to pull the poet's leg. And that was all wrong. To sum it up in two pretty adequate parallels; they made the appalling mistake of supposing that Shakespeare was like Goethe and of supposing that Shaw was like Mephistopheles. But Shakespeare was not a German, in spite of the unblessed conclusion of German scholarship in the matter; he was the very last man in the world to be cut out for a German hero or a German god. And Shaw is not a devil; far less an imp. The truth is that of the two, it is Shakespeare who is frivolous, or who is at least capable of being irresponsible and gay. It is Shaw, in spite of his real humour, who is much more cut out to be a Goethe, an earnest sage and seer, worshipped by German audiences.

The reason of the greater richness and depth of Shakespeare's gaiety, when he is gay, is in the fact that he came at the end of an epoch of civilization and inherited, however indirectly, all the best of a very ancient culture. The reason for the greater earnestness, or what might even be called the sharper morality, in Shaw and some modern moralists, is that they came after a sort of barbaric interruption that had cut off the countries of the north from Classicism and from Humanism. Goethe was serious, because he had to struggle to recover the lost civilization for the Germans. He had to stretch himself in order to balance and stagger before he could stand upright. But Shakespeare, though he had small Latin and less Greek, had much more in him of the Greek spirit and the Latin order than most of the moderns have ever had; because he received it through a tradition and an atmosphere that had been clear and uninterrupted for some time. For instance, all that light Renaissance pessimism is perfectly incomprehensible to our heavy realistic pessimists. Schopenhauer or Hardy would never be able to understand how cheerfully an Elizabethan said that all roses must fade or that life is brief as a butterfly. Modern sceptics could never understand the subtlety and spiritual complexity with which a Humanist of that age will be talking one moment about Adonis or Apollo, as if they really existed, and the next moment be acknowledging, like Michael Angelo in his last sonnets, that nothing truly exists except Christ upon the Cross. The modern free-thinkers are more simple and in a sense more serious than this. It is they who say that life is real, life is earnest; though curiously enough it is now generally they who go on to say that the grave is certainly its goal.

The Renaissance came late to England; and Shakespeare came late even in the English Renaissance. Only the brilliant accident of a still more belated inheritor, John Milton, makes Shakespeare seem to us to stand somewhere in the middle. But the Humanism, the Hellenism and the pagan

mythology mixed with Catholic theology, upon which he
fed, had been flowing together from their Italian fountains
since the fifteenth century; and long before those great
voices of antiquity, the voice of Virgil in poetry and of
Aristotle in philosophy, had spoken directly to the whole
Christendom of the Middle Ages. Shakespeare was therefore familiar with a mixture of all sorts of moods, memories
and fancies, and was not sharply hostile to any of them, save
perhaps a little to the Puritans. He could consider a
Republican hero of Plutarch, a mediaeval king, shining with
the sacred chrism as with a nimbus, a pagan misanthrope
cursing the world, a Franciscan friar cheerfully and charita-
bly reuniting lovers, a god of the Greek oracles, a goblin of
the English country lanes, a fool who was happy or a wise
man who was foolish—all without setting one against the
other, or thinking there was any particular conflict in the
traditions; or asking himself whether he was Classic or
Romantic or Mediaevalist or Modernist or black or white or
buff or blue. Culture was not one strained agony or controversy. That is what I mean by a man inheriting a whole civilization and having the immense advantage of being born
three hundred years ago.

By the time that Bernard Shaw was born, the national and
religious divisions of Europe had been dug so deep, and had
so long sustained what was at once a vigilant rivalry and a
fight in the dark, that this sort of varied and varying balance
had become almost impossible. European culture was no
longer a many-coloured and stratified thing; it had been split
into great fragments by earthquakes. Whatever virtues it
might possess, and in a man like Bernard Shaw it does possess some of the most vital of all public virtues, it had produced that curious sort of concentration which did in fact
bring forth, first the Shakespearian idolatry by the end of the

eighteenth century, and then the Shavian iconoclasm by the end of the nineteenth. Both were not only serious, but entirely serious; in other words, neither was really Shakespearian. Hence arises the paradox upon which I would remark here; that the relations between the idol and the iconoclast are really the very opposite to those which seemed obvious to the idolaters in the days of my youth. It is rather Mr. Bernard Shaw who really has the gravity of the god, or at least of the prophet or oracle of the god; seeing visions of the future and speaking words of the fate of nations. And it is really Shakespeare who passes by in the woods with the elusive laughter of a Faun, and a mystery that has something of mockery.

(*Shakespeare Review*, May 1928)

VII.
WAS SHAKESPEARE CATHOLIC?

Shakespeare Was a Christian

The conflict between the Christian tradition and the Renaissance excitement, in all the people of that period, was very deep and subtle; in none more deep and subtle than in Shakespeare. But I take it as absolutely certain that, however complex and violent was the struggle, their Christianity was perfectly sincere. Shakespeare wallowed in paganism, but there are passages in Shakespeare which I defy any independent person to read without realizing that he was what we call a Christian, that he had that particular humility of mind which was the chemical change in mankind produced by Christianity.

("Mary Queen Of Scots," *Revaluations*)

Shakespeare and Milton

It is not unnatural that there should be a certain vagueness about the personal celebration of Shakespeare in his own personal place of residence. In the very highest artist there is always a disdain of art. Shakespeare left his manuscripts loose all over the place as if they were old envelopes; and it may seem curious, and even exasperating, that the learned world should think so much of some pieces of paper of which their author thought so little. But even in this queer and casual aloofness Shakespeare is very satisfactorily

typical of the English nation. It has been said that England
created an empire in a fit of absence of mind; it is quite
certain that William Shakespeare created a drama in a fit of
absence of mind. All that is best in England is expressed in
the fact that Shakespeare has no biography; which means
that he had a very jolly life. All that is good in England is
always all the better because it comes unexpectedly,
because it comes unreasonably, as an English town appears
suddenly at a twist of an English road. . . . The things that
come to us out of our national polity we have to accept as
splendid accidents. Even Shakespeare was a splendid accident; and little as we know of his life, he seems always to
have behaved like one.

Nearly all Englishmen are either Shakespearians or
Miltonians. I do not mean that they admire one more than
the other; because everyone in his senses must admire both
of them infinitely. I mean that each represents something in
the make-up of England; and that the two things are so far
antagonistic that it is really impossible not to be secretly on
one side or the other. The difference, in so far as it concerns
the two men, can be expressed in all sorts of ways; but every
way taken by itself is inadequate. Shakespeare represents
the Catholic, Milton the Protestant. . . . Shakespeare never
went to an English University; Milton did. Milton regarded
the trick of rhyming with contempt; Shakespeare used it
even in the most inappropriate moments. Milton had no
humour; Shakespeare had very much too much: he never
lets anything else entirely run away with him, but he lets his
laughter run away with him. Milton was probably unkind to
his wife; Shakespeare's wife was probably unkind to him.
Milton started from the very first with a clear idea of making
poetry. Shakespeare started with a very vague idea of somehow making money. Whenever Milton speaks of religion, it

is Milton's religion: the religion that Milton has made. Whenever Shakespeare speaks of religion (which is only seldom), it is of a religion that has made him. Lastly, Milton was mostly blind, and took great care of his manuscripts; while Shakespeare was often blind drunk and took no care of his.

If from the above the reader cannot form a mental picture of the two men, I am sorry for him. If, however, these strictly historical facts are inadequate, I can conceive of hypothetical facts that might explain the matter. An amusing romance might be written about the everlasting adventures of the ghosts of Shakespeare and Milton passing through the world of to-day. If it were a question, for instance, of dressing for dinner, Milton would either dress exquisitely or refuse to dress on principle. Shakespeare would either remain in morning dress, lazy but embarrassed, or he would put on evening dress eagerly and all wrong. Milton would be regarded everywhere as an aristocrat, except among the aristocracy; Shakespeare would be regarded everywhere as a bounder, except among the aristocracy. They would take a hansom cab together: Milton would direct the cabman; Shakespeare would pay him. But the subject enlarges itself too magnificently before me. I cannot pause to tell you of all the other examples of the diverse and significant conduct of these great men. I cannot dwell upon the variety of their methods in dealing with a bootblack, or the highly characteristic way in which each of them behaved in the Hammersmith omnibus. How can I tell you of the Miltonian way in which Milton dealt with the post office, or the extraordinary conduct of Shakespeare in a tea-shop? It is enough that, as I say, all Englishmen are either Shakespeareans or Miltonians, and that I, for one, am not a Miltonian.

Many people have wondered why Milton described the Devil so much better than he described anything else; I think the reason is really simple: it is because he was so extraordinarily like the Devil himself. A certain Cavalier, whom some Puritan had denounced for the immorality of his troopers, replied (in a sentence that is none the worse for being certainly historical): "Our men had the sins of men—wine and wenching; yours had the sins of devils— spiritual pride and rebellion." I sympathise, politically speaking, with the republicanism of men like Milton; but I cannot help feeling that there was a truth in that answering taunt, and that the rebellion of Milton, at least, was the rebellion of spiritual pride; it was a cold anger, an intellectual violence. I do not blame him for helping Charles I to lose his head, but I do blame him for never losing his own. This strain of a stern and frigid propriety, full of scholarly memories and many dignified public virtues, does exist in Milton and it does exist still in England. Miltonic England has nearly destroyed Merry England, but not quite. The struggle is still going on, and Shakespeare is still alive, and with him all the Middle Ages. The war in us is still going on between Falstaff, who did evil stupidly, and Satan, who desired evil intelligently. Falstaff is a mocker because he is incomplete; Satan is serious because he is complete.

For this reason it is impossible not to feel a kind of mischievous pleasure in the fact that Shakespeare escaped all those formative influences which have made the modern English gentleman. Shakespeare is a sort of gigantic truant. He ran away from school and college—at least, he kept away from school and college, and I fancy he has kept away from most of his own celebrations. The lack of biographical detail about him is not, I think, a mere accident of circumstances or records. It is a part of a certain splendid vagrancy and vagueness in the daily existence of that kind of man. We do not know much of the life of Shakespeare; but I doubt if Shakespeare knew much either. Life does not consist of incidents; incidents, even happy incidents, are often an interruption to life. It may be that Shakespeare stopped living for a moment even to imagine Othello; in such a great vitality the greatest experiences are often shapeless, unconscious, and unrecorded; and it may be that the happiest hour of Shakespeare was when he had forgotten his own name. In fact, he may very well have forgotten it quite often, as he never seems to have managed to spell it twice the same. But for this reason, there must always be, as I have said, something just slightly artificial about all pomps and mysteries which celebrate Shakespeare at a particular time or in a particular place. The cant saying that Shakespeare is for all time has a double truth in it; it means that he is the kind of poet to endure for ever, and it also means that he was probably the kind of man who never knew what the time was. As Orlando says to Rosalind, "There is no clock in the forest." The poet of the wood is free from all chains, but chiefly from the most galling and oppressive of all human chains—a watch chain. And as it is with time, so it is with space. Shakespeare does not live in the forests of Warwickshire, but in the Forest of Arden. His traces may be found anywhere or nowhere; he is omnipresent, and yet he has escaped. He is hidden away somewhere under nameless woods, concealed along with the soul of England, where God has hidden it from Imperialists and thieves.

(*Illustrated London News*, May 18, 1907)

Shakespeare and Milton (Again)

A correspondent has written to me asking me what I meant by saying that Shakespeare was a Catholic and Milton a Protestant. That Milton was a Protestant, I suppose, he will not dispute. At least, he will not dispute it if he has any faint belief in the possibility of the dead returning to this earth in anger. But the point about the religion of Shakespeare is certainly less obvious, though I think not less true. The real difference between a religion and a mere philosophy is (among other things) this: that while only subtle people can understand the difference between one philosophy and another, quite simple people, quite stupid people (like you and me), can understand the difference between one religion and another, because it is a difference between two different things. The difference between two philosophies is like the difference between two solutions of a geometrical problem. The difference between two religions is like the difference between the smell of onions and the smell of the sea. Both religions may have much good; the sea is good, and onions are even better than the sea. But nobody requires to be cultured in order to distinguish one from the other. The whole practical working world bears witness to this fact, that ordinary people do not recognise a philosophy as a reality in the same way that they recognize a religion as a reality. There are real people living in real houses who will not have a Roman Catholic servant. I never heard of any people living in any houses who advertised in the newspapers that they would not have a Hegelian servant. People are really horrified if they learn that a man is an atheist; they do shrink from him morally; they almost shrink from him physically. But ordinary people do not shrink from a Hegelian: they

merely pity him. They do what they can to make his life
happier: they make him Minister of War. But about all
these things that are of the character of religion there is this
double difficulty: that, while everybody can feel them,
nobody can express them. There is no ordinary housekeeper engaging a housemaid who believes for one moment
in the modern theory that all religions are really the same.
Being a healthy-minded housekeeper, she will probably
have a preliminary and just objection to her housemaid
being religious at all. But she will quite certainly feel that if
her servant is a Salvationist she will have one sort of difficulty, if her servant is a Roman Catholic another kind of
difficulty, and if her servant is a Hindu, another. But, while
this difference is obvious to sense, it is obscure to language.
The stupidest person can feel it; the cleverest person cannot define it.

For which reason I would respectfully decline to explain
in a space like this exactly why I feel one religion in one
author and another religion in another. I think the remarks
of Aristotle somewhat too compressed to be clearly understood; still, I can understand that Aristotle was a pagan. I
think the remarks of Lord Meath, on the other hand, somewhat too diffuse and large; still, I would under any circumstances be prepared to bet that Lord Meath was born after
the introduction of Christianity into Europe. These impressions are hard to explain, because they are impressions of
everything. But here, at least, is one way of putting the difference between the religions of Shakespeare and Milton.
Milton is possessed with what is, I suppose, the first and
finest idea of Protestantism—the idea of the individual soul
actually testing and tasting all the truth there is, and calling
that truth which it has not tested or tasted truth of a less
valuable and vivid kind. But Shakespeare is possessed

through and through with the feeling which is the first and finest idea of Catholicism that truth exists whether we like it or not, and that it is for us to accommodate ourselves to it. Milton, with a splendid infallibility and a splendid intolerance, sets out to describe how things actually are to be explained: he has seen it in a vision—

> That to the height of this great argument
> I may assert eternal Providence,
> And justify the ways of God to men.

But when Shakespeare speaks of the divine truth, it is always as something from which he himself may have fallen away, something that he himself may have forgotten—

> O . . . that the Everlasting had not fix'd
> His canon 'gainst self-slaughter;

or again—

> But if it be a sin to covet honour
> I am the most offending soul alive.

But I really do not know how this indescribable matter can be better described than by simply saying this; that Milton's religion was Milton's religion, and that Shakespeare's religion was not Shakespeare's.

(*Illustrated London News*, June 8, 1907)

❖

Purgatory

Shakespeare did believe in the Roman Catholic Purgatory. He believed in the very doctrine which was considered the chief mark of a Catholic as distinct from a Protestant:

> . . . . condemned to fast in fires
> Till the foul sins done in my days of nature
> Are burnt and purged away. . . .

(*G.K.'s Weekly*, June 13, 1925)

---- ❖ ----

The Ancient Religious Unity

In so far as Shakespeare the Little Englander does reach out to something larger than England, it is emphatically not to the expanding empire of the English, but to the ancient religious unity of the Europeans. He exults not in the Schism but in the Crusades.

> Renowned for their deeds as far from home
> For Christian service and true chivalry,
> As is the Sepulchre in stubborn Jewry
> Of the world's ransom, Blessed Mary's Son.

(*G.K.'s Weekly*, June 13, 1925)

---- ❖ ----

The Medieval Religion

Medieval religion, including medieval asceticism, was totally different from Puritanism, was indeed contrary to Puritanism, and was certainly much less gloomy than Puritanism. It was different in meaning, different in motive, different in atmosphere and different in effect. The two things were so diverse that even when they were the same they were different; as different as a Catholic and an atheist vegetarian when they both refuse meat on Friday. . . . Men like Shakespeare and Ben Jonson had fathers or grandfathers who must have remembered the old medieval routine as it remained after the Wars of the Roses. Even if the Renaissance had penetrated every byway of the north (which seems most unlikely) the interruption must have been very recent and very brief. Tradition must still have been full of the momentum of the long medieval memories. Under these circumstances, if the Puritans had only been like medieval priests, they would have been noticed as being like medieval priests. The tone of the comments on them would have been "Oh Lord, here are the dismal old shavelings back again." It was totally different. The tone of the comments was "Who ever heard of such nonsense as these new religious people are talking?" So Shakespeare's characters, who accept a friar as something familiar and presumably friendly, will talk of Malvolio being a Puritan as if it were a sort of monster. It is to me simply incredible, as a mere matter of human nature, that people should speak thus of a new thing if all the old things had been exactly like it.

(*Superstitions of a Sceptic*)

Recognizable as a Catholic

I believe that recent discoveries, as recorded in a book by a French lady, have very strongly confirmed the theory that Shakespeare died a Catholic. But I need no books and no discoveries to prove to me that he had lived a Catholic, or more probably, like the rest of us, tried unsuccessfully to live a Catholic; that he thought like a Catholic and felt like a Catholic and saw every question as a Catholic sees it. The proofs of this would be matter for a separate essay; if indeed so practical an impression can be proved at all. It is quite self-evident to me that he was a certain real and recognizable Renaissance type of Catholic; like Cervantes; like Ronsard. But if I were asked offhand for a short explanation, I could only say that I know he was a Catholic from the passages which are now used to prove he was an agnostic.

("If They Had Believed," *The Thing*)

---- ❖ ----

Utterly Unmistakable

That Shakespeare was a Catholic is a thing that every Catholic feels by every sort of convergent common sense to be true. It is supported by the few external and political facts we know; it is utterly unmistakable in the general spirit and atmosphere; and in nothing more than in the scepticism, which appears in some aspects to be paganism. But I am not talking about the various kinds of Catholic; I am talking about the atmosphere of the sixteenth century as compared with the fourteenth century. And I say that while the former was more refined, it was in certain special ways more restricted, or properly speaking, more concentrated.

Shakespeare is more concentrated on Hamlet than Dante is upon Hell; for the very reason that Dante's mind is full of the larger plan of which this is merely a part. But . . . Shakespeare seems to identify himself with Hamlet who finds Denmark a prison, or the whole world a prison.

("Chaucer and the Renaissance," *Chaucer*)

VIII.
WHO WROTE SHAKESPEARE?

Quite Himself

Critics are much madder than poets. Homer is complete and calm enough; it is his critics who tear him into extravagant tatters. Shakespeare is quite himself; it is only some of his critics who have discovered that he was somebody else.

("The Maniac," *Orthodoxy*)

———— ❖ ————

The Cryptogram Again

The great Transatlantic theory that Shakespeare was not Shakespeare, but someone else with a different name, is one of those intellectual pestilences which break out recurrently in countries that do not pay sufficient attention to intellectual sanitation. In America, we may imagine, there are great cities with more than the material civilization of Paris and less than the mental civilization of Upper Tooting. In these a literary refuse accumulates, unchecked by any critical scavenger, and the result is some burst of literary disease, confounding all standards and probabilities. Two works lie before us devoted to the grotesque Bacon–Shakespeare cryptogram. The sole interest of these works lies in the opportunity they give of pointing out how little mere accumulations of detail have to do with the historic instinct. The authors of these books grab in libraries, they have dates, citations, "singular coincidences," "astonishing parallels," everything except the most glimmering conception of the nature of the Elizabethan era.

It need hardly be said that anyone who has any knowledge of the spirit and nature of that era would no more believe that Bacon wrote Shakespeare than that Lord Rosebery wrote the poems of Mr. W. B. Yeats. If all that was required were coincidences and cryptograms, we would cheerfully undertake to prove that Mr. Yeats was Lord Rosebery. The title of Mr. Yeats' chief prose work, *The Secret Rose*, is an almost clumsily transparent disguise; it indicates at once "the sky or modest rose"—hence "Prim-Rose," and again, the "Rose which is Buried"—hence Rosebery; and the word "secret" itself suggests that there is a mystery in the matter. When once we had so clear a nucleus as this, the rest might legitimately be more indirect. *The Wind Among the Reeds* would be held to mean the perturbation which Lord Rosebery's Imperialism would produce in the mind of Sir Robert Reid, while the remarkable selection of the rank in the peerage for "the Countess Kathleen" deserves serious attention. The only lesson to be drawn from the Baconian craze lies here. If any man of education were confronted with this theory about Lord Rosebery he would not trouble his head about this class of proofs. The parallels might be most ingenious, the dates consistent, the cryptogram lucid and sustained. The only objection to it would be that nobody who knows anything about Lord Rosebery, Mr. Yeats, or the life of the nineteenth century would ever think of believing it. It would be clear to anyone with any vital grasp of the literary sects and movements of our time that Mr. Yeats is the man to have written the poems, and that Lord Rosebery is not.

So it is with the American Baconians. They show their complete inability to deal with the whole question by starting with the idea that Bacon, being a learned man, is more likely to have been the great dramatist than Shakespeare, a more or less rowdy play-actor. Nay, even their opponents in the controversy take this view, and Mr. Francis P. Gervais, the author of a large book now under our consideration, called *Shakespeare Not Bacon*, appears to admit this as a difficulty. "We Shakespearians," he says, "join in the wonder that a poor player who struts and frets his hour upon the stage should have been so learned." Neither seem to realise that there are other kinds of learning besides book learning, that there are other limitations besides the limitations of ignorance, and that *Much Ado About Nothing* was quite as much above the head of a man in Bacon's position as the *Novum Organum* was above the head of a man in Shakespeare's. Of course everyone with a literary instinct can see that if Bacon had written plays they would have been exceedingly unlike those under discussion. It was precisely because Shakespeare was one of the wild theatrical group which produced a whole cycle of great plays in the same style that he had the chance of surpassing all of them.

But the real triumph of methodical madness is the work of Mr. Parker Woodward, which is called *The Strange Case of Francis Tidir*. From this we learn that Bacon not only wrote Shakespeare's plays, but those of Greene, Peele, and Marlowe, the poems of Spenser, and Burton's *Anatomy of Melancholy*. Finally, and by way of a detail, he was the son of Queen Elizabeth. We have really nothing to say to this, except that, by some curious negligence Mr. Woodward has neglected to notice that Bacon (under the transparent pseudonym of Sir Francis Drake) sailed round the world, and under the nickname of Admiral Coligny was supposed to have been murdered in the Massacre of St. Bartholomew.

With these trifling exceptions, there is hardly any eminent man of the period apparently who was not Bacon. In fact, the boasted brilliance of the Elizabethan period is seriously contracted: the Queen had, after all, only one clever man in her dominions, but he was certainly versatile and energetic.

As a specimen of the proofs offered by Mr. Parker Woodward for these we may notice that in which he points out with dark significance that, including the hyphen, there are the same number of letters in Shakespeare as in Francis Bacon. Here, again, we need only point out to Mr. Woodward, as a similarly stunning coincidence, that if he eliminates the unnecessary first R in Rosebery, he will have the same number of letters as in W. B. Yeats. Another is that in both authors the phrase "quiet conscience" occurs somewhere. When a lady declines to retire to rest "until the sun be set," it means that the truth about the plays will not be told until the author is dead. If this is the standard of argument, we ought to have as easy task in our forthcoming work on the W. B. Yeats Cryptogram. Only, in order to bring that work up to the level, it will be necessary to show that Lord Rosebery wrote not only the works of Mr. Yeats, but those of Mr. Swinburne, Mr. W. S. Gilbert, and Mr. George R. Sims, as well as Professor Drommond's *Ascent of Man*.

Shakespeare himself was one of the most voluminous authors in the English language. Peile, Green, and Marlowe between them probably wrote as many plays as Shakespeare. Spenser's *Faerie Queene* is a very long poem. Burton's *Anatomy of Melancholy* is a very large book. Add to this, Bacon wrote two huge works of philosophic research, innumerable essays, and lived a particularly active professional and political life all the time, and his industry, according to Mr. Woodward's hypothesis, is certainly creditable if credible. We think it quite possible that the whole tomfoolery might be disproved by physical and chronological possibility, but we certainly are not going to take the trouble. The whole matter belongs to that vulgar wax-work view of history which makes a certain class of spiritualists always summon the ghost of Mary Queen of Scots. Writers of this order think that all Elizabethans lived in the same street, just as persons in London sometimes think that Bombay is a little way from Calcutta. They do not realise that in the complexity of a great crisis men live side by side who are not only of different types, but almost of different centuries. There are hardly two men who had so little in common as Bacon and Shakespeare.

(*Daily News*, May 6, 1901)

❖

The Secret Rose

I remember a riotous argument about Bacon and Shakespeare in which I offered quite at random to show that Lord Rosebery had written the works of Mr. W. B. Yeats. No sooner had I said the words than a torrent of coincidences rushed upon my mind. I pointed out, for instance, that Mr. Yeats's chief work was *The Secret Rose*. This may easily be paraphrased as "The Quiet or Modest Rose"; and so, of course, as the Primrose, a second after I saw the same suggestion in the combination of "rose" and "bury." If I had pursued the matter, who knows but I might have been a raving maniac by this time.

(*Daily News*, Jan. 22, 1910)

❖

More Gammon of Bacon

For some reason not very easy to discover, books on the Bacon–Shakespeare controversy continue to be produced in great numbers and voluminous form, although the case for the Baconian cypher has been irremediably damaged by Mr. Sidney Lee's critique of Mrs. Gallup, and finally shattered to pieces by Mrs. Gallup's reply. I have read the mass of these works as they appeared down to the latest, *The Problem of the Shakespeare Plays*, by Mr. George C. Bompas, and the general impression produced upon my mind takes the form of an impassioned hope that I may never be tried for my life before a jury of Baconians. If the average judge or jury treated evidence as the Baconians treat it there is not one of us who might not be in hourly peril of being sent to prison for bigamy or embezzlement or piracy on the high seas. In order to show that any one of us was identical with some celebrated criminal nothing would be necessary except to show that we had once or twice used the same popular turns of expression. The most harmless householder in London might on the Baconian method be suddenly convicted of having committed the Whitechapel murders, and the evidence might be that one of the cousins was in the habit of calling him "Jack" and that some slangy friend of his had in an authenticated letter described him as "a ripper." Some people may fancy that this is an exaggerated parallel. Let me merely quote in answer one of the actual arguments of Mr. G. C. Bompas:

"The moon so constant in inconstancy."
—Bacon: Trans. Psalm civ

"Oh, swear not by the moon, the inconstant moon."
—*Romeo and Juliet*

It is seriously argued that two men must be the same man because they both employ the expression "the inconstant moon." I suppose that all the poems in all the ages which contain the expression "rosy dawn" were all secretly written by the same man.

If education is to be seriously remodeled and set upon larger foundations in our age, surely one branch of them into which more attention should be given is the power of valuing evidence. Almost every one of the books which have passed before me in this matter display an absolute inability to realise what is significant and what is insignificant in a human problem. There ought to be a series of text-books on evidence and arguments as to probability, in all the Schools. In the simpler text-books would be found the general principles of which the Baconians stand in need. For instance, children would be made to learn by heart the following rules:

I. To establish a connection between two persons, the points of resemblance must be not only common to the two individuals but must not be common to any large number of persons outside. Example: Thus it is no evidence of connection between Jones and Brown that they both put money on the Derby, or that they both at one particular period of London life said "There's 'air."

II. Similarly it is no proof of the connection between two persons that they both do something which, though it may actually be done by many people, might at any moment be done by anybody. Example: Thus it is no proof of connection between Jones and Brown that they both sneezed twice on Thursday morning, or that they both had a door-knocker carved with the head of a lion.

III. In order to establish a connection between two men it is necessary that the points of resemblance should be (*a*) characteristics, having something of the actual colour of an individual's character, (*b*) things in themselves unusual or difficult or dependent on a particular conjunction of events, (*c*) things, generally speaking, which it is easier to imagine one man only at a particular time doing, or two men conspiring to do, than to imagine two or more men at that time independently and simultaneously doing. Example: Thus a connection would be established between Jones and Brown, though only to a limited extent, if Brown were the only Cabinet Minister in the same social circle with Jones, and Jones had learnt a Cabinet secret.

These rules of evidence are so simple and obvious that at first sight it may seem a waste of time to summarise them even briefly. But if a reader will apply them steadily through the whole of one of the Baconian books such as that of Mr. Bompas, he will find it may be said without the least exaggeration that by the end of the process every vestige of the book has vanished.

To quote examples of this in full would be to quote the whole book. I may, however, give the following instances in order to show that I do not overstate the case:

"His purpose was to break the knot of the conspiracy."
—*History of Henry V.*

This sentence from Bacon is gravely paralleled with the line from *The Merry Wives of Windsor*:

"There's a knot, a gin, a conspiracy against me."

Again, we have:

"Wretches have been able to stir up earthquakes by the murdering of princes."
—*Bacon's charge against Owen*

"Wherefore this ghastly looking. What's the matter?
 Oh! 'twas a din to fright a monster ear
To make an earthquake."
—*Tempest*

" 'Ordinatis belli et pacis est absoluti imperii,' a principal flower of the crown. For if those flowers should wither and fall, the garland will not be worth the wearing."
—*Report 606. Bacon.*

Catesby: "Till Richard wear the garland of the realm."
—*Richard III*

And it is solemnly proposed that we should believe in a story more sensational than that of a fifth-rate historical novel upon such evidence as this, that Bacon and Shakespeare both called a conspiracy "a knot," that they both made an allusion to an earthquake and both made an allusion to a garland. If anyone will bring me two books taken at random from a bookcase, I will undertake to find in them better internal evidence than this that they were both written by one man.

The remainder of Mr. Bompas's parallels may chiefly be grouped into two classes. The first class shows that Bacon and Shakespeare both alluded to old stories that they must both have read. The second class shows that Bacon and Shakespeare both alluded to theories and superstitions that everybody in that time must have known. Will it be seriously credited as an example of the first class that Mr. Bompas makes capital out of the fact that both Bacon and Shakespeare refer to so old and banal of a story as that of Tarquin slashing off the heads of the poppies? Will it be believed as an example of the second class that he makes an argument out of the facts that Bacon refers to a toad having a jewel in its head? It does not seem to occur to him that Shakespeare's lines would be perfectly pointless if they did not allude to a commonly received story. Mr. Bompas might as well endeavour to establish a connection between all the people who ever said that it was unlucky to sit down thirteen to table. Most incredible of all is the fact that a man professing to write seriously about a problem of the sixteenth century points it out as a coincidence that Bacon and Shakespeare both compared seditions to "evil humours" in the body, the veriest catch-word of contemporary physiology. He might as well identify all the people who talk about "social decadence."

I have given a list of these quibbles because it is supremely necessary to realise with what kind of matter these immense volumes are padded; and it is not difficult to realise that where such arguments are used there is likely to be a dearth of better ones. Wherever Mr. Bompas uses a more general or vital argument it is vitiated with the same underlying evil, an absolute refusal to realise the spirit of the Elizabethan era. Let me take a single example. Mr. Bompas argues that if Shakespeare was in reality the author, it is extraordinary that all the natural history in the plays is taken from old books and stories, and none of it from the actual details of the country round Stratford. But does Mr. Bompas really know so little of the age about which he writes as to suppose that any poet in that time would have taken any notice of nature, in the modern sense, even if he had been surrounded by miles of pigs and primroses? To notice, in the Tennysonian manner, what colour a certain leaf turns in

September, what a note a certain bird utters in spring, would have been as impossible either to Shakespeare or Bacon as to write *The Origin of Species*. All their natural history was traditional; and if Shakespeare had been ten times a rustic, and had never been near London, he would have got his natural history from tradition: he would no more have written about the habits of the squirrel than Spenser wrote about the streets and shop-windows of London, where he was born. Not to realise this is to be incapable at the outset of understanding the problem of the Renascence.

Lastly, the general argument drawn from the historic personality of Shakespeare shows a failure to understand not only the time but the eternal conditions of the problem. Mr. Bompas cannot believe that Shakespeare, a common practical man who worked hard to better his position, who had several perfectly solid and temporal ambitions, who retired a rich man to Stratford and enjoyed the good things of this life, was really the author of so many miracles of thought and language. The author must have been, according to Mr. Bompas, a man like Bacon, a man who had travelled, who had seen strange countries, who had dealt with great matters, who had known violent reverses and terrible secrets of State. With this view I venture most profoundly to disagree. There is no clearer mark of the second-rate philanthropist than that he goes out to look for humanity, as if it were a race of blue apes in Central Africa. To the true philanthropist, like Shakespeare, one village is enough to show the whole drama of creation and judgment. There is no clearer mark of the second-rate poet than that he despises business. The true poet, like Shakespeare, despises nothing. Buying and selling and building a house in Stratford seem very derogatory to Mr. Bompas; they did not seem so to Shakespeare; he knew that all points on the eternal circle are equidistant from the centre.

(*The Speaker*, March 15, 1902)

———— ❖ ————

Sensationalism and a Cipher

The revival of the whole astonishing Bacon–Shakespeare business is chiefly interesting to the philosophical mind as an example of the power of the letter which killeth, and of how finally and murderously it kills. Baconianism is, indeed, the last wild monstrosity of literalism; it is a sort of delirium of detail. A handful of printers' types, a few alphabetical comparisons are sufficient to convince the Baconians of a proposition which is fully as fantastic historically as the proposition that the Battle of Waterloo was won by Leigh Hunt disguised as Wellington, or that the place of Queen Victoria for the last forty years of her reign was taken by Miss Frances Power Cobbe. Both these hypotheses are logically quite possible. The dates agree; the physical similarity is practically sufficient. Briefly, in fact, there is nothing to be said against the propositions except that every sane man is convinced that they are untrue.

Let us consider for a moment the Baconian conception from the outside. A sensational theory about the position of Shakespeare was certain in the nature of things to arise. Men of small imagination have sought in every age to find a cipher in the indecipherable masterpieces of the great. Throughout the Middle Ages the whole of the *Aeneid*, full of the sad and splendid eloquence of Virgil, was used as a conjuring book. Men opened it at random, and from a few disconnected Latin words took a motto and an omen for their daily work. In the same way men in more modern times have turned to the Book of Revelation full of the terrible judgment, and yet more terrible consolation of a final moral arbitration, and found in it nothing but predictions about Napoleon Bonaparte and attacks on the English Ritualists. Everywhere, in short, we find the same general truth—the truth that facts can prove anything, and that there is nothing so misleading as that which is printed in black and white. Almost everywhere and almost invariably the man who has sought a cryptogram in a great masterpiece has been highly exhilarated, logically justified, morally excited, and entirely wrong.

If, therefore, we continue to study Baconianism from the outside—a process which cannot do it or any other thesis any injustice—we shall come more and more to the conclusion that it is in itself an inevitable outcome of the circumstances of the case and the tendencies of human nature. Shakespeare was by the consent of all human beings a portent. If he had lived some thousand years earlier, people would have turned him into a god. As it is, people can apparently do nothing but attempt to turn him into a Lord Chancellor. But their great need must be served. Shakespeare must have his legend, his whisper of something more than common origin. They must at least make of him a mystery, which is as near as our century can come to a miracle. Something sensational about Shakespeare was bound ultimately to be said, for we are still the children of the ancient earth, and have myth and idolatry in our blood. But in this age of a convention of scepticism we cannot rise to an apotheosis. The nearest we can come to it is a dethronement.

So much for the *a priori* probability of a Baconian theory coming into existence. What is to be said of the *a priori* probability of the theory itself; or, rather, to take the matter in its most lucid order, what is the theory? In the time roughly covered by the latter part of the reign of Queen Elizabeth and the earlier part of the reign of James I, there arose a school of dramatists who covered their country with glory and filled libraries with their wild and wonderful plays. They differed in type and station to a certain extent: some were scholars, a few were gentlemen, most were actors and many were vagabonds. But they had a common society, common meeting places, a common social tone. They differed in literary aim and spirit: to a certain extent some were great philosophic dramatists, some were quaint humorists, some mere scribblers of a sort of half-witted and half-inspired melodrama. But they all had a common style, a common form and vehicle, a common splendour, and a common error in their methods. Now, the Baconian theory is that one of these well-known historical figures—a man who lived their life and shared their spirit, and who happened to be the most brilliant in the cultivation of their particular form of art—was, as a matter of fact, an impostor, and that the works which his colleagues thought he had written in the same spirit and the same circumstances in which they had written theirs, were not written by him, but by a very celebrated judge and politician of that time, whom they may sometimes have seen when his coachwheels splashed them as he went by.

Now, what is to be said about the *a priori* probability of this view, which I stated, quite plainly and impartially, above? The first thing to be said, I think, is that a man's answer to the question would be a very good test to whether he had the rudiments of a historical instinct, which is simply an instinct which is capable of realising the way in which things happen. To many this will appear a vague and unscientific way of approaching the question. But the method I now adopt is the method which every reasonable being adopts in distinguishing between fact and fiction in real life. What would any man say if he were informed that in the private writings of Lord Rosebery that statesman claimed to have written the poems of Mr. W. B. Yeats? Certainly, he could not deny that there were very singular coincidences in detail. How remarkable, for instance, is the name Primrose, which is obviously akin to modest rose, and thus to "Secret Rose." On the top of this comes the crushing endorsement of the same idea indicated in the two words "rose" and "bury." The remarks of the Ploughman in the "Countess Cathleen" (note the rank in the peerage selected) would be anxiously scanned for some not improbable allusion to a furrow; and everything else, the statesman's abandonment of Home Rule, the poet's aversion to Imperialism, would be all parts of Lord Rosebery's cunning. But what, I repeat, would a man say if he were asked if the theory was probable? He would reply, "The theory is as near to being impossible as a natural phenomenon can be. I know Mr. W. B. Yeats, I know how he talks, I know what sort of a man he is, what sort of people he lives among, and know that he is the man to have written those poems. I know Lord Rosebery, too, and what sort of a life his is, and I know that he is not."

Now, we know, almost as thoroughly as we should know the facts of this hypothetical case, the facts about Bacon and Shakespeare. We know that Shakespeare was a particular kind of man who lived with a particular kind of men, all of whom thought much as he thought and wrote much as he wrote. We know that Bacon was a man who lived in another world, who thought other thoughts, who talked with other men, who wrote another style, one might almost say another language. That Bacon wrote Shakespeare is certainly possible; but almost every other hypothesis, that Bacon never said so, that he lied when he said it, that the printers played tricks with the documents, that the Baconians played tricks with the evidence, is in its nature a hundred times more probable. Of the cipher itself, I shall speak in another article. For the moment it is sufficient to point out that the Baconian hypothesis has against it the whole weight of historical circumstance and the whole of that supra-logical realisation which some of us call transcendentalism, and most of us common sense.

(*The Speaker*, January 11, 1902)

——— ❖ ———

Sensationalism and a Cipher (Again)

In a previous article I drew attention to the general spirit in which the Baconian question must be approached. That spirit involves the possession of a thing which is scarcely comprehended in America, the instinct of culture which does not consist merely in knowing the facts but in being able to imagine the truth. The Baconians imagine a vain thing, because they believe in facts. Their historical faculty is a rule of three; the real historical faculty is a great deal more like an ear for music. One of the matters, for example, which is most powerfully concerned in the Bacon–Shakespeare question, is that question of literary style, a thing as illogical as the bouquet of a bottle of wine. It is the thing, in short, which makes us quite certain that the sentence quoted in *The Tragedy of Sir Francis Bacon* from his secret narrative, "The Queen looked pale from want of rest, but was calm and compos'd," was never written by an Elizabethan. Having explained the essentials of the method as they appear to me, I now come to the study of the mass of the Baconian details. They are set forth in a kind of résumé of various Baconian theories in *The Tragedy of Sir Francis Bacon*, by Harold Bayley. The work is an astonishing example of the faculty of putting out the fire of truth with the fuel of information. Mr. Bayley has collected with creditable industry an enormous number of fragmentary facts and rumours. He has looked at the water-marks in the paper used by Rosicrucians and Jacobean dramatists. He has examined the tail-pieces and ornamental borders of German and Belgian printers. He has gone through the works of Bacon and Shakespeare and a hundred others, picking out parallel words and allusions, but all the time he is completely incapable of realising the great and glaring truism which lies at the back of the whole question, the simple truism that a million times naught is naught. He does not see, that is, that though a million coincidences, each of which by itself has a slight value, may make up a probability, yet a million coincidences, each of which has no value in itself, make up nothing at all. What are the sort of coincidences upon which Mr. Bayley relies? The water-mark used in some book is the design of a bunch of grapes. Bacon says, in the *Novum Organum*: "I pledge mankind in liquor pressed from countless grapes." Another water-mark represents a seal. Somebody said about Bacon that he became Lord Keeper of the Great Seal of England and of the great seal of nature. The rose and the lily were symbols used by the Rosicrucians; there are a great many allusions to roses and lilies in Shakespeare. A common printer's border consists of acorns. Bacon somewhere alluded to his fame growing like an oak tree. Does not Mr. Bayley see that no conceivable number of coincidences of this kind would make an account more probable or even more possible? Anyone in any age might talk about clusters of grapes or design clusters of grapes; anyone might make an ornament out of acorns; anyone might talk about growing like a tree. I look down at my own floor and see the Greek key pattern round the oilcloth, but it does not convince me that I am destined to open the doors of Hellenic mystery. Mr. Bayley undoubtably produced a vast number of these parallels, but they all amount to nothing. In my previous article I took for the sake of argument the imaginary case of Lord Rosebery and Mr. W. B. Yeats. Does not Mr. Bayley see that to point out one genuine coincidence, as that Lord Rosebery paid secret cheques to Mr. Yeats, might indicate something, but to say that they both walked down Piccadilly, that they both admired Burne-Jones, that they both alluded more than once to the Irish question, in short that they both did a million things that are done by a million other people, does not approach even to having the faintest value or significance. This, then, is the first thing to be said to the Baconian spirit, that it does not know how to add up a column of naughts.

The second thing to be said is rather more curious. If there is a cypher in the Shakespearean plays, it ought presumably to be a definite and unmistakable thing. It may be difficult to find, but when you have found it you have got it. But the extraordinary thing is that Mr. Bayley and most other Baconians talk about the Baconian cypher as they might talk about "a touch of pathos" in Hood's poetry, or "a flavour of cynicism" in Thackeray's novels, as if it were a thing one became faintly conscious of and suspected, without being able to point it out. If anyone thinks this unfair, let him notice the strange way in which Mr. Bayley talks about previous Baconian works. "In 1888 Mr. Ignatius Donelly claimed to have discovered a cypher story in the first folio of Shakespeare's plays. In his much abused but little read. *The Great Cryptogram*, he endeavored to convice the world of the truth of his theory. Partly by reason of the complexity of his system, the full details of which he did not reveal, and partly owing to the fact that he did not produce any definite assertion of authorship, but appeared to have stumbled into the midst of a lengthy narrative, the world was not convinced, and Mr. Donelly was greeted with Rabelaisian laughter. He has since gone to the grave unwept, unhonoured, and unsung, and his secret has presumably died with him. The work of this letter was marred by many extravagant inferences, but *The Great Cryptogram* is nevertheless a damning indictment which has not yet been answered." Again on the second Baconian demonstration, "Dr. Owen gave scarcely more than a hint of how his alleged cypher worked." The brain reels at all this. Why do none of the cypherists seem to be sure what the cypher is or where it is? A man publishes a huge book to prove that there is a cryptogram, and his secret dies with him. Another man devoted another huge book to giving "scarcely more than a hunt" of it. Are these works really so impenetrable that no one knows whether they all revealed the same cypher or different cyphers? If they pointed to the same cypher it seems odd that Mr. Bayley does not mention it. If their cyphers were different we can only conclude that the great heart of America is passionately bent on finding a cypher in Shakespeare—anyhow, anywhere, and of any kind.

Finally, there is one thing to be said about a more serious matter. In the chapter called "Mr. William Shakespeare" the author has an extraordinary theory that Shakespeare could not have been the author of the works under discussion because those works rise to the heights of mental purity, and the little we know of Shakespeare's life would seem to indicate that it was a coarse and possibly a riotous one. "Public opinion," he says solemnly, "asks us to believe that this divine stream of song, history, and philosophy sprang from so nasty and beastly a source." There is not much to be said about an argument exhibiting so strange an ignorance of human nature. The argument could equally be used to prove that Leonardo do Vinci could not paint, that Mirabeau could not speak, and that Burns's poems were written by the parson of his parish. But surely there is no need to say this to the Baconians. They should be the last people in the world to doubt the possibility of the conjunction of genius with depravity. They trace their sublime stream of song to a corrupt judge, a treacherous friend, a vulgar sycophant, a man of tawdry aims, of cowardly temper, of public and disgraceful end. He killed his benefactor for hire, and the Baconians would improve this and say that he killed his brother. We know little of Shakespeare's vices, but he might have been a scarecrow of profligacy and remained a man worthier to create Portia than the Lord Verulam whom all history knows. The matter is a matter of evidence, and sentiment has little concern with it. But if we did cherish an emotion in the matter it would certainly be a hope that "the divine stream of song" might not be traced to "so nasty and beastly a source" as Francis Bacon.

(*The Speaker*, January 25, 1902)

———— ❖ ————

A Shakespeare Portrait

It is very interesting to learn that they have found Shakespeare's portrait in a tavern, especially as that is very much the place where they would have found Shakespeare. I have no knowledge, nor even any comprehension, of the subtle and minute method by which gentlemen who are art-experts are enabled to say apparently for certain what such a portrait is; but certainly there is nothing at all unreasonable in the idea of Shakespeare's being painted by some early admirer of his on the panel of an inn, or in Shakespeare's sitting still to have it painted, so long as they gave him beer enough. I see in one newspaper that a doubt has been raised about the probability of such an episode, and I gather from the context that this doubt was raised in the interests of the Bacon–Shakespeare School. I suppose that this particular Baconian thought that all portraits of Shakespeare ought to be portraits of Bacon; and if they weren't, why then they weren't portraits of Shakespeare. There seems to be something a little mixed in this line of thought; but I have no time to unravel it now. In any case, what the Baconian said about the new portrait was this; "Does it seem very likely that the raw country youth who, practically penniless and burdened with a wife and three children, joins a band of strolling players in 1587, and is heard of the year after as earning a precarious living outside the theatre doors, and who, not until four years later, takes his first essay to the publishers, has his portrait in oils done in 1588—the presumed date of the above picture?"

There may be in this school of thought swift and splendid connections of ideas which I am too dull to follow. But I do not quite understand why having a wife and three children should prevent a man's having his portrait painted. Painters do not commonly insist on their models being celibate, as if they were a sacred and separate order of monks. There is nothing to show that Shakespeare paid for it, or if he did pay for it, that he paid much; and it does not seem, on the face of it, very likely that a man would pay much for a comparatively rude painting in a wayside inn. Suppose we were talking of some man whom we knew to have been a poor actor at one time, travelling from place to place like any other actor, but whom we also knew to be a man of arresting personality, perhaps of fascination. Would there be anything improbable about some friend or flatterer of his youth having sketched him in some small town in which he stayed? Suppose we were speaking of Henry Irving. Should we be surprised to find in any lodging-house at which he had stopped when a lad that the son of the house, who had a taste for photography, had photographed him for nothing? Should we be surprised if some sentimental old lady had "done" him in water-colours? There is nothing to prevent Irving's having been quite as poor as Shakespeare; and certainly there is no reason to deny that Shakespeare was as attractive as Irving.

It may seem a trivial matter; but it is not trivial, because it is typical. The discussion touching whether Bacon wrote Shakespeare is only important because it happens to be the battle-ground of two historical methods, of two kinds of judgment. In itself it matters little whether Bacon was Shakespeare or whether Shakespeare was Bacon. Shakespeare, I fancy, would not much mind being robbed of his literary achievements; and I am sure that Bacon would be delighted to be relieved of his political history and reputation. Francis Lord Verulam would have been a happier man, certainly a better and more Christian man, if he also had gone down to drink ale at Stratford; if he had begun and ended his story in an inn. As far as the individual glory of the two men goes, the two men had this, and perhaps only this, in common: that they both at the end of their lives seem to have decided that all glory is vanity. But, as I say, the real interest of the matter lies in a certain historical and controversial method of which this paragraph that I have quoted is an excellent example.

The two arguments that often clash in history may be called the argument from detail and the argument from atmosphere. Suppose a man two hundred years hence were writing about London cabmen. He might know all the details that can be gathered from all the documents; he might know the numbers of all the cabs, the names of all the cabmen, the single and collective owners of all the vehicles in question, the fixed rate of pay and all the Acts of Parliament that in any way affected it. Yet he might not know the rich and subtle atmosphere of cabmen; their peculiar relations to the comfortable class who commonly employ them. He would not understand how paying the plain fare to a cabman is not the same as paying the plain fare to a tram-conductor. He would not understand how when a cabman overcharges it is not quite the same as if a butcher or a baker had overcharged. He would not grasp to what extent these men regard themselves as the temporary dependents, the temporary coachmen of the wealthy; he would not understand how even their bad language is an expression of that idea of dependence on the historic generosity of gentlemen. He would not comprehend how this strange class of man contrived to be insolent without being independent. It is just such atmospheres as this that history only exists in order to make real; and it is just such atmospheres as this that nearly all history neglects. But those who say that Bacon wrote Shakespeare are, so to speak, the maniacs of this method of detail against atmosphere which is the curse of so many learned men. As a matter of fact the Bacon–Shakespeare people really are learned; they do really know an enormous amount about the period with which they are concerned. But it is all detail; and detail by itself means madness. The very definition of a lunatic is a man who has taken details out of their real atmosphere.

Here is an example. I remember long ago debating with a Baconian, who said that Shakespeare could not have written the plays because Shakespeare was a countryman, and there was in the plays no close study of Nature in the modern sense—no details about how this bird builds its nest, or that flower shakes its pollen—as we get them in Wordsworth or in Tennyson. Now, the man who said this knew far more about Elizabethan literature than I do. In fact he knew everything about Elizabethan literature except what Elizabethan literature was. If he had had even the smallest glimpse of what Elizabethan literature was he would never have dreamed of expecting any Elizabethan to write about Nature because he was brought up in the middle of it. A Renascence poet brought up in a forest would not have written about trees any more than a Renascence poet brought up in a pigsty would have written about pigs; he would have written about gods or not written at all. It was not a Renascence idea to write about the homely natural history which was just outside the door. To say that Shakespeare, if he was really born at Stratford, would have written about birds and meadows, is like saying that Keats, if he was really born in London, would have written about omnibuses and drapers' shops. I was bewildered by this incapacity in a more learned man than I to capture the obvious quality of a time. Then somebody made it worse by saying that Shakespeare could describe Nature in detail because he described in detail the appearance and paces of a horse—as if a horse were some shy bird that built its nest in dim English woodlands and which only a man born in Stratford could see. If there is one thing more certain about an Elizabethan gentleman than the fact that he would know nothing about Nature, it is the fact that he would know all about horses.

I merely quote this old example as an instance of the entire absence of a sense of historical atmosphere. That horse who built his nest in the high trees of Stratford is typical of all this unnatural criticism; the critic who found him did indeed find a mare's nest. Of the same kind is the argument that Shakespeare must have been a learned man like Bacon, because he had heard so much about learning, about law and mythology and old literature. This is like saying that I must be as learned as the Master of Balliol because I have heard of most of the things that he talks about; because I have heard of the debate of Nominalists and Realists, or because I have heard of the Absolute and the Relative being discussed at Balliol. Again the man misses the whole mood and tone of the time. He does not realise that Shakespeare's age was an age in which a fairly bright man could pick up the odds and ends of anything, just as I, by walking along Fleet Street, can pick up the odds and ends of anything. A man could no more live in London then and not hear about Pagan Mythology than he could live in London now and not hear about Socialism. The same solemn and inhuman incredulity which finds it incredible that a clever lad in London should pick up more than he really knew is the same that finds it incredible that he should have had his portrait painted for fun by some foolish painter in a public-house.

The truth is, I fear, that madness has a great advantage over sanity. Sanity is always careless. Madness is always careful. A lunatic might count all the railings along the front of Hyde Park; he might know the exact number of them, because he thought they were something else. A healthy man would not know the number of the railings, or perhaps even the shape of the railings; he would know nothing about them except the supreme, sublime, Platonic, and transcendental truth, that they were railings. There is a great deal of

falsehood in the notion that truth must necessarily prevail.
There is this falsehood to start with: that if a man has got the
truth he is generally happy. And if he is happy he is generally
lazy. The incessant activity, the exaggerated intelligence, generally belong to those who are a little wrong and just a little
right. The whole advantage of those who think that Bacon
wrote Shakespeare lies simply in the fact that they care
whether Bacon wrote Shakespeare. The whole disadvantage
of those who do not think it lies in the fact that (being folly)
they do not care about it. The sane man who is sane enough
to see that Shakespeare wrote Shakespeare is the man who is
sane enough not to worry whether he did or not.

(*Illustrated London News*, March 9, 1907)

---- ❖ ----

Shakespeareans vs. Baconians

In the apparently senseless quarrel about Bacon and
Shakespeare . . . I do not propose to go over the old
ground of criticising or refuting the various contradictory
Baconian theories. I am much more interested in this moral
and almost mystical truth; that the two names have really
come to stand for suitable ideas and suitable sets of people.
There really is such a person as a Baconian. And it really is
true that his chief character is that he is not in the least a
Shakespearean.

To begin with, there is all that atmosphere of what is
called the cryptogram. Baconians proudly boast of it as a
strong argument for their case, that Bacon was profoundly
interested in cryptograms. I have not the smallest difficulty
in believing it; for Bacon was profoundly interested in a
great many things of that kind. He was interested in

conspiracies and plots and counter-plots and hidden motives of statecraft and in pretty stinking secrets of State. There was really, in a sense, such a thing as the secret of being Francis Bacon; or at least in the sense of the secret of becoming Lord Verulam or Lord St. Albans. But there was no particular secret about being William Shakespeare, beyond the great secret of why one man can say that the daffodils take the wind, when nine out of ten would merely say that the wind takes the daffodils. Now it will be noted that the two types of humanity are here divided by the sort of faults to which they are lenient. There is a kind of man who does really believe that public life ought not to be made public. He really does think that public men ought to have a special privilege; the privilege of treating their public affairs as private affairs. No doubt, in abstract theory, these people would condemn all imperfections; but men are divided by which imperfections they condemn first, and which they pardon first. When a gentleman takes bribes, in quite a gentlemanly way, it does seem to some people a sort of outrage that his little weaknesses should be dragged into the light of day. It has seemed to be like that to nearly all the apologists of Francis Bacon. But when a poacher, who happens also to be a poet, is fallen on by keepers or put in the stocks, or what not, all this half of humanity that I have called Baconian does really feel that he deserved all he got. They have a sort of cryptogrammic sympathy with anything that is naturally curtained from the common day; whether we describe the curtain as courtesy or conspiracy. On the other hand, they have no sympathy with the defiant and disreputable faults; with robbing on the king's highway or getting drunk in the public-house. And from the legend that he began deer-stealing as a lad to the legend that he died of a debauch of drink in later middle age, those are the stories which these people always tell, in triumphant scorn, against William Shakespeare of Stratford.

Needless to say, the other portion of humanity moves instantly and instinctively the other way. It starts by suspecting politicians merely because they are politic. It has its doubts about secrets of State, merely because they are secret. It feels an abstract aversion from the cryptograms of court life and the ciphers of secret diplomacy. It has some tendency to treat a rascal better than he deserves when once it knows the worst, or when once he has got his deserts. This was apparent in the case of Wilkes; but it applies in its degree to so much more valuable a person as Will Shakespeare the deer-stealer. It is their principle, in extreme cases, to give a dog a bad name and not hang him.

This and other differences arise, like everything else, from deep spiritual divisions. It will be noted that the Baconian almost always boasts of being the Modern; and praises Bacon especially for his supposed proclamation of modern scientific methods. This is not inconsistent with conspiracy; and corruption is a thing that has very modern scientific methods. Indeed, modern civilisation, that has introduced so many refinements, has brought almost to perfection this old problem of the polite way of taking bribes. Essential secrecy has rather increased than decreased in the last few centuries. I know there is a general impression to the contrary, because of the wide spaces occupied by things like advertisement and publicity. But this is to misunderstand the very nature of these things. Publicity is not the opposite of secrecy. Publicity often means only the public praise of a secret process. It means the enlargement of trademarks, but not the diminishment of trade secrets. Whether machinery and multiple organizations be good things or no, it is obvious that in their very nature they intensify the isolation of the one man who presses a button or the one man who signs a cheque. If he does these things in an unscrupulous fashion, the kind of man who wishes to excuse his action or guard his secret is the same sort of man who would guard Lord Verulam from his accusers, on the ground of his great work for science.

It will be noted that in neither case am I saying that the defence is always logical. It is not conclusive to say of Bacon: "Never mind his bribery and corruption; think of his wonderful work for experimental philosophy." It is not conclusive to say of Shakespeare: "Never mind his drunkenness or deer-stealing; think of his great work in imaginative poetry." Poetry does not excuse robbery, anymore than science excuses bribery. I am only pointing out that the poet's friends and the scientist's friends are recognizable groups and generally ready to excuse one fault rather than the other. And I am especially pointing out that the more open and casual life of the poet was, if anything, more suited to old and simple societies; the smooth and diplomatic life of the politician very much more suited to our modern society. Shakespeare had in him very much of the Middle Ages, as well as the Renaissance, and held on by a hundred links to the religious and moral life of the past. Bacon seems to be entirely of his own period, when he does not seem to be of our period; and it is a matter of taste whether we think either of them a particularly nice period. But, anyhow, out of the wild pedantry and bewildered detective fever of the old Bacon controversy there does emerge a fact of more permanent popular importance: that far deeper instincts, that set god against god, or legend against legend, were at work to set those two great names so strangely against each other.

(*Illustrated London News*, December 29, 1929)

—— ❖ ——

Shakespeare's Breakfast

I cannot imagine that Shakespeare began the day with rolls and coffee, like a Frenchman or a German. Surely he began with bacon or bloaters. In fact, a light bursts upon me; for the first time I see . . . bacon did write Shakespeare. ("The Riddle of the Ivy," *Tremendous Trifles*)

—— ❖ ——

Shakespeare and the Dark Lady (Again)

("Madame de Chambrun on Shakespeare")

I have recently read with very great interest a new book on what is not, perhaps, entirely a new subject. I refer to the subject of Shakespeare; not without reference to the subject of Shakespeare's Sonnets, of the Dark Lady, and the poet's relation to Southampton and Essex and Bacon and various eminent men of his time. The book is by the Comtesse de Chambrun, and is published by Appleton; and it seems to me both fascinating and convincing. I hasten to say that the lady is very learned and I am very ignorant. I do not profess to know much about Shakespeare, outside such superfluous trifling as the reading of his literary works. Mme. de Chambrun's book is called *Shakespeare, Actor-Poet*; and I must humbly confess that I have known him only in his humbler capacity as a poet, and have never devoted myself to the more exhausting occupation of studying all the green-room gossip about him as an actor. But it is very right that more scholarly people should study the biographical problem, and even a poor literary critic may be allowed to judge their studies as literature. And this study seems to me to be one very valuable to literature, and not, like so many of the Baconian penny-dreadfuls, a mere insult to literature. Indeed, some Baconian books are quite as much of an insult to Bacon as to Shakespeare.

I have no authority to decide the controversies of fact raised here: about the relation of Southampton to the Sonnets or the discovery of the Dark Lady in the family of Davenant. I can only say that to a plain man the arguments seem at least to be of a plain sort. Thus, I have never had any reason to quarrel with Mr. Frank Harris or Mr. Bernard Shaw about the claims of Miss Mary Fitton, or to break a lance for or against that questionable queen of beauty. I have lances enough to break with them about more important things. But to my simplicity it does seem rather notable that next to nothing is known about the Dark Lady except that she was dark; and that precious little seems to be known about Mary Fitton except that she was fair. Or, again, I profess myself utterly incompetent to consider the question of what "T. T." meant by "W. H."; and I do not think the difficulty will interfere very much with my joy in saying to myself: "But thine immortal beauty shall not fade," or "Give not a windy night a rainy morrow." But if it be true, as it is here stated, that some of these sonnets were already written when William Herbert, Lord Pembroke, was only eleven years old, he certainly must have been a precocious child if what Shakespeare says about him is at all appropriate. There may be ingenious answers to these things that I do not know, but to guileless ignorance like my own the point seems rather a practical one. As a matter of fact, I have generally found in these cases that the ingenious explanations were a little too ingenious. But, as I have said, I have no intention of dogmatising on these problems.

Madame de Chambrun's theory is that the young man for whom Shakespeare had such a hero-worship was his own patron and protector, the Earl of Southampton; for whom, indeed, she has some little hero-worship herself. But she gives very good and convincing grounds for regarding him as something of a hero. I am pretty sure she is quite right in saying that the rebellion of Essex and Southampton was essentially just and public-spirited. She says that, if it had succeeded, they would have been handed down to all history as patriots and reformers. I am also quite sure she is right in saying that it was rather a rebellion against Cecil than against Elizabeth. That alone would make it creditable. It is curious to note that, in this account, Bacon and Shakespeare, so far from being conspirators and collaborators, were two antagonistic figures in two opposite factions, one on each side of a serious civil war. Bacon was the bitter accuser of Essex; indeed, Bacon had probably become a sort of hack and servant of Cecil. Shakespeare was, of course, a friend and follower of Southampton, who was a friend and follower of Essex. According to this account, Shakespeare was presenting plays like *Richard II* as deliberate political demonstrations, designed to warn weak sovereigns of the need of greater wisdom, at the very time when Bacon was drawing up the heads of his detailed and virulent denunciation of the rebel. However this may be, it is practically certain that there was this chasm between the two great men, whom some have blended into one great man: we might say into one great monster. This theory would make an even stranger monster of the Baconian version of Bacon. Not only was he capable of leading two separate public lives, but even of figuring in two opposite political parties. He must have been plotting against himself all night and condemning himself to be hanged on the following day.

If I say that this fancy would turn Bacon and Shakespeare into Jekyll and Hyde, the partisans of the two parties will probably dispute rather eagerly about which was which. But I, for one, have very little doubt on that point. And I am glad to find that Madame de Chambrun thinks very much the same and knows very much more. If ever there was a base business in human history, it was the method of government which Burleigh and his son conducted in England in the name of Elizabeth; and, I am sorry to say, to some extent with the assistance of Bacon. The people whom Robert Cecil destroyed were all more honest than himself (not that that was saying much), and some of them were sufficiently honourable and spirited to dwarf his little hunchbacked figure even by their dignity in the hour of death. Whether it were Essex or Mary Stuart or even poor Guy Fawkes, they might have stood on the scaffold only in order to make him look small. And I am heartily glad to hear it, if it be true that this nest of nasty plutocrats, with Cecil in the midst of it, counted among its enemies the greatest of Englishmen. It gives me great pleasure to think that it was of those Tudor politicians that he was thinking when he talked of strength by limping away disabled, and art made tongue-tied by authority, and captive good attending captain ill. The last line must have described a good many scenes on the scaffold in the sixteenth century. It may be difficult to imagine Shakespeare greater than Shakespeare, but it is possible that if his friends had triumphed and his cause and faith revived, he might in some unthinkable transfiguration have been greater than himself.

I know much less of the other problem involved, which is entirely one of private life and not of public policy. I mean the question of that mysterious and sinister woman towards whom the sonneteer revives the ancient rage of inconsistencies; the *odi et amo* ["I hate and I love"] of Catullus. But even

I, as a mere casual reader of things in general, had certainly heard of the joke or scandal which is said to have suggested that Sir William Davenant was a natural son of William Shakespeare. Whether this was so or not, Shakespeare certainly knew the Davenants, who kept an inn where he visited, and where (as the writer of this book explains) Southampton himself appeared on the scene at a later stage. Her theory is that Mrs. Davenant was what we should now call a vamp; that she had at one time vamped the poet, and went on later to vamp the peer. But the poet, though his feelings were mixed, could already see through the lady, and was furious at the duping of his friend; and out of this triple tangle of passions came the great tragic sequence of the Sonnets. Upon this I cannot pronounce, beyond repeating that it is set out in this book with great cogency, comprehension, and grip; and without a trace of that indefinable disproportion and lack of balance which makes many learned and ingenious works on such subjects smell faintly of the madhouse. The writer keeps control of the subject, and we feel that, though her conclusions are definite, she would not be seriously upset if they were definitely disproved. She appeals to facts and fairness throughout, and nobody can do more. The documentation and system of references seems to be very thorough, and, in a matter which I am better able to judge, there is nowhere that sense of strain in the argument, or of something altogether far-fetched in the explanation, which continually jars us in most reconstructions of this kind, especially in the dangerous era of Elizabeth. Perhaps, after all, that era really was the great spiritual battle, and Shakespeare and Bacon really were the spirits that met in conflict. But, anyhow, it is a queer paradox that Shakespeare was an obscure and almost unhistorical figure according to some nameless or worthless, according to others impersonal and self-effacing, but anyhow somewhat elusive and secret; and from him came a cataract of clear song and natural eloquence; while Bacon was a public man of wide renown and national and scientific philosophy; and out of him have come riddles and oracles and fantastic cryptograms and a lifelong hobby for lunatics.

(Illustrated London News, October 1, 1927)

Why Indeed?

A lady writer for whom I have otherwise a warm admiration recently proposed a treaty, or at least a truce, in the war of Bacon and Shakespeare. The compromise, or what she regarded as a compromise, consisted in agreeing that Shakespeare did not write Shakespeare, without affirming that Bacon did. This rather reminds me, I confess, of some of the compromises proposed by Prussia in the later stages of the war; and especially her offer to internationalize all territories that obviously belonged to other nations. But the compromise is undoubtedly topical and in touch with the times, since there have lately appeared several rivals to Bacon as well as to Shakespeare. A procession of showy Elizabethan aristocrats now passes across the stage, each striking an attitude in turn and assuring us that he was the real author of *Hamlet*, but was too shy to say so. This is at least rather a relief after the omnipresence of the Bacon of the Baconians, who was not only Shakespeare, but everybody else too, sometimes even Cervantes and Montaigne. In fact, he was the only man of the Renaissance, and all other men were his masks. He disguised himself as a crowd. He concealed himself artfully in twenty places at once. He was certainly, as his followers say, a wonderful man; but there was something bewildering, and even bloodcurdling, about walking in that wax-work show of historical dummies, with only the one awful ventriloquistic voice calling to us on every side and out of every corner.

I only touch on this old matter as a text for some reflections on the rare art of reasoning. It does not much matter whether the man who wrote Bacon also wrote Shakespeare, but it does very much matter that the people who write English should also write sense. Now the initiators of the new attempt to eliminate William of Stratford continually fall into a strange and simple fallacy that ought to be exposed for its own sake. Even the critic already quoted fell into it, when she argued that the story of the Stratfordian actor and author is inconceivable, since he lived and died comparatively quietly as an actor, though he had produced admittedly amazing masterpieces as an author. Why, it is asked, was there not more excitement about such a sensational genius? To which the obvious answer is "Why indeed?" Why was there not such an excitement about him whoever he was, or whoever he was supposed to be? If some such explosion of ecstasy must have followed such work, why did it not follow the right man, or the wrong man, or any man? If Shakespeare had successfully stolen the glory of Bacon, why, on this argument, was there not more to steal? In that case, it is for the Baconians to answer their own question about why Shakespeare was not more admired. And it is obvious that the Baconians, on their own principle, cannot answer their own question. If, on the other hand people really knew that Shakespeare was but the mask and Bacon the master, why did they not give Bacon all the praise that is here assumed as due to the master? If it was known to be somebody else, like the Earl of Southampton, why did they not give it to the Earl of Southampton? If it was not known to anybody else, but supposed to be Shakespeare, why did they not give it to Shakespeare? This riddle remains exactly the same in whatever direction you twist it, or to whatever man you make it point. Granted that there should be a great fuss about the fame of such work, and then, if somebody did it, there should be a fuss about him; if somebody else, a fuss about him; if nobody knew who did it, a fuss about who did it. Indeed, if nobody knew, one would naturally suppose there would be the greatest fuss of all. I am only taking this as a typical current error in logic; and for that purpose I take the Baconian premises for granted. I merely point out that their own refutation can be deduced from their own premises. For the rest, I fancy it might throw some light on the mystery to throw some doubt on the data—e. g., to question (1) whether masterpieces must always be followed by this earthquake of public interest; (2) whether Shakespeare's masterpieces were so much neglected as is here implied; (3) and even whether there was not something of a case for those who, in the complexity of all contemporary quarrels, preferred to admire him on this side of idolatry.

(*Illustrated London News*, Oct. 22, 1921)

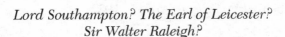

Lord Southampton? The Earl of Leicester? Sir Walter Raleigh?

I am not sure who it is who holds the cup or shield for this season as being the historical character who really wrote Shakespeare. I mean in that world of learned disputants who only agree on the first principle that Shakespeare could not write Shakespeare. When last I heard of it, it was Lord Southampton, commonly known as the patron of the poet, who was really the poet as well as the patron. Lord Southampton evidently believed in keeping a dog and then barking himself. The proverb seems to fit very exactly a nobleman occupied in keeping a playwright when he would write *Hamlet* himself. It must be somebody else by this time—the Earl of Leicester (he was dead, but that is a trifle to the student of cryptograms and conspiracies), or Sir Walter Raleigh, or Sir Christopher Hatton, or anybody else who lived in the later days of Elizabeth and the earlier days of James I. Personally, I believe the plays were written by Guy Fawkes. . . .

(*Illustrated London News*, Dec. 13, 1924)

Shakespeare Is Shakespeare

Go back another century, and we shall find the physiological doctrine of the Humours of the Body. You will also find a really learned intellectual like Ben Jonson, solemnly basing whole plays on a systematic application of the theory; while you will find a careless half-educated fellow named William Shakespeare alluding to it, but taking it much more lightly. In spite of which, somehow or other Shakespeare is Shakespeare; and Ben Jonson is only Ben Jonson.

(*New York American*, April 7, 1934)

Shakespeare Has Written Us

How can we discuss how we should have written Shakespeare? Shakespeare has written us. And you and I (I am sure you will agree) are two of his best characters.

(*Daily News*, Jan. 2, 1907)